MW00860754

THE POWER OF THE PAST

THE POWER OF THE PAST

Understanding Cross-Class Marriages

Jessi Streib

OXFORD
UNIVERSITY PRESS

OXFORD
UNIVERSITY PRESS

Oxford University Press is a department of the University of
Oxford. It furthers the University's objective of excellence in research,
scholarship, and education by publishing worldwide.

Oxford   New York

Auckland   Cape Town   Dar es Salaam   Hong Kong   Karachi
Kuala Lumpur   Madrid   Melbourne   Mexico City   Nairobi
New Delhi   Shanghai   Taipei   Toronto

With offices in

Argentina   Austria   Brazil   Chile   Czech Republic   France   Greece
Guatemala   Hungary   Italy   Japan   Poland   Portugal   Singapore
South Korea   Switzerland   Thailand   Turkey   Ukraine   Vietnam

Oxford is a registered trademark of Oxford University Press
in the UK and certain other countries.

Published in the United States of America by
Oxford University Press
198 Madison Avenue, New York, NY 10016

Library of Congress Cataloging-in-Publication Data
Streib, Jessi.
The power of the past : understanding cross-class marriages / Jessi Streib.
pages cm
Includes bibliographical references and index.
ISBN 978–0–19–936442–8 (hardcover : alk. paper) — ISBN 978–0–19–936443–5
(pbk. : alk. paper)   1. Marriage.   2. Social classes.   3. Spouses.   4. Married
people—Social conditions.   I. Title.
HQ728.S864 2015
306.81—dc23
2014021623

1 3 5 7 9 8 6 4 2
Printed in the United States of America
on acid-free paper

CONTENTS

PART III
CLASS AND THE DOMAINS OF MARRIED LIFE

PREFACE

A colleague recently told me that he was repeatedly surprised that I am passionate about class issues.[1] I nodded as he told me this because I knew what he meant. Many qualitative sociologists study groups that they are part of, especially groups that they are part of that are disadvantaged in some way. I, however, had no experience in a serious cross-class relationship. I also had no experience growing up with any sense of material need. My parents both have terminal degrees and professional jobs; by most measures, I grew up with class privilege.

I grew up, however, exposed to people located on several points on the class spectrum. Until I was 12 years old, I lived most of my life in a suburb of Cleveland. The suburb had some class diversity, but most of the people I knew were upper middle class or wealthy.[2] My neighbors' home was a historic house so big that it had what used to be a wing for servants. I had a friend with an elevator in her home. I had another friend who lived in a mansion that overlooked his backyard pool, and whose sixth birthday party consisted of a petting zoo arriving at his house. I was aware that the people around me were rich, but I was not aware of what it meant to be working class or poor.

Just before I entered junior high school, things changed. My father accepted a job as a dean of a law school, and my family moved to the rural community where his new job was located. As we drove into the town for the first time, we passed a trailer park at the town's edge. Seeing it, I asked my parents if the town we were moving to was poor. My mother replied that it was not, that the people in this town were better off than most of the people in the world. I was surprised by her answer, as my new community was much less well-off than my old one.

I spent my adolescence in my new community and learned more of the class structure. My father's job as the dean of the law school positioned my twin brother and me as the rich kids in town—a label that it took some time to understand. I became friends with some of the other "rich kids" in town—the other children of professors. I also became friends with some working-class students—the children of secretaries, janitors, factory workers, and farmers. I learned many things from these friendships, but there are two things that are most relevant for this book: I learned that class was associated with sensibilities and life chances, and I learned that meaningful relationships can cross class lines.

I thought of these experiences again as a graduate student when I read the literature on social class inequality. Before Charles Murray used the phrase in the title of his book, sociologists were documenting that the classes were coming apart.[3] They lived in different places, sent their children to different schools, and spent their leisure time in different activities.[4] Those in different classes disliked and distrusted each other. A Pew Research poll found that Americans saw class as producing the biggest divide between them.[5]

I was alarmed by the growing class segregation and animosity. At the same time, I knew from my own experiences that not all relationships were captured by these trends. I decided, then, to study those whose experiences went beyond my own—those who not only had cross-class friendships but those who vowed to have and to hold a partner from another class. I hoped that these relationships could shed light on how individuals could love each other despite their class differences—even differences that they had left behind. I hoped as well to learn about how, in a time when the classes are coming apart, people raised in different classes were also coming together.

ACKNOWLEDGMENTS

There are many people to thank for helping me write this book. First and foremost, I would like to thank the couples who agreed to be in this study. It takes an admirable amount of courage to talk about your marriage, family, and childhood with a stranger. I was constantly in awe by how much they were willing to share with me and how much they seemed to want to help the university. I hope that this book helps them understand their lives and helps other couples understand their own.

My dissertation committee—Alford Young, Jr., Elizabeth Armstrong, Karyn Lacy, Karin Martin, and Abigail Stewart—also assisted me tremendously. Each of them supported this project from its inception, answered many e-mails, and walked me through methodological, substantive, and writing issues. I want to thank Al Young in particular for pushing me to not just apply others' theories to my data but to also come up with my own. Elizabeth Armstrong has served as a wonderful mentor. The introduction of the book was inspired by her comments, and her endless work as Michigan's graduate director offered me opportunities I would not otherwise have.

I owe Karyn Lacy a special thank you for always making her office a place where I felt good about my work. As a young female professor, she also made writing a book and becoming a professor seem more real. I am also especially thankful to Karin Martin, who always read my work with amazing speed. Lastly, years ago Abigail Stewart co-authored a piece that inspired me to study social class and has been nice enough to continue to help me even though her work has since gone in other directions.

Several other professors have also been instrumental in the creation of this book. I completed my first sociological project under the guidance of Fred Wherry, and he continued to provide me with support throughout my time at Michigan. I met Howard Kimmeldorf at a meeting where we discovered our common interests in a book published almost 50 years earlier, and he has since provided amazingly detailed comments on my work. I also always enjoyed spending hours talking with Dwight Lang about first-generation student issues and social class more generally. Dwight has served as a great mentor for how to run a first-generation college students group, which I hope to be able to do at some point in the future. Nadine Hubbs also has offered much of her time despite absolutely no professional obligation to do so, and I have been extremely grateful for this. My work also owes a tremendous debt to Annette Lareau as her book, *Unequal Childhoods*, paved the way for studying class and culture in a qualitative manner.

My interest in sociology began due to my stellar undergraduate professors. Their classes taught me to develop my sociological imagination and helped me realize that nothing is ever as it seems. Many of the books I cite today are ones I read in their classes. In particular, Stephen Valocchi introduced me to studying social class and encouraged me to attend graduate school. Johnny Williams's classes were always mesmerizing. Whenever I think of conflict theory I also think of Johnny, whose life seems dedicated to understanding the roots of power and fighting for justice. Theresa Morris continues to be a great mentor and source of advice about navigating the academy as a woman.

The Michigan graduate school community has also been tremendously helpful. After each time I presented a paper in a workshop I left awed by their intelligence and good humor. My writing group—Amy Cooter, Sasha Killewald, Anju Paul, Jane Rochmes, and Jess Wiederspan—have read more drafts of my work than anyone else, including drafts that were so early that I wouldn't dream of showing them to anyone else. The idea for this project came out of a casual conversation with another graduate student—Hiro Saito— and to him I'm grateful for his offhand remark: "This would make an interesting dissertation!"

Undergraduate students also coded and transcribed some of the interviews. Lucy Alexandra Nonas-Barnes, Abigail Barnard, Andrea Fossass, Christie Low, Gina Kim, Shadmani Kushi, Matthew Shutler, and Chelsey Vanden Esschert all deserve credit for their work on these tasks. Brandon Phillips also read a few of my chapters and discussing class with him was always a pleasure. I am also grateful to Erin Peterson for her work transcribing many of my interviews. The Michigan Sociology staff—Jennifer Eshelman, Elise Harper, Tim Moore, Diana Paterno, Pat Preston, Rick Smoke, Linda Williams, and Jeannie Worrall—also deserves a huge thank you for answering all of my questions. Rackham, the Center for the Education of Women, the Institute for Research on Gender and Women, and the University of Michigan Sociology department also all provided funding which made this book possible. I would also like to thank my editor at Oxford University Press, James Cook, who has had great insights about my work from the first time he read the manuscript.

Finally, I'd like to thank my family. When I told my former neighbor that I was going to graduate school in sociology she responded that she was not surprised as I had been thinking about social justice issues since I was two years old. I'm sure this is due to my parents' influence. My father showed me that you could have an academic career in which you advocated for a subset of underdogs, and my mother's seemingly effortless concerted cultivation instilled me with the skills to achieve academically. My twin brother Noah also helped me along the way, and he has patiently listened to me talk about class inequality, usually as he beats me at card games. My partner, Rob, also deserves my heartfelt thanks. He has taught me that studying social inequality is a lot easier when you can laugh about it and that economists are, in fact, very lovable.

PART I

INTRODUCTION

[1]

CLASS AND MARRIAGE

Christie and Mike met in their junior high school's cafeteria as Christie admired Mike's rear end, and Mike admired Christie's coke-bottle glasses. They soon started dating, and they noticed their class differences. They both knew that Christie's father worked as a maintenance man while her mother did not work for pay. Christie's house was small; she shared a bedroom with her sister and a bathroom with her entire family. Her family did not buy new cars or go on vacations to other states. Due to her family's finances, Pop-Tarts were a special treat. Christie's family was happy, lively, and close but also relatively poor.

Christie felt that it was obvious that her family did not have much money, just as she felt it was obvious that Mike's family did. Mike's father worked as a professor and authored famous books, while Mike's mother took care of their large home. Mike's parents drove new sports cars and took yearly vacations to the beach. They put money aside for Mike's trust fund and counseled him on how to prepare for college. When Mike's mother asked Christie about her post–high school plans, she indicated that she never expected to have a life like Mike's. She replied: "I wanna be a grocery store clerk, checkout."

When I met them, Christie and Mike were in their mid-40s. Christie was a vivacious woman whose curly hair bounced as she laughed about the ups and downs of her life. Mike was a tall, thin, man who was friendly but more reserved than Christie. They had been married for 25 years and had been together for three-quarters of their lives. Contrary to what she expected, Christie, like Mike, earned a bachelor's degree and worked in a professional job. They raised three children together; their youngest child was leaving for college soon. They shared their degrees and their children, their home and their bank accounts, their secrets and their strategies. But despite their shared lives, their sensibilities and their marriage were still shaped by the class differences of their past. In fact, in many ways, each had more in common with strangers who shared their class background than with their partner with whom they shared their life.

This book documents the marital experiences of 32 couples like Christie and Mike—couples that are in what I call "different-origin" marriages. These are couples who share their current position in the middle class but who grew up in different classes. In each pair, one partner grew up in a blue-collar family while the other grew up in a professional white-collar family. The book shows that, though they rarely recognized it, the class of each partner's past influenced why they initially found their partner appealing and what differences they would later navigate. *The Power of the Past,* in short, reveals the hidden role that class plays in the intimate lives of married couples.

CLASS AND THE EXPERIENCES OF MARRIAGE

There are many myths about social class. One myth is that class has nothing to do with love and marriage. Subscribers to this belief assume that love is blind to class or that cupid's arrows fall randomly.

Once relationships form, those who share this conviction contend that class has no bearing on the intimate details of couples' lives. They suppose that two unique individuals begin a life together, free from the contaminating force of social class.[1]

Some social scientists hold a similar myth—the myth that class has little to do with marriage when each partner shares their adulthood class position. This subset of scholars believes that the cultural remnants of each partner's class past are washed away, or at least buried, when partners experience similar educational and occupational socialization, interact in the same networks, and have access to shared earnings and assets (Aschaffenburg and Maas 1997; Chin and Phillips 2004; DiMaggio 1982; Erickson 1996; McFarland and Pals 2005). These scholars would predict that the marriages between two highly educated individuals who share a class origin and those who do not would be largely the same, as class origin would no longer have any bearing on each partner's sensibilities.[2]

Another set of scholars emphasizes an opposing set of findings that when extrapolated too far takes the form of a myth. These scholars emphasize the enduring power of social class in personal relationships. According to this line of work, individuals from different classes mix like oil and water—put them together and they separate. This is because those from different classes possess distinct and conflicting ideas of what is normal, desirable, and foreseeable (Bourdieu 1980, 1984, 1998, 2002; Illouz 1997; Johnson and Lawler 2005; Lamont 1992, 2000). These differences not only create difficulties in finding common ground but can also result in one group using the other as a foil against which to establish their own moral worth (Bourdieu 1984; Gorman 2000; Lacy 2007; Lamont 1992, 2000; Pattillo 2007). Individuals then see those from another class as dissimilar, disagreeable, and as unlikely candidates for friendship let alone marriage (Bottero 2005; Bourdieu

1984; DiMaggio and Mohr 1985; Kalmijn 1994). Taken too far, these sound arguments result in a myth—a myth that cultural differences derived from class differences are so powerful as to block the formation of different-origin marriages.[3]

The Power of the Past exposes the fallacy of these myths. Contrary to the view of the average American—including many of those whose lives are detailed in this book—the marriages described in the coming chapters were shaped by the class in which each partner was raised. Class shaped their marriages because, contrary to the views of a subset of social scientists, those from different classes have sensibilities that were inextricably tied to the class of their past. Many upwardly mobile respondents in this study with blue-collar roots spent more time in the class they entered as adults than in the class they were born into as children, but even this did not erase the imprint that their class origin left upon their lives. Nor did an average of over 4,500 days spent with their spouse;[4] each spouse's experiences in higher education; or that husbands and wives had access to shared earnings, assets, and networks.

The book does not reject the idea that social situations are often marked by class segregation or that those from different classes tend not to get along. It does, however, demonstrate that it is a myth that this always happens, and, more importantly, it is a myth that cultural differences that are associated with class differences are always divisive. As others have demonstrated, marriages between college-educated people who grew up in different classes are not the norm but neither are they unusual (Blossfeld and Timm 2003; Charles, Hurst, and Killewald 2013; Kalmijn 1991).[5] These marriages, this book adds, are not only the result of individuals tolerating or overlooking their partners' cultural differences. Rather, *The Power of the Past* reveals that spouses believed that their love bloomed because their partner had a cultural trait that they admired but lacked. These cultural differences were associated with their class differences and were remembered as magnets pulling those from different classes together.

The Power of the Past dispels each myth—the myth that class in general is divorced from marriage, that class origin in particular has little bearing on the lives of college-educated adults, and that class differences experienced as cultural differences are necessarily divisive. In dispelling these myths, this book shows that the class individuals are born into leaves an indelible imprint upon their sensibilities.[6] It shows that although partners remembered their differences as originally drawing them to their different-origin spouse, they later felt that these and other differences became ones that they lived with but did not love. Being in a different-origin relationship then meant committing to negotiating differences, differences that were not negated by merging money, homes, and friends.

CLASS AND SENSIBILITIES

Those from different classes shared their lives but not their ideas of how to live them, their resources but not their ideas of how to use them, and their children but not their ideas of how to raise them. This book locates these and other differences in sensibilities— default ways of thinking about everyday events, such as how to use resources, divide labor, and raise children.[7] This focus moves away from the more common connection that sociologists make between class and culture—that of a focus on tastes.[8]

More so than sensibilities, scholars tend to document the connection between social class and tastes—preferences for objects and activities like art, music, literature, fashion, and sports (for example, Bourdieu 1984; Bryson 1996; Holt 1997; Lewis et al. 2007; Peterson and Kern 1996; Stempel 2005). Those from different classes often possess different tastes, differences that can be a source of conflict in different-origin marriages. But while tastes matter in a marriage (see, for example, Chapter 5), sensibilities matter more. Tastes are relatively containable because they affect a limited amount of daily activities, like what radio station to tune into on a road trip or what movie to see on a Friday night. Sensibilities, however, are less containable as they are infused into more aspects of daily life. They shape not only leisure activities but also everyday decisions, such as how to spend time or money. They are also likely to be more consequential in marriage. Differences in tastes in movies, for example, may result in debates over what to watch or, at most, unequal networks that are generated from discussing different movies with different people. Differences in sensibilities about how to spend money, attend to work, divide household labor, use time, display emotions, and raise children are likely to spark more vehement disagreements as well as to relate more to the amount of resources couples acquire.

Sensibilities may be linked to resource acquisition as institutions implicitly reward different types of sensibilities. Generally, institutions such as workplaces and schools reward sensibilities that are most associated with the middle class. Those with middle-class sensibilities are then more likely to receive recognition and to advance through institutions' opportunity structures (Bettie 2003; Bourdieu and Passeron 1977; Calarco 2011; Rivera 2011; Streib 2011). If individuals raised in different classes have different and transposable sensibilities then blue- and white-collar-origin partners are likely to have unequal abilities to obtain resources. This may create inequities within different-origin couples as well as between those in different-origin and shared-origin relationships.[9]

Sensibilities then play a key role in mapping the content of couples' differences as well as their ability to acquire resources. But what sensibilities are possessed by those with blue- and white-collar-origin spouses in different-origin marriages? No existing organizational system categorizes the sensibilities of highly educated individuals who grew up in different classes and few describe sensibilities at all.[10] Popularly, sensibilities are more likely to be thought of as related to an individual rather than to their class. Sociologically, sensibilities are connected to class in distinct domains of everyday life, such as parenting,[11] but have not been systematically linked to class origin across multiple domains of daily life.[12]

The stories that husbands and wives told demonstrate that sensibilities are systematically associated with each partner's class past and play out in concurrent ways across diverse spheres of everyday life.[13] In general, those who were born into professional white-collar families had sensibilities that I call *managerial*. They preferred to plan, deliberate, mull over, and organize their resources, their children, and their daily lives. Their partners with blue-collar roots typically had different sensibilities, those that I call *laissez-faire*.[14] They preferred to feel free from self-constraint. Rather than wanting to analyze, plan, or meticulously organize their lives, they preferred to go with the flow and live in the moment.[15] These differences played out across multiple domains in their lives. And, as the coming chapters will show, they were related to why those from different classes remembered finding each other appealing as well as the content of spouses' later discrepant approaches to money, paid work, housework, time, leisure, parenting, and emotions.[16]

Marriages, however, do not only necessitate navigating class differences but dealing with gender differences as well (Coontz 2005, 2011; Hochschild 1989). Though gender is often considered to be omnipresent in marriage, it played an uneven role in shaping sensibilities. In the highly gendered spheres of housework and parenting, gender combined with class origin in shaping spouses' sensibilities. In areas of daily life that are less associated with gender (though still not gender-neutral), laissez-faire and managerial sensibilities were associated only with class origin and not with gender. Although marriage is often thought of as a highly gendered institution, the findings in this book show that it is a highly classed one as well.

Because individuals' experiences in their class origin left an enduring impression on their sensibilities, the marriages of those like Christie and Mike were not only shaped by their own idiosyncrasies but also by the class into which they were born. Spending three-quarters of their lives together as well as sharing their earnings, degrees, home, and children did not erase the patterned ways that class related to their ideas of how to go about their daily lives. Christie harbored laissez-faire sensibilities. She wanted to feel free from the constraints of money and schedules so she spent money without thinking, decided in the moment how to use her free time, and took charge of the housework without imposing a structured division of labor. She also expressed her emotions without processing them, and, at work, she preferred to keep her eyes open for new opportunities rather than planning her career trajectory. Mike, on the other hand, possessed managerial sensibilities. He wanted to spend money carefully, plan his career trajectory, establish a structured division of labor, schedule his time, and think about his emotions before expressing them. Their marriage thus entailed negotiating these differences—differences that, unbeknownst to them, were associated with the class of their past.

THE STUDY

Class origin and marriage have rarely been studied together. Studies of marriage tend to group husbands and wives together, defining the couple's class according to the husband's position or the average of each spouses' position rather than looking at each spouse's class separately (for example, Goldthorpe 1983).[17] Research also tends to focus on adults' class location, overlooking how spouses' childhood class positions also matter in marriage (for exceptions, see Bystydzienski 2011 and Komarovsky 1962). The majority of studies also use statistics to compare couples in different classes, demonstrating, for example, that college-educated and high school educated couples have starkly different likelihoods of having a child before they marry, feeling satisfied in their marriage, and divorcing (Carlson and England 2011; Cherlin 2009; Conger, Conger, and Martin 2010; Smock and Greenland 2010). This book departs from the focus on statistical differences, adulthood class position, and assumptions that each partner shares a class, and instead draws upon interviews with highly educated adults who married a partner who was raised in a different class. In doing so, it draws attention to class differences within families, not just between them.

Interviewing individuals about such a personal topic as marriage is more feasible than one might suppose. Lillian Rubin (1976, 1994) and Mirra Komarovsky (1962) have written classic studies that detail the intimate experiences of marriage. A host of other studies document the lives of interracial couples, the meaning of gender within marriages, and even the relationship between adulthood class position and family life (for example, Bystydzienski 2011; Edin and Kefalas 2005; Hansen 2005; Hochschild 1989; Lareau 2003; Liebow 1967; Steinbugler 2012). The richness of these studies demonstrates that people are willing to talk to scholars about their relationships with the people they love. They also remind us that while the stories individuals tell about their lives may not be entirely objective, they nonetheless reveal underlying patterns in the ways that marriages are experienced and understood.

The patterns described in this book come primarily from interviews with 32 different-origin couples. These were couples in which one partner had a father who worked in a blue-collar job and had, at most, a high school degree, while the other partner's father had at least a bachelor's degree and worked in a white-collar professional or managerial position. The mothers of respondents usually had levels of educational attainment that matched those of respondents' fathers, though their education was not used to define class in this study (see Appendix A for more on this and other methodological decisions). I refer to respondents by their class origin: blue-collar-origin or white-collar-origin. Fifteen couples were composed of a blue-collar-origin woman and white-collar-origin man, while in 17 cases the genders were reversed.

I also interviewed 10 couples—20 individuals—in what I call "shared-origin" marriages. These are marriages between college-educated individuals with college-educated professional fathers. I refer to this group of respondents as "shared-origin" in order to differentiate them from white-collar-origin respondents who married blue-collar-origin partners. Though many groups could have been chosen as a comparison group, this one was chosen because it allows for an analysis of whether class origin matters in marriage or whether the marriages between two highly educated adults are largely similar regardless of each spouse's class background. Comparing different-origin and shared-origin marriages shows that white-collar-origin partners, regardless of who they married, had similar sensibilities, but they played out differently depending on the class origin of the person they married.

Though the 84 respondents in this study came from different class backgrounds, they were similar in a number of other dimensions. They were all highly educated. All had spent some time in college, and all but two had a bachelor's degree or a graduate degree. They all shared a race, nationality, and type of relationship: they were all white, United States citizens, and in different-sex marriages. Most respondents were middle-aged; their median age was

41.[18] Their marriages had all also passed the newlywed stage. On average, they had been married for 13 years.[19] These similarities were purposefully sought to understand how class background mattered in a group that is too often viewed as untouched by social forces—married, highly educated, white Americans.

Examining a group of individuals who have many homogeneous demographic traits has analytic advantages. Highly diverse, small samples are difficult to analyze as identifying meaningful patterns amongst numerous groups becomes untenable. The trade-off in creating a homogeneous sample, however, is that the findings are limited in their generality. The analysis of this sample—highly educated, married, white Americans—should not be taken to stand in for any other group. Socialization experiences, access to resources, networks, senses of self, salient sensibilities, and marriage markets often differ for those with different amounts of education; those who are downwardly mobile; and those of different races, sexualities, and nationalities (Banks 2011; Chauncey 1995; Kennedy and Davis 1993; Moore 2011; Pattillo 2005; Schwartz and Graf 2009; Seidman 2011). As such, the findings only apply to married, heterosexual, highly educated, white Americans in which neither partner was significantly downwardly mobile—a group that is both populous and, in some ways, powerful. They are the group that is often problematically set up as the standard by which other families are judged. Selecting this sample allowed me to pull back the curtain and see how class matters in these "standard" families.

That the respondents had several similar demographic characteristics, however, does not mean that the sample was entirely homogeneous. Respondents were evangelical Christians, Methodists, Catholics, Mormons, Jews, and atheists. Their politics spanned the political spectrum. They worked in a variety of jobs: seventeen respondents were stay-at-home parents; eight worked as teachers; four as lawyers; four as engineers; four as doctors; four in Internet technology fields; three as professors; and others as managers, scientists, financial analysts, social workers, politicians, or business officials. They lived in small cities, small towns, and in the countryside. Some grew up as hippies, some spent their youth singing in Klingon choirs, some joined punk rock bands, and others hunted. Some watched their parents deal with alcoholism, others with divorce. Their lives were filled with differences, although, as the coming pages will show, they were similarly influenced by class.

These interviewees all agreed to make their private lives public. They answered fliers recruiting couples with "different economic backgrounds" that were posted in their children's schools, announced at the meetings of their social clubs, and viewed through the e-mail listservs to which they subscribed.[20] Each partner then sat down with me—a young white woman with no experience in a serious cross-class relationship—and, while their partner was away, answered questions about their marriage, their children, and their childhoods.

The questions they answered were open-ended. They began by recounting the story of how they met their spouse, and, upon prompting, included their first impressions and the reasons why they felt that their partner was the one they wanted to marry. I then presented them with a list of topics, such as money, housework, paid work, and leisure, and asked them to tell me how they thought about these items compared to their spouse. They had the option of saying that they thought similarly or differently about these items, and they were asked to describe their similarities and differences using criteria that was relevant to them. In addition, I asked about their childhoods and their children. I finished by asking direct questions about their ideas of social class. In all, I spoke to each respondent, away from their spouse, for an average of 105 minutes.[21] The findings in the following chapters are the result of the patterned responses that interviewees gave to these open-ended questions.

Finally, it is worth remembering that the findings that appear in this book are drawn from a sample of respondents who remain in different-origin marriages. These are couples who are less likely to be affected by class differences than couples whose relationships dissolved before or after they married. They are also couples who agreed to talk about their intimate lives with a stranger—a feature that may have biased the sample toward those who were in especially happy marriages. Minimally, they are couples who found ways to navigate their class differences over an average of more than a decade of marriage. Given the profound ways that class structured their sensibilities, if class mattered in their marriages, it is likely that it mattered for others whose relationships did not last.

ORGANIZATION OF THE BOOK

The book proceeds by first showing how those in different-origin marriages think about class. Chapter 2 demonstrates that few interviewees who entered into different-origin marriages did so with the intention of marrying across this class line. In fact, even after years of marriage, few thought about class much at all. Chapter 3 continues the theme of the genesis of different-origin unions and reveals the reasons respondents gave for initially feeling drawn to a partner who did not share their class past.

The following chapters describe the sensibilities of white- and blue-collar-origin respondents, mapping the terrain of their differences. These chapters demonstrate that sharing a current class position and a life together did not expunge the influence of each partner's class origin on their sensibilities. These chapters examine sensibilities about money (Chapter 4), work and play (Chapter 5), housework and time use (Chapter 6), parenting (Chapter 7), and emotions (Chapter 8). Chapter 9 concludes the book by drawing out the implications of these marriages in terms of class, culture, and social relationships. It also demonstrates that even the most intimate of relationships have public policy implications.

It is also worth noting what will not appear in the upcoming pages. There is a sizeable literature about the predictors of marital satisfaction and divorce. I chose not to address these issues as they may be more appropriately studied with a larger data set collected longitudinally. The following pages also do not discuss couples' sex lives because such a personal topic may have dissuaded individuals from participating in the study. The focus is, instead, on the many ways that the broad and abstract concept of social class infuses the personal and concrete experiences of marriage. It is a study of couples like Christie and Mike—couples bound by their love for each other, their joint resources, and their children, but not by the class of their past.

PART II

ENTERING INTO AND THINKING ABOUT DIFFERENT-ORIGIN MARRIAGES

[2]

UNDERSTANDINGS OF CLASS

With a glass of red wine for him and a glass of water for me, I sat in William's inviting home—one that balanced artistic tastes with the clutter of his daughters' books, shoes, and drawings. Though he dressed in black slacks and a collared shirt covered by a pastel blue sweater, I was not surprised when William (blue-collar-origin) said he spent several years in the military. His voice boomed as if he was used to giving orders. His hair remained in a buzz cut, and he had broad shoulders and appeared physically fit. He was a captivating storyteller, and for two hours I was mesmerized by tales of his life. He spoke of growing up in a small southern town and living just blocks from his aunts, uncles, and grandparents. He talked of having a hardworking mother, an alcoholic but loving father, and a stepfather to whom he was close. He met his wife, Anneka, when they were both in the military and quickly realized that he would abandon his plans to live a bachelor's life if he could marry her. In what he described as a fantastic ceremony, he wedded Anneka, and remained very happy that he did so.

After two hours of hearing about his life, I asked William if there was anything else he wanted to tell me. His eyes filled with tears as he said that class did not matter in his marriage. In a southern accent he relayed: "I don't pay attention to any differences as to where we came from, Anneka and me. I really don't. Because I really don't think that anybody in my family loved me any less than anyone in hers."

William's reaction surprised me. His tears surprised me not just because of his military background, large build, and booming voice, but also because he had been cheerful for the majority of the interview, before my questions about class began. His statement also surprised me because I did not know why he felt that class was associated with who was loved more. My questions were about similarities and differences, but not about a hierarchy of experiences and definitely not about whose family loved who more. Nothing in his interview made me doubt that his family loved him, regardless of what class he was from.

On top of his passionate reaction, his denial that he thought about class also surprised me. The class differences between him and his wife were large enough that I imagined he would have considered how they shaped his marriage. He felt that he grew up in "the lowest" class. He grew up in a trailer, and his mother regularly borrowed money from relatives to pay their bills. He grew up thinking that everyone in his poor, rural, southern community had more than he did. His wife, Anneka, a thoughtful woman with curly blonde hair and an athletic build, did not share his childhood way of life. She felt that she had more than most of those around her, and she certainly had more than William did when he was growing up. She was raised in a townhouse, not a trailer, and never worried about whether her parents could pay the bills or if the electricity would be shut off. Her father held a PhD and was around enough other Ivy League graduates to know that he found them intolerable. Her mother held a master's degree and taught math at a school that rich children attended. Anneka did not tell her classmates about her parents' occupations and educations for fear of intimidating them.

I expected that these differences—which were shared in the stories they told each other and lived when they visited each other's families—would have led them to understand that class was not an empty category or a meaningless word. Class was something that was lived; it shaped who they were and how each wanted to attend to their lives. It shaped, as the coming chapters will show, how they thought about money, work, and play. But, contrary to my expectations, William did not "pay attention" to their class differences. Though he realized that they came from different classes, he did not think that class was a difference that made a difference.

William's opinions were representative. Most respondents entered into their relationships without thinking that their partner was shaped by class. After years of marriage, most continued to overlook the ways that class was associated with their daily decisions and dissimilar ideas. They saw their differences as stemming from their personalities, not also from the class of their past.

These findings meant that not only were those in different-origin marriages oblivious to the reasons why their marriages took the form they did but also that being with a partner from another class was not enough to produce class awareness. Contrary to the predictions of others (Blossfeld 2009; Hazelrigg and Lopreato 1972; Kalmijn 1991, 1998; Leiulfsrud and Woodward 1989), years together rarely produced knowledge of tilted playing fields or patterned sensibilities. Even in the minority of cases when increased class awareness coincided with living in a different-origin marriage, it rarely led to increased comfort in a network of those born into another class.[1] Forming a relationship with their partner rarely prompted them to want to form more relationships with people from their partner's class.

This chapter accomplishes two tasks. First, it reveals how respondents understood the role class played in their marriage. It does so by illustrating how respondents initially realized that their partner was raised in another class and by establishing how they thought class mattered in their marriage. Second, the chapter exposes that different-origin marriages should not be romanticized as conduits to class awareness or as relationships that broker more appreciation for those from another class. Usually, class shaped respondents' marriages without their knowledge.

AWARENESS OF ENTERING INTO A DIFFERENT-ORIGIN MARRIAGE

It is conceivable that individuals might have purposefully tried to marry across class lines; this section shows that this rarely happened. Several respondents were unaware that their partner came from another class and the remainder tended not to see their partner as influenced by their class background. For the majority of respondents, entering into a different-origin marriage did not entail thinking about their partner's class past.

Denying, Downplaying, or Disregarding Their Different Origins

George (blue-collar-origin), a talkative and energetic man with a loud voice, red hair, and rectangular glasses, grew up with a father who worked in a factory and a mother who worked at home without pay. He spent his childhood in a cookie-cutter house in a town that was populated by families who worked in blue-collar jobs in the auto industry. His family's income was stable but did not provide enough to cover vacations or leave his family free from financial worries. George married Norah, a gregarious and proudly nerdy woman with big glasses and a penchant for reading. She was raised by a father who presided over laboratories at a large hospital and a mother who spent her time trying to keep up with the upper-class fashions in their neighborhood. Unlike George, Norah grew up with access to balls and galas, music lessons and museums, as well as faraway vacations. By many measures, Norah and George grew up in different classes.

George, however, did not register their class differences. When I asked him when he first realized he and Norah were from different classes—a leading question, given that it did not occur to me that he would fail to notice the differences that I found so apparent—he replied that he had thought about it only when I asked the question. He laughed as he replied: "I guess we're from different class backgrounds!" In eight years of marriage, the idea that he and Norah grew up on different rungs of the class ladder had not occurred to him.

Similarly, Adam (blue-collar-origin), a reserved, competitive, former valedictorian whose parents emigrated from southern Europe, had not considered that he and his wife, Andrea, began their lives in different classes. Adam's father's earnings as an electrician were spread thin as they provided for his family of 10. Adam was the first in his family to step foot on a campus as a college student; his mother had a high school degree and his father earned a GED. Andrea's parents, by contrast, were both college educated. Her father had a position as an engineer, and his income provided her and her siblings with more as there were fewer of them. Adam, however, never considered these differences. When I asked him when he first realized that he and Andrea were from different classes, he said: "When I saw your e-mail. I never really thought of it. I thought we were just middle-class, suburban people from the Midwest. It never struck me that [my in-laws] went to college . . . I never really thought about it."

Other respondents not only did not think about their class differences but also downplayed or denied them. Eric (white-collar-origin), a handsome, warm, sociable former fraternity member, grew up in a neighborhood well-off enough that he distinctly remembered the first time he encountered a peer who could not afford to buy a school lunch. Jill (blue-collar-origin), an attractive and kind woman from an Italian-American family, was raised by a father who socialized with plumbers in order to remind himself that he earned a little more than others. Even though Jill believed she and Eric came from different classes, Eric did not. He said: "I still don't consider us from different class backgrounds today. It's funny, because when Jill told me about this research I was like, 'What? Why? How do we fit that?' And she was like, 'Well your dad was a doctor; mine wasn't.'" Though his wife thought they were from different classes, Eric had not thought about it, and when he did, he did not agree.

Mary (white-collar-origin), a tall, thin, fashionable woman who graduated at the top of her law school class, also denied that she and her husband, Ben, came from different classes. Mary's father had a PhD and worked as a professor at a small university. Her mother received a master's degree and worked as a teacher. Her husband, Ben, a laid-back, friendly, middle-aged man with red hair and a goatee, in contrast, was raised by two parents with high school degrees. His father worked as an electrician and his mother did not work for pay. Mary did not believe that these differences meant that she and her husband were raised in different classes. Neither she nor Ben grew up lacking anything, so she assumed both were raised in the middle class. Their backgrounds, she deemed, were not different.

These respondents who did not think about or denied their class differences comprised 20 percent of the sample. This group included relatively equal numbers of men and women, and those from blue- and white-collar backgrounds. Those whose class differed from their partner's in major and minor ways were also included, as were those who had a partner who affirmed their class differences. This group did not purposefully enter into a different-origin marriage, nor did their marriage provide them with insight into how class shaped their lives. As they overlooked, downplayed, or denied their differences, they did not end up considering class much at all.

Given that they stepped into each other's class worlds as they visited their in-laws and imagined their partners' pasts, their lack of class awareness requires some explanation. The first reason why they did not see their class differences may simply be that class is difficult to recognize. Race may be read from skin color, and gender from anatomy,[2] but class is more difficult to identify as it is less associated with the body. Clothes can be changed and jewelry can be bought with loaned money, making personal adornments difficult to use to interpret class position. Additionally, Americans tend to conflate whiteness with the middle class (Ortner 2003), which may lead whites to overlook class differences between themselves and other whites.

Moreover, while American social movements have positioned race and gender as differences that matter, no such social movement has revealed the ways that the class individuals are born into can shape their life chances and lifestyles.[3] Instead, the prevailing idea is that class matters little in the land of opportunity and the home of the American Dream because anyone born in the United States can grow up to become rich. This discourse obscures the fact that childhood class position shapes life chances (Corcoran 1995), and it does not even consider the idea that sensibilities are shaped by the class of one's youth. Americans are then not readily prompted to recognize class differences or even to think that class can be readily identified. They are certainly not primed to think about how class shapes the people they love.

Class differences were also denied because of the flexible and contested nature of class boundaries. Though the average person may feel fairly confident that they can differentiate women from men or whites from blacks,[4] it is less clear where the line is that differentiates the middle class from the working class or the working class from the poor. This confusion allows class boundaries to be drawn strategically, including and excluding individuals as one wishes. People tend to see the middle class as normal (DeMott 1992), and the lack of fixed class lines allows people to draw class boundaries that are wide enough to situate their own and their partner's class origin in the normalized middle class. Mary, for example, could decide that she and her husband were both middle class because neither lacked any necessities. Another respondent, John, believed that he and his wife both came from middle-class families because they each had parents who worked hard. The difficulty of seeing class and the ease of drawing one's own boundaries meant that 20 percent of respondents in different-origin marriages did not think their partner grew up in a class they did not share. Given their lack of awareness of their class backgrounds, their marriages would not result in their learning more about how class shaped opportunities and sensibilities.

Acknowledging Class Differences Without Acknowledging That Each Partner Is Classed

The remaining 80 percent of respondents believed that they were in a marriage that spanned one class divide, that of their class origin. However, the way most remembered learning of their partner's different class background is telling for how they later thought about class in their relationship. Only four respondents said they picked up on their partner's class background from the stories they told, the obstacles they faced, the tastes they displayed, or their ideas of what was to come. Rather, they said they ascertained their partner's background through their partner's *parents'* tastes, homes, and occupations. Effectively, they saw their partners' parents as shaped by class but not their partners' themselves.

Rachel (blue-collar-origin), a stocky woman with short gray hair and a large gap in her front teeth, grew up in a different class than her husband, Gordon. Rachel was raised by a mother who earned a GED and spent her time fixing fences and riding horses. Rachel's father was a gruff cop who dressed in cowboy boots and baseball caps. His aspiration for Rachel was that she not end up in jail, a fate that she once tempted when she sold drugs out of their family home. Her own aspirations shifted from being a wife to a stewardess or even a nun. She thought college was not for her and dropped out of high school before returning to get her GED and then, years later, her college degree. Rachel's husband, Gordon, grew up geographically close to her but in a family that was socially distant. Gordon (white-collar-origin), a tall, shy man who loved playing hockey, was raised by an MBA-holding father who wore cardigans and corduroys and a mother with an English literature degree who was still offended by the word "shit." Though he was a newly employed, recovering alcoholic when Rachel met him, he still carried with him his class tastes and sensibilities. His English reflected the proper grammar that his mother cared so much about, and when he walked into the rough bar where he met Rachel, he carried a tray of sushi.

Rachel did not recognize the class signals that Gordon transmitted. Instead, she said she first noticed their different class backgrounds when she met Gordon's parents. She explained how their class differences dawned upon her: "The day I met his parents, they were taking us to a play. They took us to the play *Elephant Man*. And I don't think I have ever been to the theater with my parents. My family had been to county fairs and rodeos, and Gordon's family goes to concerts or plays." Rachel was able to read the class signs that Gordon's parents transmitted. She knew that the theater was associated with a class that she did not share. She had not, however, been able to read the class signals that were associated with Gordon's sensibilities and tastes. Class was made visible by Gordon's parents, not Gordon himself.

Dan (white-collar-origin), similarly, did not realize that he and Gabriella grew up in different classes until, after a year of dating, he visited her mother. Dan, the son of an engineer and an artist, walked into Gabriella's mother's home and gazed upon a sea of crystal figurines. He remembered his reaction: "Oh my God! I don't know what to do with this!" Dan found the figurines to be tacky and distasteful, a signal of low culture and a lower class. Yet, despite that he had visited Gabriella's apartment several times and found it artistically uninspiring, he did not associate her tastes with her background. It took being bowled over by his mother-in-law's figurines for him to understand that their class backgrounds were not the same. Dan, Rachel, and other respondents like them recognized that they grew up in a different class than their partner only after meeting their partners' parents. They were able to interpret class signals that came from their in-laws but not their partners themselves.[5]

Others discerned their partner's class upbringing by asking about their parents' occupations and educations. Norah (white-collar-origin) said she first figured out their class differences "pretty much as quickly as we went over the family history." Matt (white-collar-origin) explained: "It was just the kind of thing, like [on the] second date, 'So what's your dad do?' So you kind of know that going in." Joe (blue-collar-origin) agreed: "You pretty much know after you talk to somebody for a while. You know, 'What do your parents do?' 'What do my parents do?' It comes out soon enough." They first realized their partners' class background because they asked; that they learned through asking suggests that they did not think class was readable from other cues.

Only four respondents first discerned their partners' class origin from something associated with their spouse, not their spouses' parents. Amelia (white-collar-origin) met Isaac (blue-collar origin) when they began working together as colleagues. She identified that their similar positions belied their different pasts when she first heard Isaac say "ain't." Danielle (blue-collar-origin) realized that Jim (white-collar-origin) was raised with more class privilege when he said that he graduated from a prestigious college and then moved back home. Those things, she knew, "didn't happen in my world." Jason (blue-collar-origin) concluded that he and Lori grew up in different social spheres when she recounted her vacations to Europe. To him, vacations meant rolling out sleeping bags on his grandmother's floor. He knew Lori's idea of a vacation signaled that her family could afford leisure activities that his could not.[6]

That Amelia, Danielle, and Jason were able to connect their partners' experiences to their class origin demonstrates that it was possible for respondents to use the present to understand their partners' class past. Most respondents, however, likely had similar conversations and were exposed to similar cues but did not interpret them as conveying class signals. Without seeing their partners as people who had class-inflected tastes or sensibilities, they were then unable to gain an understanding of how class mattered in their marriage.

RESPONDENTS' UNDERSTANDING OF THE ROLE CLASS PLAYS IN THEIR MARRIAGE

Four-fifths of respondents who married a partner whose father had a different type of occupation and education than their own father thought they were in a different-class marriage. But knowing that their fathers worked different types of jobs and had varying amounts of formal education is very different than believing that these differences matter. This section examines how respondents thought about the role class played in their marriages. Identifying how those in different-origin marriages think about class is important for understanding individuals' ability to grasp class more generally. If they do not understand how class shapes sensibilities after years of living with a loved one who was shaped by the conditions of their past, they are unlikely to recognize how class matters in more dynamic and less intimate relationships.

Few respondents believed that their marriages were influenced by class. In fact, many felt strongly that class did not and could not shape their identity or their marriage. Asked if they thought class mattered in their relationship, respondents often forcefully denied the relevance of their different backgrounds.

KEVIN (BLUE-COLLAR-ORIGIN): I don't see how it makes any difference. I think it's just an artificial distinction.

LESLIE (WHITE-COLLAR-ORIGIN): It's really not an issue to us, not that I know of anyway. Tom might say differently, but I'm not aware of it.

COLTON (WHITE-COLLAR-ORIGIN): No, it's not really important to us . . . It's really a non-issue.

Others just said "no" when asked if they ever think about their class differences. Most respondents indicated that their class differences were insignificant in their lives and in their marriages. They did not think about class, because, in the words of Kevin (blue-collar-origin) and Colton (white-collar-origin), it was an artificial and unimportant distinction.[7]

Respondents' denial of the influence of class recurred as they responded to questions about what advice they had to offer others in different-origin marriages. Because they thought class was inconsequential, the advice they offered was to ignore each other's class background. Tom, Rachel, and Norah gave a representative sample of this modal reply.

TOM (BLUE-COLLAR-ORIGIN): Advice. I think the best thing I could say is just don't pay much attention to it. It's really not important.

RACHEL (BLUE-COLLAR-ORIGIN): I would say it doesn't matter. I'd say marry for love.

NORAH (WHITE-COLLAR-ORIGIN): I would basically say, "Look at the person and not their family."

Most often, those in different-origin marriages were not aware of how class impacted their marriage. They denied that class had any sway on their relationship or that it was worth thinking about at all. These respondents maintained that their class origin was irrelevant to their own identity, their partner's identity, and their marriage. Their marriages did not increase their understanding of class, as they were confident that class was a category that they already understood—they understood that it was irrelevant.

A subset of respondents—about 20 percent of those in different-origin marriages—did believe that coming from different class backgrounds *could* have an impact on marriage. However, most did not see how class mattered in their own relationship. Isaac (blue-collar-origin), a stocky man with strong hands and gray facial hair, was the fifth of ten children born to a father who worked in a factory and had a fourth-grade education and a mother who rarely left their home after receiving her high school diploma. Isaac grew up in a deindustrializing city that was rough and poor. As a teenager he thought he would end up in the military or jail. His wife, Amelia (white-collar-origin), a short, serious woman, grew up in safe suburbs with a father who worked as a university president and a mother who earned a master's degree and worked as a housewife. Isaac thought that coming from different class backgrounds *could* make a difference but thought that it did not matter in his marriage as he and Amelia married relatively late: "We were older [when we met]. We both had master's degrees. We were both solid in what we were doing. Very confident. And we didn't have to change a lot. So that's clearly a different ballgame than if you're eighteen and you're marrying somebody from a different class." In other words, Isaac thought that class differences might matter for couples who married at a young age but that the influence of class was erased for those like him who married once they had stable jobs and graduate degrees.

Bob (blue-collar-origin), a short, balding middle-aged man, similarly thought that class could matter for other couples whose class pasts were discrepant but that class did not matter in his situation. Bob grew up with a father who told him that the key to not becoming like him—a truck driver who worked 16-hour days—was to go to college. His wife, Bethany (white-collar-origin), a warm doctor with pearl earrings and bangs that swept over her forehead, grew up in what she knew others thought of as a mansion and with the certainty that she would graduate from college. Bob's advice to other couples in different-origin marriages was to talk about each spouse's background: "Their experience will be different than your experiences . . . Just don't be afraid to talk about the differences." Yet, when asked if he talked about these differences with Bethany, he said that he rarely did. Their class differences, he said, were not wide enough to occasion discussion. He could see how class might matter for other people's marriages, but, he maintained, it did not matter for his own. Their marriages then did not lead to greater class understandings, as they thought class differences affected other people but not themselves.

WHAT DID CLASS MEAN TO THEM?

The following chapters reveal that class did, in fact, shape their marriages and did so quite profoundly. Respondents recounted differences in how they and their partner thought about money, paid work, leisure, housework, time, parenting, and emotions. The data in the following chapters came from the stories they told about their lives, but they still did not think that class mattered in their marriage. More strikingly, some were able to talk fluently about class in other aspects of their lives. As mentioned, many recognized their in-laws' tastes as reflections of their opportunities. Several also described how their class background limited (or enhanced) their own opportunities, and many eloquently described the ways that class mapped onto the social landscape of their high schools. But while they were able to talk about class in some aspects of their lives, most saw it as divorced from their marriage. How could they be aware of class in some aspects of their lives while maintaining that their relationship was a sacred site that class did not touch? Why, in other words, were they not able to use their marriage to learn more about how class works?

The answers lie in how respondents understood class more generally. They did not understand childhood class conditions as producing long-lasting sensibilities. Rather, some saw class as only about money and education, some simply did not think of class in relation to their marriage, and others found class to be about judgments of who was better than whom. Instead of thinking about how class shaped them, they preferred to think of themselves as unique individuals in love. Their differences, they thought, derived from their idiosyncratic personalities. They were then aware that they and their partners had different sensibilities, but they simply did not attribute them to social class.

Class as in the Past

Some respondents did not see their partners as classed people because they focused on their present circumstances, not their past ones. As such, they thought their past differences were eclipsed by their current situation, for example, by having shared degrees.

Nathan (blue-collar-origin), for instance, said: "Chelsey and I were so much alike even though we came from different backgrounds. We had both graduated from college and we were working to succeed. So her and I really weren't that different in that regard when we met." Andrea (white-collar-origin) made a similar point when asked if she thinks about her and her husband's past class differences: "At this point his education is higher than mine . . . It doesn't seem like it affects us."

Class as Unthinkable

Others did not think about class simply because it was unthinkable. When asked, many identified that they were raised with more or less class privilege than their spouse, but the lack of a broad class discourse meant that outside of the interview they simply did not think about class. When asked if she ever thought about how class played out in her marriage, Evelyn (blue-collar-origin) replied: "That never occurs to me." Anneka (white-collar-origin) regularly forgot that she and her husband, William, did not share a class background:

> I forget about it. I'm almost surprised when he'll occasionally mention something like, "Growing up we never had X." And I'm like, "Really? Oh, well of course you didn't." I haven't internalized it I guess.

Anneka realized that she and William were from different class backgrounds, but even with her personalized window into his classed past, she could not remember to think that they had class differences, let alone that they might matter. Americans tend not to dwell on class (DeMott 1992), and even with her husband's reminders of their difference she did not consider the implications of their class backgrounds. Individuals may be blind to how class shapes their marriages simply because class is unthinkable.

Class as a Signal of Moral Worth

Others did not consider class to be relevant because they believed that class was about assigning moral worth—determining who was superior to whom. They did not want to judge others, so they did not think about class. Caroline (white-collar-origin) said: "I don't think [about our class differences] because I don't think my parents raised me to be snotty." Aaron (blue-collar-origin) agreed, noting that his mother taught him "don't judge." Jim (white-collar-origin) angrily explained, "It would only be if you were looking in black and white, things were different. But we don't have a great sense that one person is better than the other person, more privileged or anything like that . . . Class doesn't make a damned difference." Ben (blue-collar-origin) was one of several blue-collar-origin men who had a similar strong feeling:

> Ultimately it comes down to I don't want to put myself in a class. I don't think I'm better than anybody else. I don't think I'm worse than anybody else. So to me, that's what the classes do. "The reason you're in this class is because you fit this criteria." Well, I don't give a shit about your criteria.

These respondents were visibly angry or tearful when making claims that class was irrelevant to their marriage as they gave little thought to who was better than whom. The question was offensive to them, as they thought that the question implied not only differences but also statements about who was morally superior.

Respondents' association of class with morality makes sense given the language that is often associated with class. Those who try hard and are morally righteous, according to the tenets of the American Dream, get ahead. Those who are poor must then be lazy and morally suspect. Furthermore, the language used to talk about class is often morally coded. People move "up" and "down" the class ladder rather than just through it. A "classy" event is a good one, and a "good family" is often one that is at least middle class. People at the top of the class ladder are at least partially celebrated while those at the bottom are called leaches, parasites, and welfare queens (Kendall 2011).

Respondents had picked up the morally coded language that is often infused in discussions of class and learned to associate class with others' moral worth. Such a conflation is problematic for the same reasons that the colorblind ideology is problematic for race relations: it masks the structural nature of class and assumes that not talking about it will make class differences matter less (see Bonilla-Silva 2003 for a discussion of colorblind racism). In this case, the moralized nature of class positioned it as a taboo topic— admitting to thinking about class would be admitting that one is a classist. This discourse then allowed some to acknowledge that they grew up in a different class than their spouse while simultaneously preventing them from further exploring the topic. The conflation of class and morality inhibited respondents from using their marriage as a launching pad to learn more about how class works.

If Class Was Not on Their Minds, What Was?

There were three key reasons why most respondents did not think that class was connected to the intimate aspects of their lives. They did not want to judge, class was off their radar, or they connected class only to their current position. How, then, did they understand their marriage? They noticed the differences, which appear in the following chapters, but they attributed them to personality rather than to class. Christie (blue-collar-origin), for example, said: "I don't think that it was the actual economic part that made the tension for Mike and I. It was personality style more than class or money." Eric (white-collar-origin) agreed: "You know, it's funny, all this talking about class, because I view people in relationships as personalities and stuff like that." When, at the very end of the interview, I explained to Scott (white-collar-origin), one of the last people I interviewed, the purpose of the study, he asked: "So those things are all predictable based on class?" He and his wife, Gina, were more different than they were alike, but to him the differences were about their idiosyncratic personalities, not about class. Most respondents thought in terms of personality differences between two unique individuals in love.

THE EXCEPTIONS: WHEN DIFFERENT-ORIGIN MARRIAGE ENABLED GREATER CLASS UNDERSTANDING

Different-origin marriages were rarely associated with gaining a better understanding of how class works, but that did not mean that such insight could not be gained. Ten of the 64 respondents in different-origin marriages did think their marriage was shaped by class and used their marital experiences to draw broader conclusions about how class shapes opportunities and sensibilities.[8] Eight of the ten who did so either had backgrounds in the social sciences or related disciplines, or were married to a partner who did.[9] This suggests that class may be easier to recognize if individuals are exposed to a curriculum that is likely to de-moralize class and relate macro class conditions to daily life circumstances. However, even when marriages served as incubators for class understandings, they rarely generated the desire to engage in more cross-class relationships.

Ian, for example, married Isabelle, a women's studies major who worked as a therapist. Before meeting Isabelle, Ian had barely considered the concept of class. In college he read Marx and Engels and came to the realization that social classes exist. His wife's teaching taught him not only that class inequality exists but also about how it plays out in everyday life. He saw the financial hardships that his wife's family faced and learned that his family was comparably well-off. He learned that his wife's entire family lived in the same small town and concluded that moving often and far-away was more emblematic of the lifestyle of his class than hers. He observed that he felt more comfortable in elegant restaurants and in graduate school, and discerned that his background gave him a sense of ease in these settings that his wife's background did not provide her. His wife, Isabelle, whose class awareness preceded his, helped Ian see these differences and attribute them to class. With Isabelle as his guide, Ian was able to use their experiences to learn more about class.

Lori and Jason, who both worked in fields related to the social sciences, also learned about how class worked through their marriage. Jason, an intelligent man and captivating storyteller, spent months during the early stages of their relationship telling Lori: "Well, look, I'm sorry. You can go on about how you really don't have any money, but it's not ordinary to go to prep school, it's not ordinary to have a family that has three homes. I don't care if two of them belong to your grandmother. It's not normal to have these servants." After Lori ended her months of resistance and realized that she grew up in the upper class, she joined Jason in interpreting her experiences through a class lens. For the first time, she admitted that her legacy status and grandmother's donations paved the way for her to enter an elite college. With Jason's help, she realized that lacking the most fashionable wardrobe did not immediately drop her from wealthy to middle class. Through her marriage, she learned to more correctly identify her position on the class ladder.[10]

Together, she and Jason also learned to connect class to culture. When Jason's younger brother teasingly asked Lori if her arm wasn't long enough to reach across the table to grab the paper towels rather than have him pass them to her, they realized that ideas of etiquette differed across classes. When Lori demanded that Jason throw out his polyester pants, they knew their fashion differences were associated with the classes from which they came. And when Lori was appalled by Jason's suggestion that they eat at Kentucky Fried Chicken—even, in a fit of disgust, calling Jason a "plebe"—they realized that the food they enjoyed was associated with their class backgrounds. They acknowledged that class was about more than money; it was also associated with the opportunities it provided and the tastes and sensibilities it cultivated.

A minority of spouses used their marriage to gain an understanding of their place in the class system and the connections between class and culture. However, the understandings that this small subset of respondents obtained should not be romanticized or assumed useful for broader class action. Jason's love for Lori did not extend to an appreciation for the upper class. He described his workplace—one that included several colleagues with upper-class backgrounds—as "enemy territory," a place where he actively hid his lower class roots. He could not imagine marrying anyone else in the upper class and found himself loathing some of the elite members of his wife's social circles. For Jason, like for others, love of a spouse from another class did not prompt him to want to form more relationships with those from his wife's class.

CONCLUSION

Married people today are meant to know each other intimately. In many ways, the respondents in this study did. They knew that their partner grew up in a mansion or in a small ranch house. They knew their partner's parents scraped up enough money for a homemade ping pong table or that they saved enough to spend a week a year sightseeing in another state. They knew that one of their sets of parents worked on a factory line and another behind more comfortable desks. They visited each other's childhood homes and recognized that one partner grew up in a much larger home, lived in a nicer neighborhood, or went to a better school. They knew these details, and they could recount them when asked. But most did not think of them often. When they did think of them, they did not think they mattered. The differences, as they saw it, were in the past and unimportant anyway. They did not shape who each person became. They certainly did not matter when it came to love and marriage.

Most respondents were like William. Though 20 percent of respondents had not thought about or denied growing up in a different class than their spouse, 80 percent, William included, observed that they and their partner were born into families in different classes. Yet, knowing this did not lead them to pay attention to it. In fact, most saw little reason to give it any thought. Most initially saw their partners as people who came from classed parents but who were not shaped by class themselves. Once married, most thought they kept love and class separate. They saw their partners as people with specific personalities, not people who were shaped by the class of their past.

As class never became etched on their minds, they missed the ways that it mattered in who they were and who they loved. Their marriages were usually not experiential learning sites; ones where they compared their partner's upbringing to their own and drew conclusions about how class influenced their lives. Rather, most different-origin marriages offered little hope that intimate exposure to a partner from another class can raise class awareness. When class awareness was raised through marriage—which occurred for a minority of spouses—it did not usually dissolve further class divides. Respondents loved their partners, but their love did not typically extend to loving the sensibilities of others from their partner's class.

Thus, respondents tended to enter into their marriage with little understanding of themselves or their partners as people who were shaped by the class of their past. Yet their lack of awareness of class did not prevent it from deeply informing their lives. The next chapter reveals the hidden ways that class was related to the stories spouses told about the beginnings of their relationships—about why they chose the person whom they vowed to have and to hold.

[3]

ACCOUNTS OF CROSSING THE CLASS DIVIDE

Vicki, a middle-aged woman who wore leggings and an oversized T-shirt during our interview at her midsized home, felt that her mother raised her to be classist. Her college-educated mother had grown up surrounded by luxuries—a mansion for daily life, an island home for vacations, maids to serve her, and the finest clothes to wear.[1] Vicki's mother taught her that such items were important and that people who possessed them were better than those without them. According to her mother, people who use Standard English are better than those who do not, and people who live in mansions are superior to those who live in mobile homes. Unlike the vast majority of respondents in this study, Vicki learned to recognize social class explicitly and to make judgments based upon it.

Vicki consciously rejected her mother's classism, but when she became involved with her future husband, John, she felt she could not suppress it. She remembered: "When I first met John's parents I had a complete reaction that was like my mom would have. How she trained us to be. Like, 'Oh, yeah, that's blue collar.' Or, 'They're blue collar. They're not well-educated. They don't speak well.'" She continued: "The way they talk and dress, the way they decorate their house, the kind of things they were interested in—all really

42

kind of stereotypically blue collar." Specifically, Vicki remembered that John's parents' home was decorated with hundreds of porcelain figurines, that his family was deeply religious, and that John's father worshipped his motorcycle. These were all things that Vicki's mother had taught her to disdain and, in turn, to disdain the people who liked them. Nevertheless, Vicki decided to marry John, a short, bearded man who talked in clichés and inherited many of his parents' tastes.

Ian and Isabelle also grew up with different exposures to luxury. Ian's mother did not believe in the superiority of her class; rather, she believed that "underneath it all we're all the same." This led her to repeatedly avow that Isabelle's upbringing in a rural community was "so idyllic and wonderful." That was not, however, how Isabelle experienced her childhood. She felt that being raised by parents who had their first child as teenagers was a struggle. She remembered the guilt she felt every time she asked for lunch money and the exclamation her mother made when handing it to her: "That school, it's taking all of our money!" She recalled shying away from classmates so they would not inhale the smell of cows that had sunk into her clothes, ones that her mom had made. And she remembered that "all of [my mother's co-workers'] kids who were around my age were all kind of fuck-ups. You know, they were dropping out of high school, getting pregnant."

Ian, a confident, youthful-looking man in his late 30s, also grew up around "fuck-ups"—those who snorted cocaine in mansions on the Florida coast. They were people who made Isabelle wonder, upon first meeting them, "Who are these people? I don't even understand this." There were other parts of Ian's life that she did not understand. Ian hailed from a lineage of academics; a building on a small college campus was named after his great-grandfather, and nearly everyone on his mother's side of the family had a PhD, MD, or JD after their name. When Isabelle met Ian, on the other hand, she did not have a sense that college was a place where she fully belonged and attending graduate school was unimaginable. Isabelle also did not know the everyday etiquette of Ian's world. She remembered asking Ian how to load his father's dishwasher and where to place the forks on the table.

Cultural matching theory would predict that when Isabelle and Ian met at a selective liberal arts college, or when Vicki and John met at the restaurant where they both worked while attending college, they would not have found each other of interest.[2] According to cultural matching theory—a theory that suggests that people like each other when they have internalized similar tastes and sensibilities and dislike each other when they have not (Bourdieu 1984; Kalmijn 1998; Lizardo 2006)—Vicki's disdain for John's language style, leisure habits, and tastes would have led her to avoid him. For his part, John would have wanted to pair with someone who appreciated his family's religion, art, and motorcycles rather than disparage them. Likewise, when Isabelle's father picked her up from college with dead chickens in the bed of his pickup truck, Ian would have felt that his own background was too different from Isabelle's to make a relationship work, and Isabelle would have preferred a partner who understood the way she was raised. If cultural matching theory applied to different-origin couples, each respondent would remember feeling solely repelled by their partner's differences.[3] Given that the couples married, this is unlikely to be the case.

Another theory, exchange theory, suggests, in contrast, that differences can be appealing. This theory predicts that pairs are formed when each person lacks a resource that the other possesses (Davis 1941; Merton 1941). Usually, researchers deductively test what resources are exchanged. When it comes to different-origin marriages, they typically test whether the more privileged partner trades their economic resources for the less privileged partner's physical resources—their good looks—or their human resources, such as their educational attainment or prestige (Arum, Roksa, and Budig 2008; Elder 1969; Schoen and Wooldredge 1989; Skopek, Schulz, and Blossfeld 2009; South 1991; Taylor and Glenn 1976). But while exchange theory offers a way to explain patterns of who marries whom, it is less able to explain why people *believe* they marry the person they do. In contemporary American society, few people talk of falling in love with their partner for their economic resources or their prestigious university degree. Instead they talk of resources exchange theorists do not examine—their partner's sensibilities or tastes (Bourdieu 1984). In this chapter, I argue that a specific type of cultural difference should no longer be overlooked as a source of exchange or viewed only as a deterrent to relationship formation. Rather, this specific type of cultural difference is what respondents believed brought them together.

ACCOUNTS OF LOVE CROSSING CLASS LINES

One theory ignores dissimilar sensibilities while another sees them as facilitating disdain rather than affection. Yet, respondents remembered specific types of dissimilar sensibilities, ones that I call "cultural complements," as a key reason why they originally fell in love with their partner. Cultural complements are the obverse of the sensibility that each partner desired but felt they lacked. Upwardly mobile, blue-collar-origin respondents often remembered that when they met their spouse they lacked a sense of stability and achievement; they said they were drawn to partners who possessed these traits. White-collar-origin respondents often remembered feeling that they lacked familial intimacy and the ability to disconnect from work and said they were drawn to partners whose sensibilities and experiences were the opposite of their own.

That these specific cultural complements resonated with these particular respondents was not coincidental. Sensibilities are internalized at an early age through repeated experiences in a particular social class (Bourdieu 1984). People who grow up with a lot of resources tend to internalize one set of sensibilities, and people who grow up with few tend to internalize an opposing set (Bourdieu 1984). Respondents drew upon these opposing sensibilities when explaining their early love of their partner. Thus, the stories they told of why they initially felt drawn to their spouse were not, as they imagined, unique to themselves and their spouse, but integrally related to the classes in which they and their partner were raised.

A Cultural Complement: A Sense of Stability

About two decades ago, Isabelle (blue-collar-origin), a blond feminist dressed in a sweater, jeans, and plain black pumps on the day of our interview, fell in love with Ian (white-collar-origin), an angry punk rocker whom she met at the selective liberal arts college that they both attended. She remembered that her attraction to him was based upon the cultural complement he provided. For Isabelle, a financially difficult upbringing on a farm meant that her childhood was unstable. Her family did not know how much income each season of crops would produce or when the next debt collector would call. Isabelle grew up feeling that the future was uncertain and that a bad event could cause a catastrophe at any time. Ian did not feel the same way. His family's history of success gave him the confidence that he, too, would be successful, and his mother's wealth and father's earnings provided him with a stable life free of financial struggle and perpetual worry. His stable life allowed him to internalize and project a sense of stability—one that Isabelle recalled enjoying. Asked why she was initially interested in Ian, Isabelle replied: "I found him to be very stable and solid, which was very nice."

Isabelle was not the only respondent who felt that she internalized a sense of instability as she grew up. Rather, this feeling was common to the women who shared her class background. Since the 1970s, blue-collar workers' wages have stagnated, and many farming and factory jobs have disappeared. Numerous unions disbanded and much of the social safety net eroded (Duncan and Murnane 2011; Morris and Western 1999). These changes made stability a precarious state for many blue-collar workers. Given that children internalize the external conditions that surround them (Bourdieu 1980), blue-collar children who grew up during this time period were likely to internalize a sense of instability.

During the same time period, children from white-collar families had more reason to internalize and project a sense of stability. The wages of college-educated workers rose, and job security was comparatively common for professional white-collar workers (Autor, Katz, Kearney 2008; Morris and Western 1999). Inequality rose as well, giving the children of college-educated parents more advantages (Kornrich and Furstenberg 2012). Children in professional white-collar families tended to assume that their lives would resemble that of their parents—they, too, would receive a college degree and work in stable jobs (Bozick et al. 2010; Goyette 2008). Thus, while blue-collar-origin respondents were likely to find a sense of stability elusive, those with white-collar-origins were not.

Madison (blue-collar-origin), a petite, pensive woman, also experienced the insecurity that her class conditions engendered and reported feeling drawn to a partner whose class conditions were associated with more stability. Madison met Evan (white-collar-origin), an introverted, thin, thoughtful man, on a high school hiking trip (see Appendix B for a table on how couples met). As Madison was introduced to her husband's family, she noticed the differences between his parents and her own. She grew up with a father who was "very much a blue-collar man." She recalled that: "My dad would do the whole guy thing, nachos and Sunday football." She compared her father to Evan's father: "Evan's dad, he would always have his shirt tucked into his jeans or his slacks with a belt whereas my dad would [have his] shirt out." Their mothers differed too. Evan's mother, according to Madison, "always sits with a straight back . . . very controlled and restrained." She described her own mother as more casual and extroverted, enjoying gossip, pointing out others' tacky shoes, and dreaming of the future. One of the things Madison and her mother dreamed of was a life like the one Evan's family already possessed: "[His family was] already where I had wanted to be . . . His parents are the people who go to the local theater and try local restaurants and . . . travel."

What struck Madison the most about Evan and his family, however, was not their clothes or their pastimes, but their sense of stability. She brought up this factor when responding to a question about why she was initially drawn to Evan.

> MADISON (BLUE-COLLAR-ORIGIN): I had a less stable childhood. My parents were trying to build a house, and we had for many years no electricity and no running water and we would go to my grandmother's house for that. And then they divorced, and he appealed to me because he was very stable, and I wanted somebody who seemed very stable.
> JESSI: What did you mean by "stable?"
> MADISON: It wasn't exactly that he had two parents. That wasn't key. It was his family is to some degree predictable and reliable. And very competent. They have it together.

Madison believed that Evan projected the sense of stability that she had wanted but found elusive. In other words, he provided her with a cultural complement.

Christie (blue-collar-origin), a cheerful, curly-haired woman with a warm smile, agreed with Madison that partners who exuded a sense of stability were appealing. She grew up in a family that scraped by on an unpredictable supply of money due to her father's small income and his penchant for alcohol. Christie met Mike when they were both in junior high school and remembered finding him appealing because he provided her with a sense of stability: "My house was chaotic . . . Mike provided some stability for me." Although Mike's parents were in an unhappy marriage, Mike did have a stable life compared to Christie's. His parents tucked away money for him in a trust fund; he knew his future would be secure.

Likely because of their divergent economic conditions, those with blue-collar-origins were more likely to lack but desire a sense of stability, while those from white-collar-backgrounds were more likely to project a sense of stability to others. Importantly, this pattern was also gendered. It was blue-collar-origin women who framed white-collar-origin men as providing this cultural complement, likely because cultural norms position men as having stability rather than in need of it (Kimmel 2006).[4]

A Cultural Complement: Achieving

About 40 percent of the blue-collar respondents—an approximately even number of men and women—reported being drawn to an additional or different cultural complement: ease or status at achieving.[5] Just as a sense of stability was desired by blue-collar-origin respondents but more easily accessed by white-collar-origin respondents, so, too, was achievement. Since the 1980s, students from all backgrounds have generally aspired to attend college and enter prestigious occupations (Goyette 2008). Whites, in particular, are likely to see college and a variety of professional careers as attainable since, for generations, people in their racial groups have had these opportunities open to them (Beasley 2011).

Yet, while aspirations of a college-degree trickled down through the class structure, the children of college-educated parents are typically given more opportunities to realize their educational and occupational goals. Teachers are more likely to single them out as achievers, providing them with further opportunities (Rist 1970). If schools have tracks for high achievers, teachers are more likely to put the children of college-educated parents on them (Oakes 1985). Parents play a role as well. Precisely because of their own educational experience, college-educated parents are usually better able to help their children step onto an achiever track by instructing them on how to use high school to prepare for college and then how to use college to prepare for a career (Armstrong and Hamilton 2013; Lareau 2011). In many ways, the children of college-educated parents often find themselves on an escalator that lands them at the gates of college and then ushers them into a prestigious career.

The children of non-college-educated parents are less likely to have these experiences, even when they share the same aspirations as their peers. Upwardly mobile students with blue-collar roots are more likely to feel that they stumble to the doors of higher education and continue to stumble once there (Armstrong and Hamilton 2013; Mullen 2010). Thus, even when the blue-collar-origin respondents in this sample made it to college, they still found achievement to be elusive. They felt their white-collar-origin partners projected more ease or status at achieving and said they were drawn to them because of this.

Aaron (blue-collar-origin), a tall son of a factory worker, was one such respondent who remembered being drawn to his wife, Alexa (white-collar-origin), because of her cultural complement of achievement. Aaron, a teacher, loved teaching. More specifically, he loved teaching high school seniors who were college-bound and already marked as achievers. When his school gave him the option of teaching a science class to the "general population" or retiring, he chose the latter as he did not want to teach lesser-achieving students. He also disliked his colleagues, whom he felt were not achievers. He vented: "People who get hired for this stuff are not the brightest lights in the chandelier." He continued: "I don't like teachers very much. I was never a teacher. I'm a physicist who happened to learn to educate and enjoy educating kids. Most of the teachers I know are very nice people, but they're not very smart, and they're not real well-educated." Aaron disliked being around nonachievers and felt that his profession prevented him from being viewed as an achiever.

If Aaron could not secure his status as an achiever through his work, he could date women who achieved. When asked if there was something he had been looking for in a person to date, he said: "Women who are going places. Or at least were making things happen as opposed to just going with the flow." He described success in dating women that fit this description: "Most of the women that I went out with over the years were people who now have careers, fairly significant ones. Now they're doctors, lawyers and dentists, professors, researchers. You name it." His wife was one of these women. They met when he was her high school teacher, though they did not begin dating until she was in a doctoral program. He identified her as "sharp" and with "intellectual stature," and pointed out that she had won national awards for her academic ability. He made contributions to her dissertation research that, decades later, still seemed to make him proud. Marrying white-collar-origin Alexa—who had a PhD, one that he helped her obtain—provided Aaron with a cultural complement. He believed that she had the achievement status that he wanted for himself but felt unable to attain.

Katie (blue-collar-origin), a short woman with kind eyes who wore a loose black sweater and jeans for our interview, also recalled appreciating her partner's ease at achieving—an ease she felt she did not have. She met her future husband, Ryan (white-collar-origin), a brown-haired class clown, when they were in high school. She remembered that after meeting Ryan's parents she gained "the sense that we were not from the same world." Her father worked the night shift at a steel mill when she was young then transferred to a daytime union position. She remembered that he "definitely worked hard for anything he ever had." They always had enough food and clothes but did not have nearly as much as Ryan's family. Ryan's father was the president of a college, and they lived in house that Katie called "immaculate," one that looked like it was "out of a Martha Stewart magazine." Ryan also remembered that Katie's father made him feel that their different worlds rendered Ryan unsuitable for his daughter: "[Her father] was very different from me and I was definitely not what he pictured for his daughter . . . He was kind of a guy's guy and could fix things. I am not."

Yet, despite their different social worlds, Ryan and Katie remained friends during high school and began dating halfway through their college careers. Katie said she wanted to start dating Ryan because of the ease at which he was achieving. She explained: "He seemed to be on a path . . . He was the kind of person who was going to continue with his education. At the time he wanted to teach. He wanted to be a religion professor . . . He had clear academic goals." Katie admired Ryan's clear academic goals but recalled that she did not have the same clarity about her own. She "tagged along" with her best friend on the latter's tour of colleges, and she then chose her college based on that friend's decision, not because she saw herself on a path to academic achievement. Her father did nothing to counteract this feeling; he tried to dissuade her from attending a four-year college. Katie ignored his wishes, but being in college did not make her feel that she had more direction. When asked how she chose her major, she replied: "To be honest, I flipped through the course catalog in college, and I was just looking for something I could do." Her career goals were also less certain. She recalled: "I never really had anything concrete . . . There was nothing I really wanted to pursue; I just wanted to do something important." Katie remembered that Ryan had more achievement-related direction and ease than she felt she had herself—a cultural complement she found appealing.

William (blue-collar-origin), the son of an intermittently employed repairman and a hardworking mother, also recalled being drawn to his spouse due to her ease and status at achieving. William grew up in a trailer in a poverty-stricken rural neighborhood. He remembered: "We were really poor. I mean there were months that we had to go and borrow money just to pay the electricity bill." He made a few attempts at mobility, entering college and dropping out, joining the military and then not working. He talked of his 20s: "I didn't have a job. I didn't have an education. I didn't really have a good direction, I guess you could say. There wasn't really much going on there I would say that was good." He eventually found a construction job to support himself while he partied. He knew he violated his town's norms of partying hard as an adult; he reported having "an image." Without direction or achievements and with an image as an immature partier, William rejoined the military. After his commander selected him to attend a special language program, William decided that he would, for the first time, strive toward academic and occupational achievement.

It was in the military language program that he met Anneka, the athletic daughter of an engineer and a teacher. She was the top student in their class. William identified her as studious, disciplined, hardworking, brilliant, and beautiful. He was not sure that Anneka would like him. He felt that they were different enough that "it was one of these things to where you wanted to know if there was something to talk about." He also knew that she viewed him as a "redneck from Louisiana."[6] Despite these obstacles, he pursued her, even inviting her out twice because she did not realize that their first evening together was meant to be a date. William found Anneka appealing partly because of her cultural complement—her position as the top student in the class and her studious habits signaled that she achieved in ways that he wanted to but had not.

Those with blue-collar-origins then typically remembered feeling drawn to their white-collar spouse due to their spouse's cultural complement. That is, they recalled that their spouse had a sense of stability and achievement that they desired but felt unable to attain themselves. But, as the next sections will make clear, memories of the appeal of a partner's cultural complement were far from one-sided.

A Cultural Complement: Familial Intimacy

For their part, white-collar-origin respondents also remembered feeling drawn to their blue-collar-origin partners due to cultural complements—ones also associated with the experience of growing up in a different class than their spouse. Many white-collar-origin respondents reported that their family-of-origin was not as intimate as they wished. This feeling likely relates to two social trends. First, many white-collar-origin children were raised by parents who used a childrearing style called "concerted cultivation" (Lareau 2003). This style is associated with having and reproducing privilege but may also be associated with perceptions of inadequate family intimacy. Children raised in this style spend a lot of time engaged in extracurricular activities that take them away from their families. Siblings end up on different schedules, and parents devote their time with their children to guiding their achievement, transporting them from one activity to the next, and figuring out the logistics of the coming days. One respondent who was raising his children using this style explained its downsides: "I spend a lot of time with my kids. But a lot of it is somewhat busy time: picking 'em up from school and getting 'em this and that and going to gymnastics, going to basketball. It's not just sitting down and talking and letting enough time pass so that you get to the important things." The children of blue-collar parents were less likely to experience concerted cultivation and its consequences as this parenting style requires substantial resources to enact (Lareau 2003). They were instead more likely to be raised in families that spend more unstructured time together (Hansen 2005; Lareau 2003)—time which may allow more opportunities to "get to the important things" and foster stronger feelings of family intimacy.[7]

Second, many white-collar-origin respondents felt that they had internalized a sense of emotional restraint from their families of origin—a sense of restraint they associated with less familial intimacy. These respondents were raised in the 1960s to 1980s, a time when white-collar workers were expected to exercise emotional restraint at work. Parents working in these jobs often used the same sensibilities at home, thus teaching their children to internalize a sense of emotional restraint (Hochschild 1983; Illouz 2008; Kohn 1969; Walkerdine, Lucey, and Melody 2001). By the 1990s, however, the now adult respondents found that emotional restraint was not only less valued but also problematic. Societal norms changed to position emotional restraint as the enemy of healthy marriages, while emotional expressivity was deemed a necessary ingredient of healthy, intimate, and successful marriages (Cherlin 2004; Illouz 2008). Many white-collar-origin respondents wanted to meet the new norms of emotional expressivity but felt constrained by the emotional restraint they had internalized in the past.[8] In general, the children of blue-collar workers were not taught to restrain their emotions but to express them (Kohn 1969; Walkerdine et al. 2001). As such, they were well-positioned to provide their partners with their desired cultural complement.

Lori, a tall, serious woman who grew up with private cooks, had three family homes, and attended private schools was one of the respondents who felt she lacked familial intimacy and said her husband was appealing because he had it. She met Jason (blue-collar-origin) at a summer academic program and married him a year later. She remembered why she felt so drawn to him: "I attributed his ability to be such an intimate partner to the fact that he comes from this household where there was so much intimacy. So that was something I obviously wanted and was looking for." She elaborated:

> There's an emotional honesty to him that I don't think you find with people from my class background.[9] So I've always really appreciated that. That's the thing I most like about him . . . And I was really struck by this idea that they were so intimate . . . The five boys, they really loved each other. They're really intimate with each other in a way that's completely unlike my family's experience . . . I sort of liked that. I was surprised by it. I kept saying, "You love each other!" To me it just seemed so—it's not that we don't love each other, but they *obviously* loved and enjoyed each other.

Lori disliked part of her background. Jason and his family provided a remedy.

Mike (white-collar-origin), a friendly man who owned a real estate business, made the same point. His father was a professor and wanted to help Mike meet his academic and career goals. But Mike met Christie (blue-collar-origin) in junior high school and remembered being drawn to her and her family because of their different focus.

Mike (white-collar-origin): My dad was like, "We've gotta get you somewhere. Let's look at what you are wanting to do and what you are interested in." But I was really drawn and impressed by Christie's family which was in so many ways closer than our family. I mean, they were more fun to be around. And definitely closer and more communicative and everything else . . . I was like "Wow, they have their issues too but just the way they communicate." It showed me that you can be closer, that you can do things and talk about stuff that we really didn't in my family.

Mike remembered being drawn to a style of emotional expressivity that he related to family intimacy—one that he felt less exposed to by his family, and, as will be evident in Chapter 8, he felt unable to produce.

Similarly, Jim (white-collar-origin), a reserved and sullen man, said he was drawn to his wife, Danielle (blue-collar-origin), a warm and exuberant woman, because her family was more intimate. He remembered:

I had little to no relationship with my siblings because they're older . . . We just did not do anything together, had very little interaction. Whereas she would relate stories about her brothers and sisters which implied there was much more involvement. Not necessarily good involvement, but there was involvement . . . I enjoyed the fact that they seemed to be a closer knit family than mine.

Jim's rejection of his family's lack of intimacy was so poignant that soon after he met Danielle they together painted a public rock with the words: "Jim Holland: born but not appreciated." In her interview, Danielle also reinforced Jim's perceptions: "His sister basically adopted another family, his brother basically adopted another family, and his other brother stayed up in the attic until he got done with school and then left. There was really no family life for them. That's what they all say. But if you looked at them, they lived in a mansion and they had all the privileges of the world. So he had that feeling. What did I have? I had my aunties . . . I always joke that Jim didn't really fall in love with me; he fell in love with the aunties. Which is fine because I loved them too."

Other white-collar-origin participants also saw their spouse as able to rectify what they saw as their family's lack of emotional expressivity and intimacy. Brandon remembered being told that when he was two, his white-collar father decided to stop hugging him because, his father believed, "showing emotion is a sin." Once an adult, Brandon found a more emotionally expressive wife. Similarly, Leslie (white-collar-origin) said that "norms of propriety" dominated her family life, silencing discussions about "how we really felt about stuff" and distorting her personality: "I really am naturally an extrovert, but I had been trained to not be by my early life." She married a man from a blue-collar background who cared less about propriety and allowed her greater emotional expression. Matt (white-collar-origin) met Jenny (blue-collar-origin) at work and began to date her after joining her family's bowling team. He remembered: "Jenny's family is in general much warmer than mine . . . Her family put more weight on fun family stuff whereas mine, it was just assumed you were going to go to college." These respondents observed that their blue-collar-origin partners had more intimate families and reported being drawn to them because of it.

A Cultural Complement: Disconnection from Work

Another set of classed experiences was associated with white-collar-origin respondents' stated reasons for initially appreciating their blue-collar-origin spouses. Since the 1960s, white-collar individuals have been especially caught between contradictory demands: They are supposed to spend more time at work and do more work at home, while also meeting the considerable time demands required by the norms of marital intimacy and intensive parenting (Blair-Loy 2003; Hays 1996). Several white-collar-origin respondents felt their parents' work overly detracted from family life. As adults, some strived to resolve the contradiction between work and family by not letting work interfere with their family time. However, their belief that they had internalized a need to constantly work made this difficult to do. Those from blue-collar families were less likely to experience this contradiction as, on average, blue-collar workers spend fewer hours at work, have hourly jobs that have clear end times, and experience less work-to-home spillover (Jacobs and Gerson 2004; Schieman, Whitestone, and Van Gundy 2006). Blue-collar workers are also more likely to identify with family than with work and to frame work as what they do for their family (Lamont 2000; Williams 2010). Several white-collar-origin partners said they initially appreciated their blue-collar-origin partners because the latter had grown up with and internalized this looser connection to work.

Vicki (white-collar-origin), described at the beginning of this chapter, met her husband John at work. One reason that she ignored her mother's classism and did not distance herself from John was that she noticed that he provided her with a cultural complement. She observed that he disconnected his identity from his work: "For him, he's just like, 'Whatever. Went to work.' And either it was a good day or a bad day, and maybe he'll say something about something happening, but basically it's just what he does to earn money." John's work ethic was refreshing to Vicki, as she resented that her single mother was part of the white-collar trend to spend more time at work and to have work dominate her identity. Vicki complained:

> My mom worked, and we went to childcare and to school. We were like latchkey kids ... I don't think [my mother] has a strong family value. She doesn't value the celebrations in families like for the holidays or birthdays. She acknowledges career things or academic, like if you do well in school or if you got a promotion. Those types of things she'll recognize. But the other things that are more traditional, she doesn't really care.

Vicki contrasted her mother's ideas of work and family to John's ideas regarding the same. She admired "the importance of family to [John] and how he structures his life around family." As we will see in Chapter 5, Vicki had not been able to stifle her own urge to work, but in terms of choosing a partner, she believed she was drawn to John because he had a sensibility unlike her own—the ability to disconnect from work.

Ian, also mentioned earlier in this chapter, felt the same way. His father was also part of the white-collar trend of spending more time at work (Jacobs and Gerson 2004; Robinson and Godbey 1997), a trend that Ian did not appreciate.

> Ian (white-collar-origin): My dad always worked really hard. He would work 16-hour days as a lawyer and get incredibly stressed out before he would go to trial. He told me one time that he had to wear three undershirts to keep himself from sweating ... And so I saw that as not at all appealing. So one of the reasons that I was attracted to anything I perceived as being countercultural had a lot to do with what I saw my parents were mixed up in and that was what I wanted to avoid.

One of the things that Ian was attracted to in the countercultural movement was his wife. Asked why he initially wanted to be with her, he said: "I liked that she was clearly nonmainstream and kind of countercultural." Isabelle also had a work ethic that differed from his own and that of Ian's father—one that was not about 16-hour days and little family time. She wanted, in contrast, to minimize the time she spent at work, explaining: "I don't want work to interfere with other parts of my life." Despite disliking it, Ian felt he had internalized his father's drive to work. Ian put in long hours at work and felt driven to repeatedly reach for the next level of career success. He appreciated that Isabelle's model of work was different than his own.

Norah (white-collar-origin), a talkative woman with short, brown hair and thick glasses, found George (blue-collar-origin), a red-haired man who shared her cheesy sense of humor, to be a suitable marriage partner partly because he helped her resolve what she experienced as contradicting ideas of work and family. She grew up with a father who was so dedicated to work that not only did he not have time for social events, but, Norah predicted, he would also die at his desk. One day at church, Norah met George, a man with a different connection to work than herself or her father. She and George dated for a few months, then Norah ended the relationship so that she could fully devote herself to her academic work. The couple stayed in touch, however, and as Norah came closer to completing her degree, she began to question if she wanted a work–life balance that resembled her father's. She thought the path for women in her field was one of forgoing children and possibly even a spouse. George, she noticed, provided a model of how she could continue to be invested in work but still have time for family. As she described it, he modeled the idea of, "Here's your work, you do it, you come home, you leave it behind. That you can be intellectually invested in what you're doing but not merged with it." His views of work allowed Norah to understand how work and family could be less conflicting.

SHARED-ORIGIN SIMILARITIES

Shared-origin respondents—those in which each partner was raised by college-educated, white-collar parents and had the same status themselves—did not report feeling drawn to partners with cultural complements. In fact, few respondents who married a partner who shared their class origin recalled growing up in unexpressive families or with parents whose dedication to work detracted from family time. Without finding an element of their past to reject, shared-origin respondents said they were initially drawn to their partners because of their cultural similarities rather than their complementing cultural differences.

Amy and Shawn, who share white-collar origins, met shortly after each graduated from separate elite colleges and entered the financial industry. Each felt that they came from close families. Amy, the confident and energetic daughter of a university president and a teacher, had moved several times with her family. She pointed to these experiences as she described the closeness of her family: "We had really close families that, like I said, the family unit was strong enough that we could uproot and go somewhere." Her husband, Shawn, a tall, formerly rowdy man who physically resembles the comedian Dennis Leary, also came from a privileged background. He remembered growing up spending time at his grandparents' "great house on a hill with vineyards and a little winery and a swimming pool" and being "keenly aware that this was not something that everybody had." Also, like Amy, he felt that he came from an intimate and emotionally expressive family. He said of his childhood: "The love of the family was absolutely number one. That's something that I always just knew and felt in my bones," and added: "My dad loves to really hang out and take time to go deep." Furthermore, both admired their parents' dedication to work. Shawn said:

> You work hard. You have to figure out what you like to work at so that you can find a way to enjoy working at it. I think that's something I learned that from my parents, watching them; I consider them to be hard workers . . . I think Amy would say the same of her parents.

Both felt that they had intimate families, and both enjoyed their parents' connection to work. They then recalled feeling drawn to their partner not because of cultural complements, but because of cultural similarities. When asked why she wanted to marry Shawn, Amy said: "We found that we had this common background . . . His family had taken them out of school, and they lived in Spain for a year, and that is the kind of upbringing I also had. We had lived abroad when I was a kid." Shawn concurred: "I remember thinking, 'Wow, she had a very similar upbringing and family experience as I did.'" Without remembering a need for a cultural complement, Amy and Shawn each focused on their cultural commonalities—ones like international travel that were enabled by their similarly advantaged backgrounds.

Carlie and Clint (shared-origin) met when Clint checked Carlie into her dorm room during her freshman year of college. They got to know each other as they shared a living community and as they discovered that they were both the children of engineers and on track to become engineers themselves. They both grew up traveling as well. Carlie had pictures from her international travels that, according to Clint, looked like those out of a *National Geographic* magazine, while Clint's travels provided him with a wide range of portraits of the United States. As well as enjoying a similar interest in travel and coming from similar backgrounds, they also enjoyed their respective family's intimate ties. When asked why she wanted to marry Clint, Carlie spoke of Clint's close-knit family:

> A strong sense of family. We had met each other's families by then, and his family is very similar to mine. You know, a strong relationship with his parents and with his siblings and the same with me.

Clint also named a close family as a reason he was attracted to Carlie: "She came from a good family, similar values . . . [Her family] had somewhat similar beliefs, you know, family oriented."

Furthermore, Carlie and Clint recalled appreciating each other's matching work ethic. Carlie explained that she married Clint partly because he had a "good work ethic. He's not one to take a sick day or skip a class or something like that—just a good work ethic." When asked what he had looked for in a spouse, a similar work ethic was among the characteristics that Clint remembered seeking: "Just someone who had similar thoughts in general about life and work attitudes . . . You get a job, you work, you raise a family, you're not a bum. You don't take advantage of society, and you have to pull your own weight." Neither Clint nor Carlie felt that they needed a cultural complement to provide an antidote to sensibilities they internalized in the past. As a result, they remembered finding each other appealing because of their cultural similarities—ones like travel that were facilitated by their similarly privileged backgrounds.[10]

CONCLUSION

Vicki married John despite that she thought he came from an uneducated family with vulgar tastes. Ian married Isabelle despite that he could not identify with her rural upbringing and, in turn, would need to instruct her on things that were obvious to him—how to load a dishwasher, and what one does in graduate school. They also found their partner appealing even though they did not talk of trading their privileged class background for their partner's good looks or educational attainment. Thus, cultural matching theory is incomplete as it explains why respondents would remember feeling reserved about a partner from another class background but not why they would remember wanting to spend their life with them. Exchange theory's prediction that couples match when they have complementary resources fared better. However, the theory cannot explain how individuals construct their own accounts of being drawn to their different-origin spouse. Exchange theorists tend to analyze resources such as wealth, beauty, and educational attainment rather than sensibilities. They therefore miss the more common criteria that appear in contemporary Americans' accounts of falling in love.

Overall, respondents told stories of love crossing class lines for reasons that previous theories could not fully foretell. Many recalled being drawn to their spouse because of their spouse's cultural complement. The cultural complements they spoke of were not idiosyncratic but patterned according to each partner's class origin. It is relatively difficult for people who grow up in blue-collar environments to find stability or ease at achieving; it is easier for people who grow up in white-collar families to do so. Similarly, given the parenting styles and workplace expectations of the time period, it was relatively difficult for white-collar-origin respondents to experience family intimacy and learn to disconnect from work; it may have been easier for college-educated adults with blue-collar-origins to do so. These types of oppositions are built into the class system. Though other theories suggest these cultural oppositions act as social repellents, respondents instead reported that they served as magnets, drawing the different-origin couple together.

Shared-origin respondents shared more similar upbringings with their spouse. They then explained the initial appeal of their partner by talking of cultural similarities rather than cultural complements. They also framed their pasts differently than did most white-collar-origin respondents in different-origin marriages— perhaps because they did not have a blue-collar-origin partner to compare themselves to or perhaps because the two groups really had different experiences and looked for different things when selecting a spouse. Either way, their accounts showed that the class origin of each spouse related to their explanations of falling for their spouse: shared-origin couples focused on their cultural similarities while different-origin couples focused on their cultural differences.

These findings are encouraging as cultural differences were previously framed only as barriers to inclusion, not also as justifications of it. However, it is important to remember that respondents' stories of appreciation focused only on some factors, ignoring other ones that also likely brought them together. For example, for the respondents to appreciate their spouse they had to meet. Schools, colleges, workplaces, religious institutions, and friends facilitated this. They also had to see their partner as a potential spouse, and their partner's similar race, education and, for many, age and religion, helped make this possible. In addition, the couples all shared some general similarities. They often talked of shared but vague values—they shared a belief in treating others well or that marriage was a valuable institution. These concurrent cultural similarities also likely helped the couple cement their relationship and allowed some cultural differences to be viewed as complementary rather than divisive.

The following chapters turn to the married lives of those who recalled being united by cultural complements. They show that, although respondents believed that cultural complements initially drew them to their spouse, their perceptions shifted so that differences that were appreciated became differences to manage. As Isabelle observed, "The things that you're drawn to sometimes become the things that drive you crazy."[11]

PART III

CLASS AND THE DOMAINS OF MARRIED LIFE

[4]

MONEY

Aaron felt that with a "factory rat" father and homemaker mother, he had a typical blue-collar childhood. As a teenager he donned Frankie Avalon hair and a black wardrobe; he identified as a smart geek who hung out with punks. His parents ended their formal education after their sophomore years of high school, and Aaron remembered that they celebrated him as a child prodigy. His friends also celebrated his academic success; they were in awe of the atom smasher and linear accelerator he built in high school and encouraged him to apply to the nearby state university. Aaron followed their advice and was accepted to college and awarded a scholarship. Combined with his job in the university food service department and the money he made playing in a band, he supported himself through college and became a high school teacher.

That was over 40 years ago. When I met Aaron he was 63 years old and had spent two-thirds of his life in the middle class. He still identified as a cross between a geek and a punk, and he still spent as much time as he could reading and performing music. His ideas of money, however, both reflected his past and distanced himself from it. He explained that his parents "didn't have money" but that they "tried real hard to get me stuff that I really wanted, a bicycle and that kind of thing. But you didn't just go out and buy the latest fancy gadget because everybody else had it. It didn't work that way."

Now that he earned more money, Aaron used it to prove he was no longer bound by the constraints of his past. He relished that he could spend what he wanted, and he purposefully did not keep track of his expenditures. He explained: "I go out and spend twenty-five, thirty, or fifty dollars. I don't care. It's my walk-around money. But then I need to account for it [to my wife], and I just I can't do that. This is sort of like quality of life. You want this, you need this. It's important. Well, I'll get it." He continued: "If I decide I need something and it's important, then I don't care what it costs. It's irrelevant. Cost is irrelevant." He summed up his approach: "Money should be spent, in my opinion."

Alexa was a quiet, plain woman, with long gray hair and strong morals. She never had many friends but took comfort in hard work, school, and, unlike her husband, God. Her childhood was unpleasant. Alexa's father was a mechanical engineer, and her college-educated mother worked in the tax industry. For years, her father commuted several hours to work, coming home every other weekend for what Alexa called "weekends from hell." Her father would yell that nothing his wife and kids did was right, deposit his paycheck, and then return to work. Eventually he found another job, and the family moved. She remembered that in those years she "got a real good education in cooking, cleaning, keeping house, and dealing with grumpy dad." Despite her father's steady job, his grumpiness was related to worrying about money and spending frugally. Alexa, however, thought much of his worry was self-imposed. She said: "I got this boatload of inheritance from someone who was wearing clothes and sleeping in sheets that would make bad rags for poor people. Miserly would be a good description of our upbringing."

Alexa met Aaron in high school; he was one of her teachers. Neither she nor Aaron could pin down exactly when they began dating but think it was sometime when Aaron was helping Alexa on her doctoral thesis. When I met her at age 44, Alexa had spent more time living with Aaron than with her father. Yet, despite questioning her father's financial decisions, her ideas of money were more closely aligned with his ideas than her husband's. She described Aaron's financial sensibilities: "His goal has always been to have enough money that he didn't have to worry about it, because he was raised worrying about it... [Now] he's finally got enough he doesn't have to worry about it, and he is damned if he's going to worry about it." This was not her view of money: "I treat it carefully. I don't want to waste it." She refused to spend much on her appearance, preferring to shop at Value World and avoid make-up. She did not think they needed a bigger house, as Aaron did, and cooked homemade food to avoid paying to eat out. Alexa did not think it was appropriate to take a laissez-faire approach—a relatively unmonitored and unplanned approach—toward money. She favored a more cautious and managerial approach—one in which she "treated money carefully," monitored expenses, and saved when possible.

Danielle (blue-collar-origin) was an adventurous and lively woman with a colorful past. The daughter of a chemical worker and a stay-at-home mother, she grew up in a stable but modest working-class family before hitting more severe hardships. She described growing up as a dorky, fat kid who found school to be an upsetting place. Her best friend was black, and she kissed a black student in a school play—both of which resulted in her getting assaulted in her recently integrated school. She became pregnant as a teenager and her parents sent her away to hide the pregnancy, then forced her to sign away her rights to motherhood. The civil rights and hippie movements caught her attention as well, and the combination of it all made school seem both unpleasant and irrelevant. A year and a half from graduation, she dropped out of school.[1]

Danielle then married a man she called a lunatic and had a daughter. In their six years of marriage, they moved 17 times. She remembered constantly wondering: "Are we going to have enough food?" She stood in welfare lines and dreamed of going to coffee shops to steal toilet paper. She learned that thinking about money was not helpful when there was too little to meet her needs: "I just pretended like it didn't exist, and I would just spend what I needed to and never think about it." She elaborated: "I was afraid to face the realities of it, which is that it's limited. You only have so much. And you have to budget, and you have to think about it, and you have to plan ahead, and you have to save. I just thought, 'I don't want to do all that.'"

It was at the end of this period in Danielle's life—when she was living in poverty and divorcing her first husband—that Danielle was introduced to Jim, a tall, thin man with a low ponytail and a dry sense of humor. She first heard of Jim when her boss said that he was the employee raised with a silver spoon in his mouth. Jim's family was well-off for generations. He had a great-grandfather who was general, a grandfather who was a famous writer, and a father who was a successful scientist. He grew up in a mansion in a wealthy neighborhood and never faced the material struggles that his wife did. Danielle liked that he was not jaded like most of the people she knew. He was also hopelessly shy, so much so that she got to know him by asking about their colleagues' shoes—something she knew he noticed more than their faces. When I met them, they had been married for 27 years.

For 27 years, they had differences about how to spend money. Danielle tried to start doing what she dreaded—thinking about money, budgeting, and believing that it was real and limited. She felt she made great progress but would still spend impulsively and pretend they had more than they did. She convinced Jim to go on a vacation when they did not have the money to pay for it, and she still believed that life is short so they should spend money even if it may not be wise. Jim did not adopt Danielle's views. He did not spend without thinking but researched purchases until Danielle would exclaim: "I can't stand it! We're just going to buy this! Stop researching it!" He also did not spend excessively, nor did he stand by his wife as she did. Jim returned Danielle's purchases so often that she resorted to spilling soda on their new sofa to prevent him from returning it and falsely telling him that there were bans against returning cologne. He did not buy many things for himself either. He drove cars that strangers called "death traps" and wore shoes that prompted his wife to joke: "I think a homeless guy gave them back to us." He spent hours trying, in Danielle's words, to "save eleven cents." Jim's preferences were then to save, meticulously think through purchases, and use money to live for tomorrow. Even after nearly three decades of marriage, Danielle took a more laissez-faire approach—one characterized by the freedom to spend without thinking and to spend to make the most of the current times.

Alexa's and Jim's (both white-collar-origin) ideas of spending were then more similar to each other's than they were to the partners with whom they spent their lives. They both thought that money should be actively managed—that purchases should be researched, carefully considered, and documented, and that financial security required saving for the future rather than spending freely to enjoy the present. Their ideas were likely influenced by their pasts—they grew up with enough money left over after paying their bills that they could save and actively manage their surplus. Despite their years together, their partners, Aaron and Danielle (both blue-collar-origin), however, favored a different approach. Aaron and Danielle both thought money should be spent and preferred to take a laissez-faire approach to their purchases—to spend without careful thought, to use money to enjoy the present, and to assume their financial situation would be fine now and in the future. Though blue-collar-origin respondents left their parents' financial situations behind as they joined the class their spouses had always known, their ideas of money were related to their past. Their financial sensibilities both replicated the strategies they learned in the past and distanced themselves from their past constraints.[2]

BLUE-COLLAR-ORIGIN RESPONDENTS' FINANCIAL SENSIBILITIES

Even after years of marriage, blue- and white-collar-origin partners in different-origin marriages tended not to share ideas of how to use money. Those with blue-collar origins replicated the strategies that had worked for their parents and also distanced themselves from them. Their sensibilities toward money derived from a class location that their spouse did not share, routing them to have different financial sensibilities than their spouse.

Replicating Strategies That Were Used in the Past

Blue-collar-origin interviewees named different ways that their parents responded to having limited means, but, despite these differences, they tended to develop the same ideas of money: Money should not be carefully managed or saved but spent without too much thought and as if there were few constraints.[3] Some, like Jill (blue-collar-origin), a local politician who resembles the soap opera actress Susan Lucci, grew up with parents who "were in debt up to their eyeballs." Jill maintained that they used their money to buy new RVs, houses, and diamond rings that allowed them to pretend to be in a class that they were not. Jill watched her parents spend money continuously and felt that she learned to do the same: "I'm very comfortable spending money. That's what we did."

Her current monetary goals were to "indulge and live in the time." She tried to convince her husband, Eric (white-collar-origin), to do the same: "He worries about money more than I do. I'm okay with spending money and enjoying ourselves. He's always worried that we don't have enough . . . I've got to make him spend a little more. Live life a little more." Jill's parents borrowed money to live the life they wanted, and, while Jill felt she was more restrained than her parents, she still adopted some of their laissez-fair approaches; she spent freely and without worry.

Isabelle (blue-collar-origin), an introspective therapist, also grew up learning financial strategies from watching her parents manage their debt. Unlike Jill's parents, her parents, however, did not attempt to pass as middle class but simply tried to survive. She learned that taking a laissez-faire approach to money made sense because thinking about money and trying to manage it would not improve their financial situation. She also learned that spending money was wise, as, if it was not spent, someone might take it. She explained: "Coming from the family that I came from, it's like, 'If you have money, spend it, because someone's going to want it [like a debt collector]'.[4] And so I think historically I have been very unconscious about money and nervous about it but not really knowing what to do, how to make it different, impulsive with money . . . For my family, it's, 'You can buy groceries, you can pay this bill, you can pay this bill. You can't do it all, so why bother trying to do it all?'" She said she still bought things "without thinking about whether we could afford it or whether it was okay." Isabelle's family situation taught her that money should be spent when it was available and that worrying about finances was point-less as they would always have financial difficulties. She learned to use money in a laissez-faire style—to spend without too much thought, not impose constraints on her spending, and use money to live for the day.

Other blue-collar-origin respondents learned from their parents' precarious financial situations that a small amount in their savings account was normal. They learned that there was little reason to worry about limited savings as they had gotten by on shoestring budgets in the past. For example, Jenny (blue-collar-origin), a petite, soft-spoken stay-at-home mother, grew up with financially stable parents with modest incomes. Because having little savings did not pose major problems in her childhood, she, unlike her husband, did not mind maintaining a near-empty savings account. She explained: "I just have faith things will work out . . . [My husband] frets about retirement and college costs. And I tend to think, 'We'll get there. It will be okay' . . . And just the week to week stuff. I'm okay if we only have forty dollars in the checking account, but he worries more about that kind of stuff than I do." Jenny's background positioned a small checking account as normal and not a reason to worry. She also believed that not thinking too much about money was fine. Things had worked out in the past with parents who earned less. It would work out for her and her husband too.

Christie (blue-collar-origin), a warm, open, social worker, also grew up learning that a small savings account was normal and not a cause for concern. She was raised by a father who worked on a maintenance crew and a mother who worked at home. Though her family's financial situation meant that they sometimes rationed food, she learned that worrying about money did not help: "[My husband] Mike worries about finances so much more than I do which is so weird. Money is so important to Mike. And he had it growing up, and I didn't have it growing up. I just always assume things are going to be okay. I don't know if it's because my family made it through . . . I've just always assumed the money would be there." With faith that their financial situation would continue to work out, in conversations with her husband, Mike (white-collar-origin), she regularly found herself repeating: "Live for the day!"

Blue-collar-origin respondents' idea that money should be used to live for the day likely derived from their observations of their parents' response to having limited means. If financial situations would never be fully resolved and there was never enough to amply stock a savings account, then not worrying and living for the day made sense. No amount of careful planning and no amount of worry could make up for the fact that there was simply not enough. Respondents may have *had* to "live for the day" as there was little money left over to pay the bills and also "live for tomorrow." Even though respondents left their class origin and parents' financial situations behind, some still used the financial strategies that they learned in the past. Simultaneously, some also used their new money to distance themselves from their past. This again meant taking a laissez-faire approach—spending money freely, as if there were few constraints.

Distancing Themselves from the Past

Spending and spending without great thought were also strategies that respondents used to distance themselves from the past. Madison (blue-collar-origin, a stay-at-home mother), a soft-spoken, thoughtful, academically inclined woman, grew up dreaming of making it. She described her mother as a social climber, and together they envisioned what it would be like to leave behind their half-built house, sporadic electricity, and outhouse. With her college degree and college-educated husband, Madison now had the financial ability to live the dream she and her mother imagined. This meant buying things that were not strictly necessary—decorative items, gourmet foods, and items that would make her life a little bit easier. In short, it meant spending. She told: "I am a spender. I tend to go over the budget by a couple hundred dollars each month . . . For me, it's important to indulge and live more in the time." Madison dreamed of the things that money could buy. Now that she had money, she wanted to use it to distance herself from the poverty of her past. This required spending, not saving.

Simply spending money also allowed respondents to feel unbound from their pasts. Madison received a thrill from spending money and buying extra things—a practice she could not do before because there was never enough money for things that were deemed extras. Christie (blue-collar-origin) similarly remembered that her parents could only occasionally afford Pop-Tarts, and even then she had to split them in half to share them with her sister. She now enjoyed buying Pop-Tarts and chided her husband for buying generic food. Elliott (blue-collar-origin), a cheerful stay-at-home father in his late 30s, grew up eating government-provided cheese and swearing he would never work in a factory like his father. He now got a thrill out of being able to spend large sums of money: "I still think a hundred dollars is a lot of money. Growing up that was a ton of money. It's cool that I can now go out and spend a hundred dollars and not necessarily think twice about it." Now that respondents had money, they enjoyed being able to spend it without worrying. Doing so proved that the constraints of their childhoods were not the constraints of their adulthoods.

Several respondents received a thrill from purchasing a specific item: a large home. Such homes "proved" their position in the middle class, symbolized that they achieved the American Dream, and distanced themselves from the stigma they attached to the homes of their past. Chelsey (white-collar-origin), a teacher, wanted to downgrade from what her husband, Nathan (blue-collar-origin), called their "McMansion light." Chelsey struggled to convince Nathan to move out of their large home—but to him the house advertised his upward mobility.

Chelsey: Another reason that Nathan is so attached to the house is that for him, a big house is a sign of success—that he's overcome his background, class, etc. So it's much more important to him as a status symbol than it is to me. It doesn't even matter to him what the inside looks like as long as people seeing it from the outside are impressed with its size.[5]

In their new position, blue-collar-origin respondents may spend to show they made it. They bought homes to show the world that they had arrived.

Thus, for upwardly mobile blue-collar-origin respondents, living for the day and spending without careful thought were both responses to their past and to their mobility. From their past, they learned that they needed to spend—partly because saving was infeasible, but also because not spending might mean that someone else would take their money. They did not fear a small stockpile of savings as this was normal to them. They also learned that worrying about money did not allow them to change their financial situation and as such there was little reason to think carefully about their budgets. They also spent in ways that responded to their mobility. As youths, they imagined how they would *spend*, not save, money once they had it, and now that they had it, they spent to fulfill their dreams. They also spent to get a thrill—to show themselves they had made it—and spent on large homes to show others they had made it. Though their financial situations were very different than that of their parents, the laissez-faire spending strategies they used both resulted from and responded to the class of their past.

WHITE-COLLAR-ORIGIN RESPONDENTS' FINANCIAL SENSIBILITIES

Just as Alexa's marriage to Aaron and Jim's marriage to Danielle led them to merge bank accounts without merging their financial sensibilities, so too was this the case for many white-collar-origin respondents. They grew up in families that were able to meet their basic needs while also saving, and they were accustomed to having a larger family safety net. Their childhood financial security meant that they did not spend their youth repeatedly imagining what they would do with more money, nor did they feel the need to use money to distance themselves from unstigmatized pasts. They instead wanted to save—to use money to "live for tomorrow"—and to meticulously manage their money so that they felt secure that they and their children would stay in the class in which they had always lived, the middle (and sometimes upper) class.

Evan (white-collar-origin), a thin, introverted, software engineer was the grandson of a wealthy couple and the son of a doctor and a nurse. He grew up understanding that his parents' finances were stable and more than enough to cover his basic expenses as well as vacations, theater visits, and his college tuition. He had no need to distance himself from the past and instead wanted to save for his own future and his children's future. Unlike his wife, Madison (blue-collar-origin), who regularly spent more than they budgeted, spent to get a thrill, and used money to realize her dreams, Evan focused on their future financial stability. He said: "My philosophy on money is very much to save . . . I get concerned about not really having enough for retirement. We are saving some for the kids' college . . . I have no idea what the future will bring, and I am afraid that we will not have enough."

Vicki (white-collar-origin) also felt the need to save. She wanted to manage her money to prepare for her future and that of her children. Her husband, John (blue-collar-origin), did not grow up assuming he would always be in the middle-class, and he was fine with taking a riskier approach. Vicki explained:

Like retirement and savings, saving for college. Just all those things that I know are so important. For him that's just not important. He doesn't think twice about [saving]. He thought even less about it when we first met. Now he'll think a little bit about it, like planning for college [for our children]. But at the same time he just goes, "They could get student loans. We had student loans." I go, "No! No! They can't get student loans!" He has an answer for everything. Like: "You don't have to plan for retirement because everyone's going to have to work until they die. That's just how the economy is." And it's like, "Okay, but you can't count on that."

Vicki did not share her husband's idea that it was okay to not fully plan for their children's college tuition or their own retirement. Though John never had a large family safety net, Vicki had grown up in an environment where there was always a safety net—her wealthy grandparents, and later her mother's large income—and not having one was not something she wanted to consider. She wanted to manage her money—to think carefully about how to use it—so that she and her children could stay in their class.

Leslie (white-collar-origin, an office worker), a self-described science fiction nerd who also ran marathons and contributed to a cooking blog, felt the need to save as well. She explained: "I'm the saver, and he's the spender." Leslie tried to convince her husband, Tom (blue-collar-origin), to save more but felt that her efforts were fruitless: "I'm trying to plan and budget, not that I'm doing a very good job by myself right now. I try not to spend more money than we need to, try to actually determine what the needs are. If the kids say they want something or need something, it used to be he'd just do it no matter what it was. Now he checks with me, except it's still me having to decide."[6] She called herself the "superego"—the one who decides what to buy and what to forgo. Leslie's call was usually to carefully consider their budget and save; Tom's was to not think about budgeting and spend. Leslie thought about retirement, their children's college funds, and a family safety net. She took steps to make sure they remained in the class in which she had spent her life.

White-collar-origin and blue-collar-origin spouses then tended to disagree about how to use their money. White-collar-origin partners wanted to save and budget, while blue-collar-origin partners were more likely to want to spend and avoid thinking about their expenses. The former, in other words, wanted to take a managerial approach to money, while the latter favored a more laissez-faire approach. Shared lives did not lead to shared ideas of money.[7]

EXCEPTIONS: WHITE-COLLAR-ORIGIN SPOUSES WHO OUTSPENT THEIR BLUE-COLLAR-ORIGIN PARTNERS

Deviating from the primary pattern, a few white-collar-origin partners were more inclined to spend money than their blue-collar-origin spouses. Each of the white-collar-origin respondents who outspent their partners lived a current lifestyle that was less privileged than the one in which they were raised. While their education levels and occupations resembled those of their parents, their financial situations did not. They then spent more to try to reproduce the lifestyle they had grown accustomed to living. However, it should be noted that this was not a sufficient condition for wanting to spend more— many white-collar-origin savers also had less in their bank accounts than their parents had in theirs.

Anita (white-collar-origin), for example, a frumpily dressed, cheerful marketer in her early 40s, regularly outspent her blue-collar-origin husband. Her father was a dentist, and her stepfather was a professor. Their incomes, combined with her mother's income from working as a nurse, meant that Anita grew up living in

MONEY

a privileged environment. Her husband, Todd (blue-collar-origin, a retail salesman), described Anita's situation: "Her mom and step-dad's house would probably be a two or three million dollar house. Everything was state of the art. It had a Viking range and subzero fridge, swimming pool in the backyard." Anita and Todd lived in a much smaller home, one that did not have the newest appliances or a pool.

Anita spent more than Todd as she tried to emulate her parents' home and as she tried to offer her children the same advantages that she received. She explained: "I expect, hope, to get to the same point that my parents are at. Whether it's home comfort level and that kind of thing ... I'm trying to create a similar feel or quality to our home." In addition, she spent more on their children's education than Todd thought was wise. She sent their children to private preschools and then, without telling Todd, enrolled them in a public elementary school outside their district—one that was not free. She admitted that this meant "not compromising on things when compromising might be a better idea." Todd, who grew up in a trailer and received a rural public school education, was not convinced that the items Anita found necessary really were. He recalled: "When we were talking about where to put them [in school], I was like, 'Honey, there's got to be cheaper places,' She's like, 'No, these places aren't accredited. They're not licensed.' I'm like, 'This is our situation. We can't do that,' But what are we doing? We're spending money we don't have." Anita wanted to use their money to pass on the advantages that she had—advantages that Todd never had, did not feel entitled to, and did not feel were necessary to hand down to their children at all costs.[8]

Parker, a tall, confident, artistic manager was also one of the few white-collar-origin respondents who spent in a laissez-faire manner. He had not replicated his parents' lifestyle though he hoped he would. He grew up with very wealthy parents. His father owned a watch worth $25,000, bought expensive cars, and covered Parker's attendance at a private boarding school. Parker grew up assuming "I'm going to be a corporate attorney and work in mergers and acquisitions, and I'll have a Ferrari by the time I'm thirty." His life veered from his goals; though he passed age 30 years ago, he had not met any of his original goals. He reported that he now spends much more than his blue-collar-origin wife and had a different understanding of what is necessary. Parker explained: "I've never really worried about money. I've always figured I can always work and it will always work out. But I think she does worry about it and gets a little freaked out sometimes." Parker's wife Lillian worried in part because Parker did not only spend on small things which she would not have foregone but also on large things. For example, shortly before their son was born, Parker found he could not fit the new car seat in their current car. Without consulting with his wife, Parker went out and bought a new—his wife emphasized, not used—SUV. While Lillian thought that this purchase was unnecessary as they could have purchased a new car seat instead, Parker felt it was justified. His parents had regularly bought new cars when they did not need them, and now he was simply doing the same. Although his financial situation was more limited than his parents', he acted as though it was not. His ideas of spending were derived from his childhood class position, even if they did not correspond to his current financial situation.

WHEN IDEAS OF MONEY CHANGED

Most respondents were unable to change their partners' financial sensibilities. A few, however, were able to find more common ground when one partner could correct the other's incorrect information. For example, though Leslie (white-collar-origin) could not convince Tom (blue-collar-origin) to become a careful saver, she did eventually persuade him that a budget determined the *maximum,* and not the minimum, amount they were supposed to spend. Colton (white-collar-origin) similarly taught Evelyn (blue-collar-origin) about the perils of carrying a credit card balance, and she began to charge only items that they could pay off. Providing new information, however, was not a surefire way of changing their partners' views. Mary (white-collar-origin) was still trying to convince her husband, Ben (blue-collar-origin), that bills should be paid on time. She said that he regularly asked: "What's the worst that could happen? It's late. We'll pay a late fee. Oh well." She found herself repeating: "Oh, no. Think credit report."

Most of the differences that couples had, however, were not small differences about the definition of a budget or the dangers of a bad credit report; rather, they were more philosophical differences about the purpose of money, how much needed to be saved to feel secure, and if there were joys of spending without thinking. Only three respondents reported changing their financial sensibilities in major ways. One was William, who grew up with limited means. After obtaining a graduate degree and marrying a partner with a graduate degree, William's sensibilities shifted.

> William: That is something that's changed tremendously. Not [my wife], but me. I used to spend money, a lot, and had no concept of saving, period. And, this didn't come strictly from her. Her family never thought like that. So over the years that has been a major difference in me, the way that I approach our finances and the way that I spend money, the way that I budget things, all of that has changed a lot.

William now saves for retirement and vacations. He said this shift was not hard: "She pretty much takes care of that. I put aside the money in certain places but all of it's pretty much automatic. If it's not there, you don't really depend on it. It just goes somewhere . . . It moves in different directions, and so it's not necessarily difficult." Yet while the change may not have been difficult for William, no other blue-collar-origin respondent made such a large shift in how they spent their money. This suggests that the change is often hard, or, more likely due to the evidence above, unwanted.

William's change may be explained by two factors. First, William used to spend more of his income on entertaining: "It wasn't a problem for me to go out and spend three hundred dollars on a meal for friends because I worked eighty hours a week. It was nice to have somebody to actually hang out with that didn't swing a hammer." For William, having a wife and children meant entertaining less and therefore spending less. Second, William, who worked in construction at the time, was intent on socializing with people who "didn't swing a hammer." After marrying his college-educated wife and then graduating from college himself, William could socialize with white-collar people without having to foot the bill. The way he used to spend money was no longer necessary given his mobility.

Only two white-collar-origin respondents reported changing their financial practices due to their partners' influence. One was Ian,[9] the son of a lawyer. He spent his early 20s believing in his wife's view of money: "When I first started dating Isabelle, the idea that you could buy stuff on credit cards, and you could just be in debt and not really worry about it was really a novelty. And so I was like, 'Well, this is really cool.'" Ian felt that his parents divorced, in part, because his mother was a spendthrift and his father was miserly. Given his attributions for their divorce, he concluded that thinking about money was unappealing. Ian was then susceptible to adopting Isabelle's view that one could not think about money, as it would resolve the problem of being in a relationship in which people had different spending habits. He now regretted that this approach put them in debt but also continued to follow it: "Both of us are extremely uninterested in making and maintaining a budget . . . We definitely come together on the fact that we'd like to be totally unconscious about money and not think about it."

Adopting their partners' financial sensibilities was possible if uncommon. Most others needed to negotiate their differences. The strategies they used varied, and it was not the case that class origin or gender was associated with what strategies were used. Blue-collar-origin respondents often kept spending more than their partners wished they would, but some also tried to save more to please their partners. White-collar-origin partners sometimes opened long-term savings accounts despite their partners' view that it was unnecessary, continually asked their partners to save more, or simply rolled their eyes and sighed when their partner purchased items impulsively or, they thought, unnecessarily. In general, their strategies were necessary because their financial sensibilities did not solely replicate their partners' or respond to their current incomes.

SHARED-ORIGIN COUPLES AND IDEAS OF MONEY

Shared-origin couples reported possessing financial sensibilities that were similar to those of white-collar-origin respondents in different-origin marriages. They wanted to save their money and felt that they did not spend without careful consideration. Leah (shared-origin), a deeply religious homemaker with a 1980s fashion sense, who married Luke, a Christian IT professional, said: "Neither of us are really big spenders on ourselves. We're not really into buying a lot of clothes or expensive stuff or jewelry or any of the big ticket items." Clint (shared-origin), a tall, funny, engineer married to Carlie, also an engineer, presented himself as frugal: "We both believe in saving for a 401(k). I mean, you save for retirement, you save for big purchases, save for vacation. You try and live within your means." Phil, a laid-back architect, married to Rose, a stay-at-home mother with a more serious demeanor, said: "I don't think we have a whole lot of differences in the way that we approach how we spend money . . . I think we're both the type of people that consider our purchases before we make them." Shared-origin respondents like Leah, Clint, Phil, and their partners typically preferred not to spend a lot or spend without thinking. Their preferences, like most in shared-origin marriages, were similar to those of white-collar-origin spouses who married a partner raised in another class.

Even among shared-origin couples, however, there were differences in the circumstances in which they grew up, and therefore differences in how they thought about money. Adrienne (shared-origin), a short-haired, feminist, computer-scientist turned law student, grew up with a college-educated father who was frequently without work. When she was 16, her family's financial situation worsened as her parents divorced, and her father left the country, she thought, to avoid paying child support. Adrienne's husband, Paul, a middle-aged, curly haired, computer-scientist turned journalist, grew up in a much more financially secure environment. While he did go through a short financial hard spell as a child after his father died, his mother had a job as a scientist, and she remarried a professor. He did not experience as many income fluctuations as his wife had.

Both Adrienne and Paul described themselves as frugal. Adrienne said: "We never really spent anything. We bought a house, but other than that, we really just didn't spend money." However, while their ideas about money were similar when their finances were stable, they relied on strategies that they learned in their past when money was tight. Paul once lost his job, and they responded to his unemployment in different ways. Adrienne explained Paul's position: "Paul grew up in a family where there was always enough. His family is much better off than mine is. And he just can't imagine not having enough, even when there is no income coming in . . . I'd say, 'Maybe you should pack a lunch instead of going out to lunch every day.' And he just wouldn't. He couldn't fathom that that was something that most people do when money is tight . . . He just thinks there will always be more." Adrienne, however, was used to income fluctuations from her father's sporadic unemployment and subsequent desertion and took an approach that she learned when she was younger: "It's natural to me at the first sign of trouble to say, 'Okay, we are going to bat down the hatches, we are going to stop buying this, this, and this, and we are just going to make do.'" Though they both claimed to be frugal when times were stable, their ideas did not coalesce when times were tough. Adrienne bemoaned: "It's difficult in a relationship when one person is sacrificing a lot and the other person just goes right on. And I just haven't been able to reconcile that. I don't really know what to do about that . . . It's just a difference that I don't think that we will ever be able to overcome." Respondents learned different financial strategies in response to their childhood class conditions, and even couples with minor class differences—those who both had college-educated parents who worked in professional white-collar jobs—rarely merged their financial ideas after many years of marriage.

CONCLUSION

Shared bank accounts and shared lives did not lead those from blue- and white-collar backgrounds to share their ideas of money. Those with blue-collar-origins typically wanted to take a laissez-faire approach to their money. They enjoyed the freedom to spend without thinking and to use their money to live for the day. Those from white-collar backgrounds, by contrast, usually wanted to manage their money. They wanted to set a budget and research their purchases. They were not used to depleted savings accounts and tried to avoid them; they also wanted to make sure that their future in the middle class was secure. These differences meant that those in different-origin marriages lived with a spouse who spent or saved more than they would have on their own.

Respondents then tolerated living with a spouse who had different financial sensibilities. Though it is beyond the scope of the data to know for sure, it is possible that respondents' tolerance for their partners' financial sensibilities was facilitated by the widespread valuation of both sets of sensibilities. On one hand, there are cautions against thinking too much about money and guarding it too carefully. On the other hand, there are cultural rewards for being frugal and financially careful. Because both ideas receive widespread validation and because spouses are likely to see financial differences as part of normal marriages, respondents may have been tolerant of living with a spouse whose ideas of money they did not share.

Of course, for some couples, this was easier than for others. Alexa was frustrated with Aaron's laissez-faire spending style but felt they had so much money that how he spent wasn't worth fighting about. Aaron, for his part, knew his spending style was hard on his wife but felt that spending without thinking was too important to him to compromise. Danielle and Jim had less money and fought over it more. They learned to compromise to some extent, but Danielle still pushed to spend more and Jim to save more. For most of the couples, each partner learned to tolerate their partner's style though they did not always appreciate it.

The patterns of financial sensibilities may have critical implications for class reproduction. Those from white-collar backgrounds tended to want to save and carefully budget. These tactics are likely to help them maintain their class position in retirement and in the case of a job loss. They are also likely to help their children attend college, as the amount parents have in savings is a key predictor of whether their children attend and complete college (Conley 2001). Conditional on income, different-origin couples are also likely to have less saved than shared-origin couples given that the latter have two partners who prefer to save more. The former are also are less likely to have two sets of parents who can act as financial safety nets and contribute to their own and their children's finances. The combination may disadvantage different-origin couples compared to shared-origin ones. Thus, even though they shared a class position as adults, the class individuals were raised in may have lingering implications for the position they are able to maintain for themselves and pass on to their children. This was also the case, as we will see in the next chapter, concerning ideas of work and play.

[5]

WORK AND PLAY

Vicki (white-collar-origin) felt that she could not shake her mother's ideas of work. She explained: "[My mother was] always working, that's all she does. That's where she validates herself and gets her self-esteem and self-concept from. So it definitely wears off on you as a child that you have to be the same way." Though it was decades since she had lived with her mother, Vicki found herself also seeking self-esteem and validation through work and putting in long hours to reap those rewards. She automatically signed up for leadership positions at the school where she worked as a teacher, instinctively joined new committees, and continually strategized about how to become a superintendent. She liked the idea of working from when she woke up to when she went to bed. She derived a great deal of satisfaction from her job and felt that her work provided her with self-esteem and purpose.

Though Vicki enjoyed wrapping herself up in her work, she often thought that other approaches to work were better.[1] Since the time when they met, 17 years ago, she had admired her husband John's (blue-collar-origin) very different ideas of work. John called his work as a restaurant manager "just a job." It was not, he felt, part of who he really was. He had little interest in advancing his career or even thinking about work when he was at home. Vicki admired that John so easily put his family ahead of his career, a priority that she

intellectually believed in but found difficult to internalize or practice. Even though John asked her to focus more on family, she found
her time and identity more tied up in work. Though she preferred
her husband's ideas of work to her own and to her mother's, she had
not learned to replicate them.

Vicki's and John's sensibilities regarding work were likely
rooted in their backgrounds.[2] Vicki's mother received her MBA
before becoming the vice president of a chain of hospitals.[3] Like
Vicki, those who grew up with parents in white-collar professional
positions observed that dedication to work could lead to climbing
the company ladder and that work offered self-esteem, status, and
power. It is no wonder that as adults, white-collar-origin respondents then felt that driving to succeed would bring them validation
and prestige. Women felt this as well as men; by the time respondents were coming of age, women were graduating from college at
higher rates than men, and the feminist movement promised that
identifying with work would yield personal satisfaction (Buchmann
and DiPrete 2006; Gerson 2010).[4]

Of course, work is not rewarding for everyone. John grew up
with two parents who worked in factory jobs. Work in factories and
other blue-collar settings can be less intrinsically interesting as the
work is more routine. Such jobs also tend to offer fewer opportunities to feel accomplished because workers have little say in what
tasks are selected or how they are completed. Creativity, independent thinking, and personal touches are also less likely to be valued,
as everyone is expected to make the same product or provide the
same service. Many blue-collar workers are also promoted based on
years with the company; ambition and drive are less often the basis
of increased wages or prestige. There is then little reason for those
who grew up in blue-collar communities to think that ambition
would be rewarded or that paid work offered validation and personal recognition. Those who grow up in blue collar communities

are likely to learn that validation is more tightly connected to family than work (Williams 2010).

At the time of the interviews, most respondents from both white-and blue-collar backgrounds worked in professional or managerial positions—those that typically offer opportunities for validation and status. White-collar-origin respondents tended to enjoy these aspects of their jobs, saying that their work provided a sense of accomplishment and identity. Blue-collar-origin respondents, however, usually did not. They discursively distanced themselves from their careers and were more interested in creating physical and emotional boundaries between work and home.[5] They also felt less driven and less interested in managing their career paths. Instead, they preferred to take a laissez-faire approach by keeping their eyes open to spot new opportunities that came their way. These differences in how white- and blue-collar-origin partners thought of work created inequalities in their relationships, ones that were different than the inequalities that shared-origin couples experienced. This chapter illustrates the link between class origin and partners' ideas of work as well as the resulting implications for inequality. It then turns to how they thought about their time outside their work—their play.

BELIEFS ABOUT THE PURPOSE OF WORK

Those who grew up with white-collar parents tended to see work as part of their identity. Eric (white-collar-origin), a business developer, revealed that his identity was deeply connected to his work: "I've worked so much for so long that it's tough to really get asked: 'What are your activities? Who are you out of work? What's your identity outside of work?'" To Eric, his identity was inside his work. He did not know how to answer questions about his identity outside of his job. Mary (white-collar-origin) felt the same way. In high school she was a straight-A student and voted most likely to succeed. She sailed through law school, landed a job as a lawyer, and assumed she would become a CEO. Her identity was tied to her academic and workplace success, so, when she temporarily stopped working for pay after having her first child, she felt she lost her identity. She wondered: "Who am I? I'm not really me. I'm a mom or I'm a wife. I'm not really me." She planned to return to work so that she could "find herself" again. She knew who she was when she was working.

Many white-collar-origin respondents identified with work in part because it gave them a sense of accomplishment. Alice (white-collar-origin), a lawyer, felt that her sense of self was tied to work. She enjoyed her job because she accomplished things: "I'm a working person at heart . . . I like going to work everyday. I really like doing something for somebody else and being accountable for it." Leslie (white-collar-origin) left her PhD program after having her first child and then became an office worker at her children's school. Despite that her job was not as prestigious as the one she originally imagined, she still enjoyed that she felt accomplished at work. She said, "I like working, a lot." She liked it because "it's [easy] to say, 'I've checked this task off.'" Alexa (white-collar-origin), a systems administrator, enjoyed the same feeling, despite that her husband, Aaron (blue-collar-origin) had different ideas: "I'd like to say he's taught me how to play, but I don't think he's succeeded. I actually have more play doing work than I do doing things that are play because the things I enjoy the most have end results. They're for a purpose. They achieve things. They accomplish something. I don't think he's been able to change that."[6]

Not surprisingly, given that white-collar-origin respondents tended to feel that their identity was tied to work and that they enjoyed getting things done, they also tended to feel very driven—more driven than their blue-collar-origin partners. Nathan (blue-collar-origin, a laid-off salesman) prided himself on his work ethic, but still felt that his white-collar-origin wife, Chelsey, a teacher, was more driven: "My set point is surviving. Whereas hers is excelling . . . She's really driven. She's more driven." Ian (white-collar-origin, a professor) also felt that he was more drawn to work than his wife, Isabelle (blue-collar-origin, a therapist). He described: "I think that our ambition plays out very differently. I am really driven . . . I will stay up for four days straight to meet a dead-line, and I am constantly driven to try to achieve the next thing . . . And she's just not really driven in the same way." White-collar-origin men and women then felt that work was a part of their identity and a place where they felt accomplished. They felt highly driven, more so than their partners.[7] Work offered their parents the opportunity for validation, autonomy, and a sense of accomplishment, and they felt the same about their jobs. This was despite that many, like Vicki, remembered being initially attracted to their partners because they were better able to dis-identify from work.

Blue-collar-origin respondents' ideas of work were typically different than those of their partners. To them, work was something they did, and even something they enjoyed, but it was not a part of who they were.[8] Kevin (blue-collar-origin, a student in a master's program) emphasized that unlike many white-collar respondents, work was not integral to his identity: "I'm not one of the people who's necessarily defined by what I do. I've never defined myself that way." Sue (blue-collar-origin), a physician's assistant and the breadwinner of her family, also felt strongly that her identity was not in her work: "I am not a career woman. Even though I work in a career I struggle at it at times . . . There are days I just want to go through the motions and get my paycheck."

Not identifying with their job, blue-collar-origin respondents also drew firmer boundaries between work and home. Some, like

Joe (blue-collar-origin, an accountant), limited their hours so they could be home with their families: "You have to make a living. But I don't think you need to be totally driven and spend your life at a job, you know, get there at six and home at nine and totally ignore everything else that's going on. Life has to be a balance . . . And I've never wanted a job where I had to work late. I always wanted to leave at five o'clock so I could be home and be with the family."⁹ Others, like William (blue-collar-origin, an operations analyst), limited their hours and also created emotional cut-offs from their jobs: "My ideas of work are you go, and you do your thing, and you come home. It's a way to earn a living, and outside of that I don't put much more into it. I enjoy what I do, but I don't want to bring it home. It belongs there when I'm here." Vicki (white-collar-origin, a teacher) explained that John (blue-collar-origin, a part-time restaurant manager) also made these emotional cut-offs: "I think even if he had a job that would technically be consuming, it wouldn't be for him. I think [that because of] the things he says to me about 'just leave it at work' or that kind of thing. That you don't let work get in the way of your family and your time at home, which I do all the time." Blue-collar-origin respondents were then more likely to find work to be "just a job." They distanced their identity from it and created clearer boundaries between their work and home lives.

White-collar-origin and blue-collar-origin respondents generally held different ideas about what work meant to them and how large a role it should play in their lives. Given these differences, it is then not surprising that white-collar-origin respondents tended to want to manage their career trajectory while blue-collar-origin respondents did not. Leslie (white-collar-origin, an office worker), for example, described that she strategized about how to advance her career while her husband, Tom (blue-collar-origin, a computer programmer), took a more laissez-faire approach: "He's been at the same job for quite awhile and only moves when forced to, which has happened a couple of times since we've been married. Whereas I want to get somewhere."[10] Anita (white-collar-origin, a marketer) also felt that she managed her career trajectory in ways that her husband, Todd (blue-collar-origin, a retail salesman) did not: "I think [I am] more driven in actively reaching for what I want. Whereas I feel Todd is a little more, 'Let's see what comes.' And the right thing will come."[11] Leslie and Anita (both white-collar-origin) planned how to move their careers forward, while their husbands, Tom and Todd, responded to opportunities that arose but did not actively seek them out. They took more laissez-faire approaches, ones in which their careers would unfold relatively free from self-management.

Of course, these patterns did not cohere perfectly to the class of respondents' pasts. Two white-collar-origin men described taking more laissez-faire approaches to work. Both experienced challenging mental health situations. One was Jim, whose wife said of him: "He settled for basically the second job he got, and he's never moved . . . And his argument was, 'Well I'm comfortable here.' His dad used to tell me, 'Don't pressure him because if you do, he's not stable. He might go into a depression.' " The other, Brandon, also had mental and physical health challenges that were debilitating to the point where he often went without paid work. He also did not manage his career trajectory, which he attributed to his observations of his father's experience as an engineer: "Growing up it seemed to me that work must have been torture for him because he was always ticked off and tired . . . I didn't even know what an engineer was when I got to high school. All I knew was sitting behind a desk and coming home angry at your family, and I knew I didn't want to do that." Brandon explained how his perception of his father's experience influenced him: "I revolted against that. I rebelled against that. So for me work is just a way to pay for life, and if I didn't have to work I wouldn't."[12] Likewise, a few blue-collar-origin respondents took a more managerial approach to their work. Aaron (blue-collar-origin), for example, called himself a workaholic who would not work at a job he did not love and who was driven to do his best at work and to win accolades. However, despite these exceptions, it was usually blue-collar-origin respondents who favored a laissez-faire approach to work and white-collar-origin respondents who preferred a managerial one.

INEQUALITY AND IDEAS OF WORK

"He's definitely changed jobs and career paths a couple times because of me," Anneka (white-collar-origin) said about her husband, William (blue-collar-origin). After they married, William followed Anneka across the country, from California to Washington, DC, and then again to the Midwest when Anneka found new work. He left the military because she asked him to, did not return to the oil rigs where he previously worked because it would require being away from the family for long periods of time, and left a professional white-collar job after six months in order to follow Anneka to her new job. He gave up promotions and work that he enjoyed for the sake of his wife's career.[13]

It is generally thought that women move for their husband's careers (for example, Bielby and Bielby 1992; Shauman and Noonan 2007), but in this sample of different-origin couples gender was not the main factor in who moved for whom. In total, 15 respondents moved for their partner's career. There was gender parity in how many men and women moved for their partners: eight women and seven men said they moved because of their partner's job opportunities. But there was not parity in who moved for whom in terms of class origin. Thirteen blue-collar-origin respondents moved for their partner's career, while only two white-collar-origin respondents— one man and one woman—moved for their spouse's job. If moving is a sign of prioritizing one partner's career over the other—a reasonable assumption, as moving requires the other partner to leave their current job and possibly forgo promotions or endure a period of unemployment—then it was white-collar-origin respondents' careers that were most often prioritized. In this sample, class origin, more than gender, was associated with who moved for whom.

Such inequality may follow from respondents' ideas of work. Blue-collar-origin respondents were most likely to think of a job as just a job—a route to a paycheck but little more. If this is the case, then absent losing a job, it makes little sense to leave a community and uproot a family for another job that will be just a job. It makes much more sense if work is a main component of one's identity and a route to personal fulfillment.

White-collar-origin respondents' more managerial approach to their career may also have made it more likely that their partners would move for them. They were more likely to actively seek new opportunities—opportunities that may be farther away. Those who kept their eyes open for new positions but did not go out of their way to seek new information would be less likely to be aware of job openings in other cities.

Moreover, white-collar-origin respondents were more likely to hold the idea that moving for their job was something that people like them did. College-educated people are more likely to move for their jobs than high school educated people (Finch 1989); the former are then more likely to grow up with the idea that moving is a route to career advancement. Thus, Ian (white-collar-origin) believed it was normal to move to the West Coast for graduate school and then to the Midwest for a career. His wife, Isabelle (blue-collar-origin), had less knowledge of what graduate school was and how to choose between different universities, and also "didn't have the wherewithal that somebody would go somewhere with me or that I could be making such lofty decisions." To Isabelle, such decisions were lofty in part because it was unusual to think that men might move for their wives' careers, and in part because her entire family lived in the same town. Her parents still called to ask when she was moving home. Moving away from home was not what people like her did.

Blue-collar-origin respondents also moved for their white-collar-origin partners simply because it seemed like the economically rational thing to do. Those from blue-collar backgrounds are more likely to move through college in nonlinear ways, taking more time to earn their degree (Goldrick-Rab 2006). As such, their careers in professional industries may be less advanced than those of similar aged white-collar-origin respondents. This is what happened to Rebecca (white-collar-origin), a talkative woman who grew up spending summers at a country club, and Joe (blue-collar-origin), a quiet man who spent his summers working for vacationers in the resort town where he was raised. The couple met at a bar when Rebecca was visiting friends. Though Rebecca was four years younger than Joe, she already had a job as a teacher in another state, while Joe had recently graduated from college and was looking for work. As she had a job and he did not, they decided that it only made sense that he moved for her. Blue-collar-origin respondents then often moved for their white-collar-origin spouses' career because of the latter's tendency to manage their career trajectory, consider moving for a job, and graduate from college in a shorter timeframe.

TRYING TO PAY IT BACK: WHITE-COLLAR-ORIGIN RESPONDENTS AS THEIR PARTNERS' JOB COACH

While couples prioritized white-collar-origin partners' careers, white-collar-origin partners, especially women,[14] also tried to help their spouses with their careers. Having the knowledge of how to help their partners succeed, however, was often not enough to persuade their partners to act on it. When white-collar-origin spouses' advice conflicted with their partners' ideas of work, their efforts often failed.

A few white-collar-origin women paired with blue-collar-origin men who had not finished college before they married. They all tried to convince their husbands to finish their degrees. To white-collar-origin women, completing college was simply what people did and how they showed that they valued education. They had not considered, however, that their husbands may view a college degree differently—as a way to improve their earnings. As their families were financially stable, many of their husbands saw no reason to enter or reenter higher education. It was then difficult for white-collar-origin women to persuade their blue-collar-origin husbands that college was necessary.

Alice (white-collar-origin), a confident and friendly lawyer with short blond hair and glasses, was part of a family in which graduate degrees and high-powered careers were normal. Her siblings included a vice president of a marketing company, a plastic surgeon, and a radiologist. She grew up dreaming of becoming a successful career woman, originally one who would be so devoted to her career that she would only spend 15 minutes a day with her children—time that would, however, be of the highest quality. Alice became a lawyer and opened her own practice. She married Elliott (blue-collar-origin), a man she met when she was in college and dated for nearly a decade before they married. Elliott was a waiter at a chain restaurant when they met, and, after moving to be closer to Alice, became a car salesman before they married. Alice tried to convince Elliott to do what had worked for her and her siblings—obtain a college degree to find a more prestigious career. But Elliott simply did not see the point, because to him, education and jobs were avenues to making money, and he was already making enough. He explained: "I didn't want to [go to college] initially. We had talked about why do I need to go to school when I'm making eighteen, nineteen, twenty dollars an hour? Why go to school?" Elliott did eventually attend college to appease Alice but dropped out after realizing that his future wages as a teacher would not differ dramatically from his current wages as a car salesman. Alice's encouragement could not override Elliott's idea that the purpose of education was to earn more money, and, as such, he did not need a college degree.

Vicki (white-collar-origin) also tried to convince her husband, John (blue-collar-origin) to finish his degree, but, like Alice, she failed. John stopped attending college when he found a well-paying job in internet technology, and, for years, remained a semester shy of finishing his bachelor's degree.[15] Vicki spent years telling him that she was "dead set" that "you have to finish your degree." Being college educated was part of Vicki's identity, and a part that she wanted to pass on to her children. As such, she pleaded with John to obtain his bachelor's degree—a symbol, to her, of valuing education. But, to John, a degree was not necessary as their family finances were stable, and not having a degree may have been a way of taking pride in his past. He refused to finish his last semester of college because, he said: "My dad didn't go to college, and he was able to support his family." Given that their finances were secure and that John believed a job is just a job, Vicki was unable to convince him to finish his degree and find a different job..

Lori (white-collar-origin) also struggled to help her husband, Jason (blue-collar-origin) forward his career. They both had advanced degrees, so Lori did not need to convince Jason to enroll in higher education. She did, however, model a style of work that he admired but felt he could not replicate. Both were professors, but he felt that she managed her career by creating new possibilities, while he approached his job as if he were in a blue-collar position that required completing tasks others assigned.[16] He explained: "[Lori] just had a sense of possibility that she could go out in the world and do things. And she would. She'd go out and start programs." He admired Lori's ability to manage her career but felt he was unable to follow her lead: "I still don't have this ... People like me think that the world is out there and is structured already, and I've got to adapt myself to it. It's still to this day very hard for me to think of the university as a place where I can just play, where I can go start a program. I'm usually given something to do, and I try to do it well."

Lori's modeling of how to manage a career path was not one that Jason felt he could follow. Nor did he follow Lori's advice to network in order to advance his career. Lori wanted to help Jason in a traditionally gendered way—to entertain his colleagues. But Jason refused. He refused not because he was uninterested in advancement, as some blue-collar-origin respondents were, but because he worried that his class origin would be exposed. Dinner parties with colleagues are a middle-class ritual (Rubin 1976), and he worried that he would make a faux pas that would reveal his class roots. Though Lori felt it was important to socialize with colleagues, Jason's anxiety about his past meant that he would not accept Lori's advice.[17]

White-collar-origin respondents were only successful in helping their partners' career when their partner was in crisis. Crises are times when Bourdieu (2000) predicted that changes in class sensibilities are most likely to occur, and when Swidler (2001) suggested that new ideas may be more closely followed. Anneka (white-collar-origin) created a crisis to encourage William (blue-collar-origin) to return to college. William had started college before he met Anneka and found it a great place to party but not a place where he received high grades. When he and Anneka married, he had a job in the military, one that paid well without requiring a college degree. His classed ideas of work as well as his gendered ideas of breadwinning suggested to him that he should work rather than attend college. He remembered: "I was very much brought up in, 'You need to go out there and earn a living, and you need to take care of your family.' My initial thoughts were, '[Going to college] isn't taking care of your family.' And there were opportunities for me there to earn a good living, even without a degree." His family called regularly to tell him not to go to college and asked questions such as: "How could you go back to school when your wife's pregnant and you're not going to work?" Sensing that she was losing her fight, Anneka created a crisis. She protested his decision loudly and repeatedly. She argued with him and enlisted her family to call and tell him the benefits of a college degree. She was clear that their marriage would be much, much happier, if he attended college. In a state of crisis, William left his breadwinning ideas behind and attended and graduated from college.

Ian (white-collar-origin) also helped Isabelle (blue-collar-origin) in a time of crisis. After the couple had moved across the country for Ian's job, Isabelle applied for a new state-issued license to practice therapy. Seven months after submitting her paper work, she had not heard about her application and therefore could not work. Isabelle remembered that Ian tried to give her what he called "entitlement lessons" as he firmly pushed her to call the licensing agency. Being delayed in earning money for months, she eventually worked up the courage to call, all the while thinking: "Oh, God. I'm such a pain. I can't." Her call worked, as the president of the board apologized for the delay and approved her license. But, even so, when asked about Ian's entitlement lessons, she said she still did not easily act on them: "I definitely haven't internalized that. I think it's something that I am aware of. Sometimes. But it's never a comfortable thing."

Thus, when white-collar-origin respondents tried to help their blue-collar-origin spouse advance at work their advice was usually only taken in crisis situations and even then was not regularly internalized. White-collar-origin respondents' advice rubbed against decades of acting in different ways and believing in different strategies. This suggests that actively transferring cultural capital from one adult to another is difficult at best. Even advice from a respected and loved partner was not often trusted, acted on, or internalized if it conflicted with already internalized ways of thinking.

SHARED-ORIGIN COUPLES AND IDEAS OF WORK

Shared-origin marriages were often characterized by a different dynamic. Unlike in different-origin marriages, both partners often expected to find work validating, fulfilling, and a key part of their identity. Women in shared-origin marriages, however, had such high expectations of finding validating work that they left or never joined the full-time paid labor force when they could not find it. Thus, in order to meet their expectations about work, the majority of women in shared-origin marriages, decided, paradoxically, to leave full-time jobs and become part-time workers or full-time stay-at-home mothers.

Amy (shared-origin) was an energetic 39-year-old woman with straight blond hair pulled back in a low professional ponytail. She always thought that fulfilling work was in her future. In fact, she remembered telling her family that she would have a powerful and exciting job: "I wanted to be the president [of the United States]. My grandfather was actually involved in politics and he was a state senator, and I remember telling him that I was going to be president and he said, 'Oh, you could be the president's wife.' And I said, 'No, I'm going to be the president.' " Amy's belief that she would become the president of the United States was not a childhood fantasy, but a belief that lasted until adulthood; her husband said that she is still disappointed that she is not on track to reach that goal.

Amy has not made it to the White House, and, in fact, struggled to find a fulfilling career at all. She spent her first years out of college working in the financial industry but quit after thinking: "This isn't what I want to be when I grow up. And you should certainly not spend this many hours doing something you don't really like." She then turned to a career she thought she would enjoy more—photojournalism. But her ideas of photojournalism were very romantic—traveling the world to snap pictures of faraway places. She again felt unfulfilled as she instead found herself at the public library taking pictures of children's storytimes.[18] Amy never imagined she would be a stay-at-home mother, but after being unable to find a validating career it went from being unimaginable to being preferable: "We had decided to have a child when I was not happy with where I was professionally. It made sense in a way to not go back to work because I didn't have any work that I wanted to go back to." Amy did not view work as "just a job" or as a financial necessity. Work was supposed to be something she wanted to do and something that would bring her prestige, adventure, and fulfillment. Lacking these options, she left the labor force to become a stay-at-home mother and to search for a more fulfilling career.

Jen (shared-origin), a short, curly-haired, spritely woman, similarly recalled, "When I was growing up I never thought I wanted to be a mom." She wanted to be an art professor, and after obtaining a master's degree she landed a job as an adjunct. The job did not go as she expected because she found that it was not adding to her self-esteem. She remembered: "I just thought, "You see the time that I am putting into this job and the effort that I am putting into this? If you don't think it's worth it to advocate for me, then you know what? I'm okay. You really just pay me gas money to get here." Given that her career was not validating, and, in addition, that her son was having trouble in elementary school, she decided it made sense to remove herself from the paid labor force.

Perhaps ironically, dropping out of the paid labor force allowed the majority of shared-origin women to find more fulfilling work. Not burdened by needing to earn money, they could pursue their interests regardless of the pay.[19] After Jen quit her job as an adjunct art professor, she created and sold her own art from home. Leah, a drama major in college, left the labor force after disliking the politics at her workplace. She took up freelance writing and videography, both of which she found more fulfilling. Alisha found that her passion was in volunteering, so she cut back her paid work to 15 hours a week. These women assumed that their jobs would be validating and enjoyable, and found work outside the full-time labor force that made this possible.[20] Like white-collar-origin women in different-origin marriages, not only did they expect to find work that could be part of their identity, but they also felt that they had the agency to find a way to do so.

Shared-origin men were constrained by their breadwinning role, and therefore did not feel that they had the option of leaving the labor force when their careers were unrewarding. Brad (shared-origin) went to law school because, according to his wife, "His parents wanted him to follow in the family footsteps and there was a lot of pressure." He is now a lawyer with his own private practice but does not enjoy what he does: "If he had it to do again, he would have done another pathway. I think he's good at what he does because he's smart, but I think if he had it to do again, he'd be captaining a charter boat or fishing or a nature guide or an engineer." Brad, however, did not have the option of leaving his job as a lawyer to become a charter boat captain as gender norms cast him in a breadwinning position. Thus, while shared-origin women risked financial instability should they divorce, they had the option to look for fulfilling work in more part-time and untraditional venues. White-collar-origin women in different-origin marriages sometimes also lacked this option as their husbands were less interested in career advancement and their own income was needed to make ends meet. Thus, similar ideas played out in different ways depending on the class origin of each partner.

PLAY

Blue- and white-collar-origin respondents not only had different sensibilities regarding work but also regarding how to spend their time outside work. Scott (white-collar-origin) was a short, curly-haired man who seemed comfortable in khakis and a button-down shirt. We met in the house he and his wife designed—one with bold colors, high ceilings, and art selected from the local fair. He convinced his wife that building their own home was a good idea—she thought an existing home would be just fine. Over the jazz playing in the background, Scott also told me that he had just returned from a ski trip to Utah—one that he went on without his wife. This was not the first vacation he had taken without her. Though he loved his wife, their ideas of leisure were so different that he sometimes went away without her.

Scott had not originally thought he would marry Gina. They met through an online dating site, and he remembered being initially drawn to her because of her close ties to her parents and her love of skydiving. He later realized, however, that he misread Gina's passion for skydiving as a passion for adventure. He figured out: "She wasn't necessarily those things that I was looking for. She definitely was not interested in traveling the world. She wasn't all that interested in what was going on in the larger world around her." When Scott was not traveling or at least reading about international events, he wanted to get out of the house. He wanted to go to local parks, walk downtown, sample new restaurants, explore museums, and attend sporting events. His wife, Gina (blue-collar-origin), had no interest in these activities—she saw leisure as a time to relax, and preferred her local neighborhood over international places, familiar white bread over exotic foods, and spending vacations unwinding at resorts over skiing down slopes or backpacking through Europe. Scott could not imagine a future with a person who preferred using leisure time to relax rather than explore and who was more interested in her corner of the state than in countries far away. So, before they married, Scott dumped Gina.

Scott then pursued a woman who lived a cultured life in Manhattan. He realized, however, that she would not leave her career to follow his, so he returned to the Midwest and to Gina. He figured that he could persuade Gina that together they could travel across Europe, cook exotic foods, and hike through national parks. On weekends they could follow politics, learn about new cultures, and attend local events. After marrying, he persistently pressured her to adopt his leisure habits and denigrated her for wanting to stay in her comfort zone. After nearly a decade of marriage, however, Scott realized that Gina was not going to change. He reduced the amount of pressure he put on her to enjoy what he enjoyed. He told himself that her ability to resist his pressure was admirable. He tried to respect her for being able to be happy without getting out of the country or even the house.

Scott's and Gina's different ideas of leisure were emblematic of the differences described by many different-origin couples. Many white-collar-origin respondents, like Scott, had sensibilities that suggested that leisure time should be busily managed in order to include many activities. Their tastes tended to be those of cultural omnivores (Peterson and Kern 1996), meaning that they enjoyed both highbrow and middlebrow activities, things like international travel as well as football games. In contrast, those with blue-collar-origins, like Gina, tended to have sensibilities that were more laissez-faire. They preferred not to use their free time to expand their cultural repertoire but instead to relax and see what happened.[21] Their tastes were those of cultural univores—they enjoyed a smaller range of activities and their tastes tended not to include highbrow activities (Peterson and Kern 1996).[22] They were happier staying home and relaxing rather than attending the theater or visiting a museum.[23] These differences likely stemmed from their childhoods, as white- and blue-collar children grow up doing different things for fun and using leisure time in different ways. White-collar children tend to grow up packing their free time with cultural activities (Lareau 2003; Vincent and Ball 2007), which gives them the sense that leisure time should be busy and planned time that occurs, at least in part, outside the home. The activities they participate in also tend to be a mix of middlebrow activities that are accessible to many as well as highbrow activities that are accessible primarily to those in their class. They then learn to be busy cultural omnivores whose leisure activities overlap with widely rewarded activities.

Children raised in blue-collar families are less likely to be involved in many activities, especially those associated with high culture (Lareau 2003). Their parents tend to have tighter budgets that prevent them from being involved in a plethora of organized activities, and they also have less incentive to do so. Knowledge of poetry or the ability to play the violin may help children succeed in middle-class settings, but do not typically help people get their foot in the door at the local factory or help them make connections with local service-sector managers. In blue-collar settings, being normal and fitting in are often prized, not showing off unique skills or being active in a large range of highbrow activities (Stephens, Markus, and Townsend 2007). More time is also spent spontaneously hanging out with friends or relaxing with family (Lareau 2003; Rubin 1976)—family that are more likely to work in physically demanding jobs and who may prefer relaxation to leaving the house. These differences likely carried over into respondents' adult lives, as white-collar-origin spouses often preferred to spend their leisure time busily accumulating cultural capital through participating in highbrow and middlebrow events that were inside and outside the home, while blue-collar-origin respondents favored taking a laissez-faire approach that prized relaxing at home and going with the flow.

White-collar-origin respondents then spent their time trying to convince their partners not to take a relaxed, laissez-faire approach to leisure but to leave their home and become more involved in cultural events. Lori (white-collar-origin) learned that she would need to do this the first time she visited her husband, Jason (blue-collar-origin), at his childhood home. After spending the week sitting in a room that she described as a cave— a wood-paneled room with dark curtains that were kept closed— she realized that her husband and his family had no desire to get out of the house or to be involved with cultural activities. She tried to persuade them to do something else—explore the nearby city, go to the beach, or even just take a walk. She failed in convincing them to leave the relaxation of their home behind, and, a quarter-century later, she usually failed to persuade Jason to leave the house with her. She called getting him out of the house her "lifetime ordeal." He still preferred to spend his leisure time relaxing at home, while she still preferred to manage her leisure time so that she would be more involved with cultural events outside their home.

Mia (white-collar-origin) also was interested in being involved in more cultural events than was her husband, Kevin (blue-collar-origin). She grew up traveling on the weekends and wanted to do the same as an adult. She also wanted to go to the local theater, spend time ice skating, and take her children to community events. She was a cultural omnivore—one who enjoyed highbrow events like theater as well as middlebrow events like ice skating. Her husband, however, was more of a cultural univore. He enjoyed sports but refused to attend the highbrow (and feminized) theater and had little interest in taking weekend trips. He preferred to stay home and watch football on TV—to spend more time relaxing than accumulating middle-class cultural capital.

Even when they were at home, white-collar-origin respondents preferred to spend more time in engaging in highbrow activities than did their blue-collar-origin spouses. Ryan (white-collar-origin) grew up spending weekend afternoons going to lunch, to a bookstore, and then settling on the couch to read with his family. As an adult, he still spent his leisure time reading as well as listening to new music. Katie (blue-collar-origin) grew up playing in her backyard and watching TV. Ryan tried to share his interests with Katie, but, after 12 years of marriage, she still did not appreciate his highbrow tastes: "She likes Shell Silverstein [a poet who writes for children] a lot. That's where she draws the line."

Dan (white-collar-origin) also preferred to spend his weekends involved in a variety of activities. He wanted to spend part of his weekends exploring parks and hiking outside. When he was home, he preferred to spend time "doing something creative, something I can lose myself in." He tried to involve his wife, Gabriella (blue-collar-origin), in some of his artistic endeavors but found that she had trouble accessing some of the cultural and artistic skills he already had. She also simply did not want to spend her weekends creating new things but instead wanted to relax: "I'd rather sleep late in bed, read a book. That's my downtime. I don't want to be moving around."

Vacations followed the same patterns for different-origin couples. White-collar-origin respondents wanted to use their time to expand their horizons. As such, they wanted to manage their time in order to pack in as many sight-seeing events and museums as possible. They wanted to explore cities, travel across the country or out of the country, and learn about new places. They also enjoyed beaches and lake houses but often not for long periods of time, as the slower pace left them bored.[24] Blue-collar-origin respondents, however, often preferred spending a week on a beach relaxing. They had no need to engage in a wide range of cultural activities—years of marriage had not turned them into cultural omnivores or those who tended to manage their cultural capital accumulation.[25]

Couples resolved their differences in a variety of ways. Some white-collar-origin women took their children to plays and musicals while their blue-collar-origin husbands stayed home. White-collar-origin men sometimes took their children to sporting events while their blue-collar wives relaxed at home. On vacation, couples spent one day relaxing and the next sight-seeing, or went on vacations that one would enjoy more than the other. They also found movies they could agree on and friends and family they both liked to visit. Much of their time was also spent at their children's events, which each spouse enjoyed.

One activity, however, regularly led to passionate disputes. White-collar-origin women tended to deeply dislike how much their blue-collar-origin husbands watched television, a leisure activity that was both part of "low" culture and contradicted their ideas of using leisure to accumulate an array of cultural capital.[26] Chelsey (white-collar-origin) found her husband's love of television to be incomprehensible and distasteful: "I just can't stand how much TV he watches. It drives me crazy . . . And he watches the same movie over and over again. There are about five movies that he likes, and they are on all the time, and he watches them every single time they're on. And I don't get that at all." George (blue-collar-origin) said that his wife, Norah (white-collar-origin), had such disdain for TV that he reduced the amount he watches: "I was willing to watch TV, but she pointed out that TV is a lot of mindless entertainment that really doesn't enrich us very much. So we cut back on that." To white-collar-origin women, watching television may be the antithesis of using leisure time for cultural capital accumulation as well as being a symbol of low culture. Several women hated that their husbands engaged in it and convinced them to stop when they could.[27]

Shared-origin couples had few disagreements or differences about their leisure activities. Most spoke of how busy they were with their children's activities, household improvements, and vacations that balanced relaxing beaches with national parks and hurried sight-seeing. None talked of highbrow interests that left their partners disinterested or felt that they had hours to relax. In general, they did not take a laissez-faire approach to leisure, but managed their free time through busy schedules and many events.

CONCLUSION

After years of marriage, respondents from different class backgrounds did not share their preferences regarding work or play. Those with white-collar-origins, like Vicki, tended to be driven to advance at work and see work as part of their identity and a source of validation. Those with blue-collar-origins, like John, were more likely to understand their jobs to be routes to paychecks more so than validation, and, as such, made clearer cut-offs between work and home. They also took a more laissez-faire approach to career advancement, while those with white-collar-origins were more likely to actively manage their career trajectories. These differences meant that couples tended to prioritize the white-collar-origin partner's career.

Couples also had differences in terms of what they wanted to do with their time outside work. Those with white-collar roots were more likely to favor managing their leisure time to participate in a wide variety of highbrow and middlebrow activities that occurred both inside and outside the house. Their partners had less interest in highbrow activities and in leaving the house; they saw their leisure time not as an opportunity to expand their cultural horizons but to simply relax.

That these differences persisted after years of sharing resources suggests the improbability of taking the class out of the person after taking the person out of the class. The differences also remained even as spouses actively tried to get their partners to change—to drag them out of the house and into the theater or a college classroom. Even respected and loved partners were unable to transmit their cultural capital to the person with whom they spent the most time, suggesting that cultural capital may not be easily transferred from one adult to another through even the strongest of ties. Individuals, rather than couples, were the holders of tastes and sensibilities.

These differences in sensibilities have potential consequences, both within couples and between them. As blue-collar-origin partners were more likely to put their spouse's career first, they may be in more precarious positions should their relationships dissolve. This disparity may be compounded as blue-collar-origin respondents were more likely to keep their eyes open for career opportunities rather than searching them out, making it more difficult for them to advance or find new work. Their lesser interest in using leisure time to get out of the house and into a range of activities may also have economic consequences as some employers reward active leisure pursuits and as social connections made through play can facilitate advancement at work (Lizardo 2013; Rivera 2011).[28] Inequality between couples, not just within them, may also arise as couples in which two partners are from white-collar backgrounds may engage in more leisure activities that are rewarded by workplaces.

However, though the nonassimilation of upwardly mobile respondents may have negative consequences for their own career advancement, it may benefit a younger generation of potentially upwardly mobile individuals. Hiring decisions are often influenced by the sharing of sensibilities and leisure activities (Rivera 2011, 2012). To the extent that upwardly mobile individuals are on hiring committees, they may be better able to appreciate the work and leisure preferences of those who share their class origin. Their nonassimilation may then help upwardly mobile individuals who come after them succeed in their new class.

Gender inequality also played out in different ways depending on the class composition of the couple. In different-origin marriages, gender was less associated with who moved for whom than was class origin. In shared-origin marriages, couples tended to have more traditional gender dynamics. Men's careers were ostensibly put first as they tended to stay in the labor force while women were more likely to leave it. However, absent a divorce, women experienced some advantages as they had more freedom to look for an enjoyable career.[29] They thought that work should be fulfilling, and because their husbands were breadwinners, they had the space to search for a job that would be intrinsically satisfying.

More so than in shared-origin marriages, those in different-origin marriages then lived with a partner whose ideas of work and play differed from their own. Though it is a proposition that cannot be proven with the data at hand, it is plausible that the widespread cultural support for both sets of sensibilities allowed each partner to tolerate the other's differences. Blue-collar-origin respondents' ideas of work were not only initially appreciated by their partners (see Chapter 3) but are also appreciated in the broader culture. Prioritizing family and refraining from making work one's life are popular sentiments, ones crystallized in one blue-collar-origin respondent's favorite saying: "Nobody ever put on their tombstone that they wish they could have spent more time at the office." At the same time, white-collar-origin respondents' idea that work should be a vocation is an old one with widespread appreciation (Weber 1905). Likewise, using leisure for enjoying cultural activities and for relaxing are both widely valued.[30] The differences they navigated were then ones that were not easily put in a hierarchy. In some ways, the same can be said for the differences discussed in the following chapter, those that center on housework and time.

[6]

HOUSEWORK AND TIME

Lillian (blue-collar-origin, a stay-at-home mother), a soft-spoken, artistic woman told her husband that it was okay for him to avoid housework. She said: "[He's learned] that he doesn't have to clean up the house. That it's safe. I'm not going to come down on him if his clothes aren't picked up even though it's sometimes an irritant." Anneka (white-collar-origin, a doctoral student), an athletic and studious woman with short curly blonde hair, had a different take on the same phenomena: "I get annoyed with him for leaving his clutter around the house because I always feel like it's left there with the implication of 'Anneka's going to come through and pick that up later.' I know deep in his heart he's not thinking his maid service is coming through; he just leaves clutter around. But that's probably the other thing we argue about most."

Both Lillian and Anneka had husbands who left things around the house, and both did end up picking up after their husbands. Their common practices, however, did not produce common feelings about them. Lillian, like many blue-collar-origin women, saw housework as her responsibility and told her husband it was fine to do less. Anneka, like many white-collar-origin women, however, felt resentful that she cleaned up after her husband and argued with him about the division of labor. Both women did more housework than their husbands, but they felt very differently about the inequality.

This chapter adds to existing literature on housework—literature that repeatedly finds that women do more housework than men (Brines 1994; Gupta 2006, 2007; Hochschild 1989; Killewald and Gough 2010; Lachance-Grzela and Bouchard 2010; Tichenor 2005). This chapter shows that while women usually do more work than men, their class background is related to how they feel about the unequal division of labor. The second half of the chapter also reveals that planning—one form of housework—does not simply fall along gendered lines but is divided according to class origin as well.

CLASS ORIGIN AND FEELINGS ABOUT THE DIVISION OF LABOR

Women do more housework than men (Brines 1994; Tichenor 2005). Yet, not all women do the same amount of housework. Low-income women tend to spend more time on housework than high-income women (Gupta, Sayer, and Cohen 2009). Assuming that this was true during respondents' childhoods, blue- and white-collar-origin women would have been exposed to mothers who performed different amounts of housework. They may also have been exposed to different gender norms about who does chores. Those in blue-collar families tend to believe in a more gendered division of labor while those in white-collar families tend to profess a belief in a more egalitarian split (Deutsch and Saxon 1998; Hochschild 1989; Pyke 1996).[1] As gendered ideas of housework formed in childhood can follow individuals into adulthood (Cunningham 2001), those from different classes may have different orientations toward housework.

For the couples in this study, class origin mattered little in who was in charge of the housework. Gender, unsurprisingly, mattered much more. Two-thirds of couples agreed that the woman did more housework; only in one case did a couple agree that the man did more.[2] But, while class origin did not matter in respondents' attributions for who did how much around the house, it did matter in how they felt about the inequality. Here, as others have found, it was not inequality in the division of labor that by itself led to specific feelings but was instead the intersection of women's expectations with what their husbands were willing to do (Hochschild 1989). Women with white-collar-origins were likely to expect their husbands to be equal partners. When they were not, they typically became upset about the uneven division of labor and tried to manage it. Women with blue-collar-origins tended to expect to do the majority of the housework themselves. They were then less disturbed about the unequal division of labor and took a more laissez-faire approach to who did which chores.

Many white-collar-origin women, such as Vicki (white-collar-origin, a teacher), started their marriages prepared to manage the division of labor. Vicki remembered that when she married John (blue-collar-origin, a restaurant manager) she studied the book, *Halving It All,* to learn how to create an equal division of labor. She recalled: "I was adamant that if we both work, then we both do half of everything." Yet, the lessons from the book were not enough; Vicki spent the next decade trying to arrive at a more equitable division of labor. She stated: "It took us seven years to get it right, or maybe ten years. It takes a long time. A lot of negotiating and fighting." As part of her managerial efforts, Vicki allocated and reallocated tasks, taught John to clean more thoroughly, and monitored his progress. Vicki cared enough about the division of labor to read about it and spend the first 10 years of their marriage searching for a split that would feel equal.

Inequality in the household division of labor also bothered Mia (white-collar-origin), a lively brunette who began her career as a banker and then became a stay-at-home mother. She remembered feeling bothered about the division of labor from the beginning of her marriage: "When we first bought the house, I was doing all of the cleaning, and Kevin was watching a lot of football. And I was like, 'This is a bunch of B.S.'" Kevin would not do more household work and instead recommended that they hire a woman to clean their home. This worked until their finances changed, and they could no longer afford to pay others to clean their house. Ten years later, Mia, now a stay-at-home mother, again tried to prompt Kevin to do what she considered a fairer share of cleaning but found herself failing: "Just last week we had a discussion and I said, 'Since we're both home [Kevin is now a master's student], I don't think I should be doing all of the cleaning. You could clean the master bathroom.' I am still waiting for him to clean the master bathroom so we don't agree on that." Mia tried to manage the division of labor, though she did so unsuccessfully.

Regardless of whether they were in the paid labor force, white-collar-origin women typically were conscious of real or perceived inequalities in the division of labor. Stay-at-home-mother Mary (white-collar-origin), a serious and ambitious woman, also tried to negotiate an equal division of labor: "My impression [of his idea] is that he goes to work and does nine to five there and then I do kids and house. But those hours tend to be in my mind a lot more than his job. So that's something we're still negotiating." Caroline (white-collar-origin, a researcher) had a similar problem. Her husband worked full time while she worked part time, but she did not feel that their different hours of paid work should mean that the housework was all her responsibility. After years of negotiating, she decided that she could not convince her husband to change and so she hired help. She felt it was necessary as "a cleaning lady is definitely cheaper than a marriage counselor."

Even in couples in which the woman worked for pay and the husband was home, the unequal division of labor was a source of stress for the white-collar-origin woman. Alexa (white-collar-origin, a systems administrator) worked full time; her husband, Aaron, had recently retired. Alexa did not hide her anger when speaking of housework:

> There's so much sitting and staring at me every time I walk into that house that I can't sit for two hours. He considers that to be a failing on my part. I consider it to be a failing on his part that he doesn't see the stuff. I went down the stairs with the broom today, and I got this God awful pile of dust just going down the stairs. And I said, "Does nobody besides me see these piles of hair inside the stairs?" He says, "You know, I do clean that but probably not as often as I should. Builds up awfully fast, you know." And all I hear is, "No, you don't see it. Builds up real fast my eye. Builds up 'til I sweep it."

White-collar-origin women wanted to manage their household division of labor so that it would be equal. As their blue-collar-origin husbands did not go along with their plans to the extent that they wished, they spent years researching, negotiating, reassigning tasks, monitoring their husbands' work, and complaining about the unequal division of labor.

White-collar-origin women in shared-origin marriages did the same. Diana, a feisty, energetic teacher, spent longer than she wished trying to create a more equitable division of labor. One day, sick of being the one to clean, she did something she later regretted. She narrated: "He had this pile of laundry sitting on the floor, sitting on the floor, sitting on the floor. So he'd left his long underwear on the floor, and I kept saying, 'Could you just pick it up?' So he came home finally and he goes, 'Where's my underwear?' And I said, 'I threw it away. I'm done. I was tired of looking at it.'" Adrienne (shared-origin) also felt that her differences with her shared-origin husband, Paul, made her take steps that she felt were drastic. When they "were financially in the worst possible shape" she hired a housekeeper "because otherwise it would've been on me." She explained: "I was tired of being angry about that. He just doesn't think about it, and I think about it all the time." That both white-collar-origin women who married blue- and white-collar-origin men spent years and tears trying to manage an equitable division of labor suggests that the perceived inequalities were not based on the class origin of their husbands, as neither blue- nor white-collar-origin men met their standards. Rather, they believed that gender inequalities existed, and they felt compelled to try to change them.

However, while the distribution of labor may be unequal regardless of the class origin of the men, not all women were angry about it or tried to manage it. Women with blue-collar roots tended to take a much more laissez-faire approach to housework. They tended to believe in going with the flow to get housework done and were not as upset if this meant they did more than half. Unlike white-collar-origin women, Gina (blue-collar-origin, a stay-at-home mother) did not read about housework or try to manage their division of labor. Concerning housework she said, "I don't think we really discussed it. We just fell into roles." Gabriella (blue-collar-origin, a librarian) also did not enter her marriage with ideas about how to manage the housework. Instead she said: "We didn't really talk about it . . . It's naturally divided itself."

Taking a laissez-faire approach to housework—falling into roles or letting them divide themselves—meant falling into gender roles. Not only was this the case, but their nonmanagerial style also meant that they did not try to reassign roles later. They did not see the need to, as they did not expect their husbands to take an equal role. Sidney (blue-collar-origin, a stay-at-home mother) credited her husband not with doing an equal amount of the housework but with being cleaner than other men: "He never leaves clothes on the floor. I have to hand him that, he's really clean compared to some guys." Christie (blue-collar-origin, a social worker) did not try to convince her husband to do more housework but counted herself lucky that he did not complain about the housework that she did: "It's my responsibility pretty much. In terms of doing the dishes, all of that. But the nice thing about Mike is he doesn't get upset about it." Jill (blue-collar-origin, a local politician) also told her husband not to worry about the housework: "I'll say to him, 'Let that go. Hang out with the kids today instead.'" These blue-collar-origin women did not manage the division of labor but took a more laissez-faire approach, one that meant that they did the majority of the housework without assigning tasks or negotiating roles.

The economy of expectations was then different for women with different class origins. Women with white-collar and blue-collar roots both usually said they did more housework than their husbands, but women from white-collar-roots felt more perturbed by this inequality. Of course, these patterns were not absolute. Andrea (white-collar-origin, a stay-at-home mother), for example, sometimes resented that her husband did little around the house but also said: "I don't think we talk about it, we just tend to gravitate towards things we like to do, and it's okay." Jill (blue-collar-origin) reported that she often told her husband not to worry about the housework, but at the same time, once a year she would become frustrated and ask him to do more. The managerial/laissez-faire divide then represents the general pattern of how class origin relates to housework, but the pattern neither captured every respondent nor every moment in time for a particular respondent. And, as shown below, blue-collar-origin women who felt their homes were potentially stigmatizing carefully managed the appearance of their house, even if they did not manage the division of labor.

HOUSEWORK AND CLASS SENSIBILITIES

Feelings about housework were not only about the division of labor but also about the projection of class identities. Beverly Skeggs (1997:90) observed the following about white working-class women:

> When a visitor enters the house they see their most intimate environments through the eyes of the other and they apologize. They continually doubt their own judgments . . . They care about how they are seen in the eyes of the other. They feel they have to prove themselves through every object, every aesthetic display, every appearance. Their taste in furniture and aesthetic organization becomes along with their clothes, body, caring practices and every other aspect of their lives a site of doubt. A site where they are never sure if they are getting it right. They assume that certainty exists elsewhere, that others have it . . . The working class are never free from the judgments of imaginary and real others that position them, not just as different, but as inferior, as inadequate . . . Class is lived out as the most omnipresent form, engendering surveillance and constant assessment of themselves.

Homes are then sites where people—especially women, who are viewed as responsible for the domestic sphere—may feel judged for their class position and where they try to prove that they are respectable despite their lower class position. As upwardly mobile women moved into the middle class, they gained the financial resources to use their home to display their new station in the middle class. However, having financial resources did not always give them a sense of security that their house—and, by extension, themselves—would not be judged.

Madison (blue-collar-origin), a petite, soft-spoken woman who wore a fashionable red top with her jeans rolled up around her shins during the interview, worried about how her home reflected her class position. She grew up in a home that was constantly under construction and in disrepair. She spent afternoons with her mother dreaming about how to improve their home when more money came in. But the money did not arrive fast enough to avoid social stigma. Some of Madison's peers knew the state of her home and ostracized her because they thought she was poor. As a child, Madison learned that the state of her home was related to the state of her social network.

As an adult with more resources, Madison wanted to create a home that would turn away stigma. Her goal was to create an upper-middle-class home, a home which distanced her from her past. But, like the working-class women whom Skeggs interviewed, she could not seem to get it right. She made tables and charts of where each dish would go, only to decide that the system was wrong and start again. She organized and reorganized the linen closets so that her home looked respectable and neat. She read home decorating magazines and watched home improvement television shows so that she could pick out the right ornamental items. She felt she tended to obsess about the appearance of her home. Her obsession had a goal: "For me it's about creating this atmosphere that I thought, 'This is what a nice, comfortable kind of middle-class home looks like, or upper-middle-class' . . . And it's not so much for me keeping up with the Joneses. It's just creating this image that's in my head."

Yet, Madison's research into creating an upper-middle-class home did not make her feel that she was getting it right. She tried to gain the approval of her white-collar in-laws—those who had the type of home she always wanted—but she appeared to them be trying too hard, doing too much. She felt judged and as if she was getting it wrong when they would say to her: "Why would you do that? Why is that necessary?" Her in-laws were less emotionally invested in their home—they proved their class position through their inherited wealth, prestigious jobs, and educations. To Madison, however, her home was a site where she felt particularly vulnerable for being judged for her class background. If her home did not look "classy," then Madison could be exposed as coming from a lower class. Madison understood the consequences of that—she remembered feeling rejected because her home represented her poverty, and some of her classmates did not play with the poor. As an adult, Madison obsessed over housework, as she tried to create the "upper-middle-class image" in her head but did so without the background to feel confident in her choices. She tried to do too much, at least according to her white-collar in-laws, and still felt that she could never get her house to be "right."

Isabelle (blue-collar-origin, a therapist) also worried that her home could be harshly judged, and, by extension, so could she. Her husband, Ian (white-collar-origin, a professor) described how deeply she cared about the state of her home, a feeling that he did not share: "She can't be happy if the house isn't nicely decorated, all put together. It was actually a source of conflict when we first moved because she wasn't working and she was spending all of her time and a lot of money that we didn't have on furnishing the house. And I would have preferred to do that more slowly and have her focus on getting a job. But she sort of felt like she couldn't even go out and do that until she felt like her house was a home . . . I don't particularly like the house to be messy and grimy, but it doesn't make me crazy. And with her it's incapacitating."

To Isabelle, unlike to her husband, the upkeep of their home was urgent because it was not only about aesthetics but also about judgments of her class past. She explained: "I like things to be clean and orderly. I think that comes from wanting to be different than my background. I get really paranoid people are going to think we're really trashy." Isabelle worried that people would conflate having trash with being trashy. Though no one in her adult life had accused her of this, her childhood class position meant that accusations of being white trash were ones that she wanted to preemptively fend off.

Jason (blue-collar-origin, a professor) also felt a connection between housework and his class background. But, unlike the women whose class origin led them to do more housework, Jason's interpretation of his class origin and his gendered responsibilities meant that he did less. He grew up in a small home that was not well maintained. For five years, his parents' kitchen cabinets lacked doors. For 15 years, his family walked on concrete floors because they ripped out the linoleum without replacing it. To Jason, this became normal, and less a source of embarrassment than it might have been to Madison and Isabelle as his gender shielded him from the notion that it was his responsibility to care for the house.

Jason and his wife, Lori (white-collar-origin, a professor), currently live in a beautiful home that they purchased with the help of Lori's inheritance. The house is situated in a neighborhood where long driveways lead past well-maintained front lawns and children safely ride their bikes on the sidewalk-less roads to the racquet club down the street. Jason, however, had trouble appreciating his home and neighborhood as the distance between them and those of his past made him feel alienated from his current residence. Lori explained: "He would say, 'I haven't done anything to deserve this house!' He doesn't even in his deep psychology see the house as being his."

Feeling like the house wasn't his meant, partially, that he felt unable to care for it. Lori revealed: "There is an idea about how you keep up the yard, how you maintain things, that he feels is foreign to him. It intimidates him. He doesn't want to make decisions in these areas." He also felt like he might do simple things regarding the house wrong, like calling the wrong snow-plow company or selecting the wrong mailbox. Yet, unlike Madison and Isabelle, who also worried about getting household maintenance projects wrong, his gender relieved him of feeling that he was responsible for the house. He then opted out of tasks that he felt he might get wrong, rather than obsessing over them. Feelings about housework then are related to the class respondents grew up in but men and women act upon them in different ways. As with ideas of housework, ideas of how to use time also related to experiences with gender and class origin.

TIME

Gabriella (blue-collar-origin), an affable, out-going librarian, and Dan (white-collar-origin), a financial analyst with long gray hair and an artistic flair, were married in a small ceremony at a church not far from where they lived. Despite the careful planning that a wedding entails, a theme arose that they had not planned: their differences in their ideas of time. Dan remembered that during the wedding the minister "pointed out that I tended to plan a lot and Gabriella tended to wing it." Gabriella recounted the story that the best man told: "Dan loves to make jack-o'-lanterns for Halloween . . . He plans out the face and then he carves it. I'm not a big jack-o'-lantern person, but 'Oh I love you, honey. Let's make jack-o'-lanterns together.' But I didn't want to plan it out, so I just started cutting and ended up with this pumpkin with this big hole. That exemplifies it. Dan's like, 'Plan it out' and I'm like, 'Just start cutting!' "

On the day they married, Dan then was one who wanted to plan and manage time while Gabriella preferred to "wing it"—to take a more laissez-faire approach to time. These differences, after eight years of marriage, had not disappeared. Dan revealed that he is now more willing to "allow things to happen" but does this to please his wife rather than because his sensibilities had changed. Generally, Dan felt that their differences remained. Dan described: "I tend to plan a lot and Gabriella tends to wing it. That's been a continuing dynamic in our relationship. I've got a budget all set out and I write notes about what we need to do on the weekend and what we need to plan for, and she's just kinda: 'Whatever, we'll deal with it when it comes up.'"

Differences in ideas of time management are often attributed to gender. Women are viewed as responsible for planning children's doctor's appointments, play dates, the couple's social time, family meals, and extracurricular activities (DeVault 1999; Tichenor 2005). But, as some have noted (Burton and Tucker 2009; England, McClintock, and Shafer 2011), planning may also be related to class destination. In this section I argue that ideas of planning and time use are neither entirely attributable to gender nor to adult class position. As Dan and Gabriella's case begins to suggest, planning is also related to class origin. White-collar-origin respondents tended to want to manage their time, while blue-collar-origin respondents typically preferred to take a more laissez-faire approach to time by going with the flow.[3]

Time and Class Origin

Blue- and white-collar-origin respondents felt that their parents had very different ideas of time. Ian (white-collar-origin, a professor), for example, described that his mother planned carefully before he and his wife, Isabelle, visited: "My mom, she's very planned out. So she'll start talking to us three weeks before we're going to go visit and telling us about the menus that she's picked out and exactly who's going to sleep where and 'Well, I've got this air mattress. I think it's going to be okay. If that doesn't work out, I've got this back up plan.'" Ian's wife, Isabelle (blue-collar-origin), did not have parents who planned: "Whenever we visit Isabelle's mom, it's like we never know when we're supposed to go where, and there are many times when it's not clear if we need to go get dinner ourselves or if she's going to make it . . . Her father can't even tell us where he's going to be the next day. He can't make plans and say, 'I'll meet you at someplace for lunch the next day.' . . . Her mom and stepfather will tell us on very short notice that they're coming to visit us. And they won't tell us how long they're going to stay."

Ian and Isabelle were raised by parents with different ideas about if they should plan time in advance or take a more laissez-faire approach to their time. Ian's mother was a social worker and her first and second husbands were both well-off. Their financial stability allowed them to plan as it was unlikely that an unforeseen event would disrupt their ideas of what was to come. Isabelle's father was a farmer and her mother was a bartender. Making plans for them was less feasible as her father's work depended on the whims of the weather and her mother's work schedule was set by others. Their income also depended on the yield of their crops and the tips of patrons, meaning that it was neither constant nor predictable. With income and work fluctuations, going with the flow, rather than planning, was a useful skill.

In addition, planning differences may stem from childhood socialization patterns. Other research finds that blue-collar children tend to grow up without many planned activities; they become skilled at spontaneously filling their time. White-collar children, on the other hand, often grow up attending a series of planned activities and do not develop the skills to entertain themselves during unplanned time (Lareau 2003). Each of these factors may have contributed to the pattern that white-collar participants typically wanted to actively manage their time while blue-collar respondents more often wanted to avoid managing time.

Such patterns continued to the present. Matt (white-collar-origin), a thin, introverted manager, and Jenny (blue-collar-origin), a busy stay-at-home mother who was constantly involved in at least a half-dozen volunteer groups, were married for 20 years but still had differences in how they thought about time.

> Matt (white-collar-origin): I tend to be a little bit more of a planning person. Jenny tends to be a little bit more opportunistic. So if we need to buy an old used pickup truck or something, I'll tend to say, "Well, think, too, what do we need? And what year should we look at, and what features do we want?" And she would be more of, "Let's just keep our eyes open. If we see one that looks good, let's go buy that. And don't do all of this planning."

> Jenny (blue-collar-origin): His need to figure out everything before you get there took me some learning. I got irritated with that. But I finally just understood his need, and now I'm better with it. [It could be] small things like where are we going to park, directions, how are we going to get there. I tend to be like, "We'll read the signs." He has to know ahead of time. That kind of thing. Being hugely prepared. He doesn't like to do things on the fly.

Alexa (white-collar-origin, a systems administrator) and Aaron (blue-collar-origin, a recently retired teacher) had similar differences. Alexa felt she planned much more than Aaron: "Sometimes we like to plan things together, but it's gotta be something that I'm already fired up about. I don't think he ever comes to me and says, 'I want to do this. How about we do that?'" Aaron did not believe in actively managing his time: "I remember people having planned ahead for the future. And it's like, 'Well, no, if you live properly right now, each minute to minute, the future's going to take care of itself.'" Thus, blue-collar-origin respondents such as Aaron, Gabriella, and Jenny preferred to take a laissez-faire approach to time—they enjoyed spontaneity and going with the flow. Their white-collar-origin partners, however, favored managing their time through careful planning. They wanted to feel prepared for what was coming.[4]

Differences in planning ethics were experienced in different ways by blue- and white-collar-origin respondents. Blue-collar-origin respondents often found their white-collar-origin partners' planning ethic to be simultaneously annoying and helpful. Jack (blue-collar-origin, an engineer) told his wife, Caroline (white-collar-origin, a researcher), that he no longer wanted to know her plans for their menus next week or for their lives in six months. At the same time, he attributed her planning ethic to their ability to go on vacations, finish household projects, and find their relatives appropriate gifts. Similarly, while Jenny found her husband Matt's need to plan small details in advance to be frustrating, she also found his skill useful and admirable. When she was in charge of a preschool's relocation, she turned to Matt for help with the move because of his planning proclivities: "He's good at thinking through the logical order of things. If a problem occurs, what are your options and what would be the best step. He's real good about all that." She could also see how her husband's planning ethic helped their daughter in school: "My daughter, she's fourteen . . . She's got a project due in a week and she knows how to divide it into pieces so it will get done. She's way better at that than I am." Jack and Jenny, as well as other blue-collar-origin respondents, then found their partners' planning ethic to be both irritating and useful. Such an ethic was implicitly a rejection of their own more laissez-faire style but also sometimes helped them succeed.

White-collar-origin respondents, especially women, were more likely to see their partners' planning ethics as a problem to try to fix. Leslie (white-collar-origin, an office worker) viewed planning as a necessary part of housework and a form of labor. As such, she was offended that her husband did not do it: "I can't think of an area in our lives where he takes the lead in planning. I plan the vacation. I plan the budget, such as we do, which is not very well at this point . . . If it's a goal that needs both of us, it's like having a weight sometimes. He doesn't mean to be a weight but . . . I'm a planner, and he's just not. He's a reactive person." Though Leslie disliked that she did all the planning, she could not get her husband to change: "If you plan, if you're a planner, you do that mental projecting all the time . . . You're thinking ahead, saying, 'What's going to happen if I do this?' I really don't think he does that. I don't know if it's because he doesn't want to, it's too hard, he doesn't have the capacity, I don't know. But he just doesn't do that." To Leslie, her husband's laissez-faire approach to time was a problem that she could not fix.

Vicki (white-collar-origin, a teacher), felt the same way. She wanted to manage time, while her husband, John (blue-collar-origin, a part-time restaurant manager), wanted to take a more laissez-faire approach. Vicki described her own sensibilities as: "We need to plan! We need to schedule! We need to be neurotic!" Her husband, however, took the opposite approach: "For him, it's 'It will always work out. It will always get done. Don't worry.'" Vicki saw John's approach as deficient and as such tried to change it: "At the beginning of the marriage I thought, 'This is something we'll work on, and I can change him. I can turn him into a neurotic type-A person.'" Like Leslie, however, she learned that her efforts would not change her husband's approach to time: "I understand that that's who he is and he's not changing . . . Having to accept that was a big thing."

White-collar-origin respondents, especially women, may have been more likely to view their partners' approach to time as problematic because they were not confident that going with the flow would allow them to get things done. Many women were contending with the second shift, and, as they saw planning as necessary, they felt that their husband's lack of planning added more to their shift. White-collar-origin men found their wives' lack of planning to be irritating as it left them feeling unprepared and unable to get as much done. Dan, for example, tried to relinquish his planning in order to do what Gabriella wanted—to go with the flow—but then would find himself thinking: "Grrr. I haven't been able to do what I wanted to do." Thus, while blue- and white-collar-origin respondents tended to have different ideas of time, it was the latter who typically found their differences to be solely problematic. Planning ethics were often divided by class origin, but such divisions did not produce uniform conflicts.

Shared-Origin Couples and Time Use

For shared-origin couples, planning was a gendered endeavor, as respondents claimed that women did the majority of the planning. However, men did not feel that going with the flow was best. Rather, they believed that managing time through planning was necessary, but thought their wives were better at doing it than they were. Phil (shared-origin, an architect) said that his wife, Rose, "has such a handle on what she is doing on any given day at any given hour." He was pleased that she taught him, to some extent, how to do the same. Paul (shared-origin, a journalist) admired his wife's ability to organize and plan: "She is much better at organizing and planning than I will ever be . . . Not that I am bad at it, I end up getting a lot of things done, but I am much more likely to follow a tangent than go down a straight line." Men and women from white-collar backgrounds then tended to think managing time through planning was best but that the wives were better at it.

CONCLUSION

Women from white-collar backgrounds tended to want to manage the division of labor, and men and women with white-collar roots typically wanted to manage their time. Women from blue-collar backgrounds instead favored taking a laissez-faire approach to the division of labor. They more often reported falling into gender roles and not trying to manage their partners' housework. Men and women from blue-collar-origins also tended to want to go with the flow. Managing time, they thought, was not desirable.

The class divide in ideas of housework and time has implications for gender inequality. White-collar-origin women most often tried to get their husbands to do more around the house, including more planning, but their attempts may have added to the second shift as it entailed research, negotiations, and fights. Blue-collar-origin women did not feel the burden of equalizing the household division of labor but may have put themselves in danger of a more unequal relationship as they fell into gender roles that they felt little need to challenge. Neither strategy— working to equalize the gendered division of labor or letting it go—was related to perceptions of achieving gender parity in household labor.

Individuals' sensibilities about time may also have implications for class reproduction. The ability to plan is not part of many schools' or workplaces' explicit curriculum, but, as Jenny (blue-collar-origin) noted, is useful for succeeding in them. A preference for managing time may be viewed by gatekeepers as efficient, organized, and purposeful; a preference for a laissez-faire approach may be viewed by gatekeepers as inefficient, disorganized, and unmotivated (Rivera 2015). Respondents' ability to reap the full rewards of these institutions may then be tied to an environment that shaped them long before they said their vows.

[7]

PARENTING

Leslie (white-collar-origin) identified as a geeky tomboy with too many interests and not enough time. Her hair was cut short, her clothes were plain, and she wore large glasses that she removed to wipe away the tears that formed as she explained what happened that morning. She came downstairs after getting ready for work and found her husband, Tom (blue-collar-origin), a stout, balding introvert with a goatee, on his hands and knees, wiping up the milk that their seven-year-old daughter spilled. Leslie questioned him: "Shouldn't you be supervising her doing that instead of you doing it and her watching?" She explained her reasoning: "If you do this, where you just tell the kid to get out of the way, you're telling them they're not competent. You're telling them they can't handle this. You're telling them that they won't be able to handle this, that only an adult can handle this. So you're both pushing down their self-esteem and their ability to handle things. You're also not lifting them up in showing them how to do it and giving them the tools to be able to handle it in the future." I asked Leslie why she thought that Tom had not asked their daughter to clean up the spill. She told me that it was because he did not like to manage their children: "If he's in charge he just feels better doing it than delegating. He feels less comfortable supervising someone."

For 11 years, Leslie tried to convince Tom to change his parenting style. Just as she asked Tom to manage the clean-up of a spill, she also asked him to manage their daughters' use of time. She asked him to initiate family reading times rather than allowing their seven- and eleven-year-old daughters to spend their evenings as they pleased. She asked him to implement routine bedtimes and structured bedtime rituals rather than going with the flow each night. She tried to show Tom how to become the managerial parent that she thought was best but felt she had failed. Speaking of her efforts, she said: "The implementation is just not always there. He just doesn't know how. It doesn't fit with his natural style or his natural inclination." I asked Leslie what she thought Tom's natural parenting style was. Her reply: "Laissez-faire!"

The example of Leslie and Tom—a couple who shared a love of their children but not an agreement on how to parent—demonstrates both the intractability of parenting styles and the deep meaning of them. Leslie's intensive instruction was ineffective at goading Tom to shift from his more laissez-faire parenting style to her more managerial one. Her inability to change Tom's parenting habits was perhaps unsurprising considering that Tom not only took a laissez-faire approach to parenting but also to his own time, money, work, and leisure. Yet, as Leslie's tears indicated, their disagreements were intense as they were not only about how to live their own lives but how to raise their children as well.

Their disagreements, of course, were not unique. Some may see Leslie's and Tom's differences as those that typically fall along gender lines. It is, after all, not unusual for women to think more about the hidden curriculum of mundane family events and family rituals (Lareau 2000; Walzer 1998). However, if gender alone shaped parenting styles then Leslie's parenting sensibilities would be emblematic of all women in this sample. In fact, her managerial parenting sensibilities represented only those of women who shared her class origin. Women with blue-collar roots were also in charge of parenting but typically talked of having different sensibilities. They were more likely to favor a laissez-faire style, one that meant taking a more hands-off approach toward their children's time use and behaviors. Though they also loved their children, they had other ideas of what was best for them.

Of course, that women from different classes displayed different parenting sensibilities is not to say that gender did not matter. For women, their gender positioned them as being in charge of parenting, while their class origin was associated with their ideas of how to parent best—either in a more managerial or laissez-faire manner. For men, despite the recent uptick in father's involvement with their children, their gender positioned them as their wives' helpers in parenting (Coltrane 1996, 2004; Townsend 2002). Thus, even though their class origin was associated with whether they preferred to manage or take a laissez-faire approach in their own lives, they were also expected, regardless of their class origin, to not disrupt their wives' parenting practices and to not take primary responsibility for parenting. As a result, white-collar-origin men typically took a more laissez-faire approach to raising their children than to navigating their own lives. Blue-collar-origin men, like Tom, took a laissez-faire approach in much of their own lives and approached parenting in the same way.

This chapter demonstrates that years of co-parenting did not lead respondents to share parenting sensibilities. It also reveals that, contrary to the dominant discourse about parenting and social class, white-collar-origin women were largely alone in their preference for managerial parenting. White-collar-origin men as well as blue-collar-origin men and women more often discussed a preference for a laissez-faire parenting style.[1] These patterns were revealed in four aspects of parenting: expectations of childrearing, ideas about organizing children's time, notions of strictness, and aspirations for their children's future. The chapter also incorporates the parenting sensibilities of those in shared-origin marriages in order to demonstrate that parenting sensibilities cohere around class origin as well as to highlight how they played out in different kinds of marriages. The chapter first, however, shows how these new findings augment past scholarship on parenting.

PAST SCHOLARSHIP ON PARENTING

College-educated, white-collar professionals tend to have a parenting style that scholars refer to as "concerted cultivation" (Lareau 2003). These parents believe that children can be shaped by adults' efforts and that it is adults' responsibility to see to it that their children become (academically) successful adults. In this effort, they fill their children's time with enriching activities that they believe will develop their character and build their skills (Hoff, Laursen, and Tardif 2002; Lareau 2003; Vincent and Ball 2007). And, although they tend to believe in fostering their children's independence, they regularly undermine this belief by micromanaging their children's daily life (Weininger and Lareau 2009). They are hands-on parents who dedicate countless hours to their children's careful development (Hays 1996; Lareau 2003).

High school educated parents who work in blue-collar jobs love their children just as much as college-educated parents but typically have different beliefs about what children need and what it means to be a good parent. They are more likely to believe that their children have the capacity to develop on their own. As such, adults provide their children with love and material necessities but do not see the need to organize their children's time or micromanage their lives. Children, they believe, should be allowed to mature without a great deal of adult intervention (Lareau 2003).

This typology is useful in depicting broad differences in classed parenting styles but it ignores two key characteristics of parents. First, the prevailing wisdom overlooks that parents who are currently in the middle class may hold beliefs that correspond with the dominant beliefs of the class *in which they were raised*—a position pointed out by sociologists Josipa Roksa and Daniel Potter (2011). Parents may intentionally and unintentionally parent how they were parented, and these styles are likely to be different depending on whether respondents were raised in white-collar or blue-collar families. Their different backgrounds may offer them different ideas of what skills they want their children to possess and what class they want their children to enter into as adults.

Second, this analysis of classed parenting styles ignores that men and women are not usually equal contributors to parenting (Coltrane 1996; Townsend 2002).[2] Some men may be highly involved as parents and maintain independent ideas about how to parent, but, in general, men are expected to follow their wives' lead rather than developing their own parenting plans (Walzer 1998). As such, men who take a self-management approach in most aspects of their lives may not take as much of a managerial approach when parenting.

This chapter demonstrates that ignoring class origin and gender means misunderstanding the ways that parenting sensibilities play out. Parents' college educations did not provide them with a homogeneous set of parenting beliefs, nor did shared parenting resources or spending years together co-parenting the same children.[3] Instead, respondents' recollections of their initial expectations of parenthood suggest that a divide along lines of class origin and gender may have appeared even before their children were born.

EXPECTATIONS OF PARENTHOOD

White-collar-origin women, unlike all groups except shared-origin women, remembered their plans to be managerial parents. They remembered that before their children were born they had visions of who their children would become and what parenting strategies they would use to effectively shape them. Some were going to give birth to doctors, others to musicians, and most to academic achievers. They were going to have structured reading times, routine bedtimes, and cook only healthy food. Their children would not watch television, scream in a restaurant, or need to be bribed. They spent countless hours reading parenting books and scrutinizing their peers' parenting practices. They had a vision and a plan. They expected, in some of their words, to be a "perfect parent."

It had not occurred to many white-collar-origin and shared-origin women that being a perfect parent did not only depend upon their own managerial strategies but upon their children's agency as well. They remembered their surprise that their managerial strategies were not as effective as they had imagined because their children had other ideas of who they wanted to be. Anneka (white-collar-origin, a graduate student) reflected: "I realized that a lot of it is dependent on the child and not the parent. As much as a parent can will something to happen with children, they're their own people too." Vicki (white-collar-origin, a teacher) similarly remembered: "Before you have kids you really do think that you can control so many variables. Then you realize there are things that you can control, but not a lot. And of those things that you do control, there's still a lot of compromise." Asked how her ideas of parenting had changed over time, Bethany (white-collar-origin, a doctor) offered a similar response: "You have all of these expectations of what they're going to do, and you realize they have other ideas of what they want to do . . . You can't control everything she does or everything she thinks." Shared-origin women also tended to plan their managerial styles without consideration of their children's agency. Carlie (shared-origin, an engineer) said: "You always have these great ideals . . . You learn that you have to adapt your ideals around the personalities of your kids."

With the exception of a small number of white-collar-origin and shared-origin men, women with white-collar roots were alone in recalling that they had assumed that carefully thought-out parenting practices would yield compliant children. Despite their similar class destinations, no other group of respondents consistently expected to be managerial parents. Most, in fact, entered parenthood with few ideas at all. Lillian (blue-collar-origin, a stay-at-home mother) recalled that before her children were born, she only knew that she wanted to have children. She had few visions of who they would be or how she would raise them: "I had an idea that I would have a lot of children. The reality after having the first one—I realized it takes a lot more than just the desire to have a lot of children. It's hard. I saw it in a general dreamy kind of way. Oh yes, a farm full of children."

Gina's (blue-collar-origin, a stay-at-home mother) vision of parenthood was much more aligned with Lillian's than with women from white-collar backgrounds. The daughter of a metalworker, Gina imagined taking a laissez-faire approach to parenting. She did not imagine who her children would be or how she would shape them:

> How have my ideas changed since before I had kids? I think getting on the floor and playing with them more than just providing for them and making sure you know what's going on in

their lives. Involved parenting . . . I never realized how much really goes into it. All you picture is the baby. You don't picture them growing into kids.

Other blue-collar-origin parents and white-collar-origin men also did not plan who their children would be or what managerial strategies they would use. John (blue-collar-origin, a part-time stay-at-home father and part-time restaurant manager), for instance, said: "I didn't have any [expectations] before they were born. You just have no idea before your kids are born. And then once they're born, you figure it out." Madison (blue-collar-origin, a stay-at-home mother) concurred: "I don't think when we had them I had a lot of expectations." Nick (white-collar-origin, a stay-at-home father) similarly recalled: "I don't know that I had any ideas about parenting when we first had [our first child]." Paul (shared-origin, a journalist) reiterated this point: "I don't think I really had any strongly formed opinions about what it would be like to be a parent . . . It's been eye-opening to figure out how much time you spend and how small things you do have a big impact on how they behave."

Thus, it was primarily white-collar-origin women and shared-origin women who entered parenthood with the idea that carefully considered parenting strategies would shape their highly malleable children. Such women were raised by parents whose jobs entailed managing others, and, as the previous chapters have shown, they managed most aspects of their own lives. As women, they were expected to take charge of parenting, and they did so in a manner that made sense to them: They envisioned who they wanted their children to be and strategized about how to create the child they imagined. No other group had both a general predilection toward management and the idea that their children's development was primarily their responsibility.[4] As a result, blue-collar-origin women and men, as well as white-collar-origin and shared-origin men, did not remember preparing their managerial strategies before their children were born. Once their children were born, in terms of structuring their children's time, similar divides held.

CURRENT IDEAS OF PARENTING

Structuring Time

A hallmark of contemporary middle-class parenting is organizing children's time (Lareau 2003; Hoff et al. 2002; Vincent and Ball 2007). But the idea that middle-class parents structure their children's time neither takes into account the class origin nor the gender of parents who currently reside in the middle class. Not all parents were raised in a milieu that put a premium on structured time, and not all currently organized their own time (see Chapter 6). Moreover, in any given family, both parents are not expected to be equally in charge of organizing their children's time—if this duty is deemed necessary, it is often considered the responsibility of women and not men (Lareau and Weininger 2008). Again, it was the group who was raised by parents who worked as managers, who managed their own time, and who were expected to take charge of parenting who most fervently believed in organizing their children's time: women who grew up in white-collar households.

White-collar-origin women typically believed that structured activities were necessary for their children's development. Zoey (a stay-at-home mother) enrolled her four-year-old daughter in swimming lessons, creative movement classes, story time, sign language classes, and music lessons, all with the idea that they supplemented her child's preschool curriculum. Zoey's goal was to identify and cultivate her daughter's skills: "I think it's important to expose your kid to a lot of different things and see where they fit and what they like without investing too much. You know, is your kid a natural athlete? Is your kid a natural brain?" Mary's (white-collar-origin, a stay-at-home mother) ideas of parenthood were the same. Her four- and six-year-old daughters were enrolled in gymnastics, swimming, foreign language classes, and sports so that they could learn teamwork and to "set goals and win things." To white-collar-origin women, organized activities outside the home helped them identify and build their children's skills.

White-collar-origin women also typically believed that time in the home should be organized. Alexa insisted that her children have a set routine: wake up, make the bed, pack their own lunch, walk to school, do well in school, come home and complete homework, attend music and religious lessons, and go to bed at a set time. Most white-collar-origin mothers insisted on at least some of these: set bedtimes, structured reading and homework times, and routine mealtimes. They thought that children succeeded when their routines allowed them to know what was coming next and when they had daily time to focus on their academic endeavors—both completing homework and doing extra reading.

Even time that was seemingly unstructured could be used by white-collar-origin women to shape their children's character and build their skills. Norah (white-collar-origin, a stay-at-home mother) had filing cabinets that overflowed with newspaper clippings, cartoons, and research reports on parenting. She adapted a school curriculum that was "not mainstream yet" but that had "a carefully thought out rationale" and "good research to back it up" to implement at home. This style, according to Norah, "involves ways to teach self-regulation through children's natural activities," such as play, and teaches "how to set goals and follow through with them." Thus, even time at home that appeared to be unstructured could be used by white-collar-origin mothers to teach skills, especially the skills that replicated their own—the skill of being a self-manager.

Shared-origin women preferred to parent in much the same way; they preferred to structure their children's time in order to build their skills. Leah (shared-origin, a stay-at-home mother) said that her children's time outside school was so filled with soccer games, church, piano lessons, foreign language classes, and trips to the zoo that it required a lot of effort to "just let the kids stay in pajamas for half the day and play and not be structured." Alisha (shared-origin, a stay-at-home-mother) also mentioned that her children's schedules were both filled and structured: "Our kids are so busy, and they're doing so many things, and we have a very structured home life." Rose (shared-origin, a stay-at-home mother) entered parenthood planning on implementing "a structured learning time and a structured play time and a structured time to read," and while she gave up on some of this structure, she still made sure that her children were involved in music lessons, sports teams, and a series of enrichment activities. These women also wanted to use this structured time to build their children's character and skills. Leah, for example, explained her children's involvement in sports by saying: "[The coach] is really teaching the kids life lessons as much as he is teaching them to play soccer."

While organizing children's time is often viewed as the dominant practice of college-educated women, blue-collar-origin women, despite their college degrees, did not share the idea that structured time should be used to build academic or life skills. Only a few blue-collar-origin respondents involved their children in many activities, and these mothers reported doing so not to conscientiously cultivate their children's skills but to provide them with opportunities that they lacked in the past. Isabelle (blue-collar-origin, a therapist), for example, disliked that she was raised by laissez-faire parents. She was often alone as her father farmed and her mother bartended; she gravitated toward school as it provided her the structure she craved. Now, as a mother, she saw it as her responsibility to make sure her three- and five-year-old sons did not feel the same way. She enrolled her children in gymnastics lessons and soccer teams, and tried to find the perfect balance of "being out in nature, letting them bake things with me, pulling out art supplies, having some magical combination of spontaneity and planned activities." She did this not to cultivate their skills but because, Isabelle explained, "I don't want them to be deprived. I want them to have the best possible thing that they could have."

Sidney (blue-collar-origin, a stay-at-home mother) felt the same way. She remembered that her childhood felt lonely as she was an only child, her parents did not have the idea that they should play with her, and she did not have the opportunity to participate in as many activities as she wished. Her five- and six-year-old children were now in a wide array of organized activities, and at home she threw dance parties, played board games, and baked with them. Her goal was not to have her children learn to set goals or become chefs, but to make sure that they did not feel as lonely as she did. For Sidney and Isabelle, good parenting involved relieving their children from the burdens of their own pasts rather than seeking to cultivate their skills.

Other blue-collar-origin women were more ambivalent about structuring their children's time, both in the home and outside it. They tended to enroll their children in at least one organized activity while simultaneously questioning their necessity. Lillian (blue-collar-origin, a stay-at-home mother), for example, said about her six-year-old daughter: "We have done dance. She's enjoyed dance . . . I want to support her in doing the best that she can and that doesn't necessarily mean jamming her full of activities." Madison's (blue-collar-origin, a stay-at-home mother) philosophy was similar: "We just try to let them be free range and let them play and have fun. We try to give them stimulating experiences, but we don't want them to be overscheduled." Gina (blue-collar-origin, a stay-at-home mother) was married to a white-collar-origin man, Scott, who strongly wanted to enroll their three- and six-year-old children in organized activities, but she ignored his pleas as she thought they were unnecessary: "He thinks they should get out of the house more, and I think they're happy being home a lot of the time. If you're playing with them, they're happy." Blue-collar-origin women were more likely to question the necessity of organized activities and to not mind when their children had unstructured play time. This finding may be surprising given prevailing ideas about college-educated women's parenting style, but it was consistent with blue-collar-origin women's tendency to take a laissez-faire approach when using their own free time.[5]

Blue-collar-origin men, despite their college education and white-collar jobs, also did not want to structure their children's time to the extent that their white-collar-origin wives did. No blue-collar-origin man said that he implemented his own system of organized time, and many did not agree with the systematic use of time that their white-collar-origin wives imposed. Some simply did not see the point of extensive structure. Tom (blue-collar-origin, a computer programmer) revealed: "Though I know the kids need structure, I think Leslie thinks they need more structure than they really do." Adam (blue-collar-origin, a manager) agreed: "With signing up the kids for a lot of sports things, it seems like there's always something for them. I guess I don't think they need to do so much."

Others more actively resisted the idea that their children needed so much structure. Ben (blue-collar-origin, a sales director) begged his white-collar-origin wife, Mary, not to have their four- and six-year-old daughters involved in an organized activity every night. He also questioned the need to organize their children's time at home: "[Mary] feels like if the kids are left to do something of their own imagination, she's failing. She has to keep 'em busy all the time. That's where we're very different . . . I tell 'em, 'Go find something to do. You can draw, you can play, you can watch a cartoon. You can do whatever.'" He also questioned the need to cultivate their children's cultural skills, calling German lessons a "waste of time" and believing that violin lessons were unnecessary: "You're not trying to raise someone to play in the symphony."

John (blue-collar-origin, a stay-at-home father and part-time restaurant manager) also resisted his wife's, Vicki (white-collar-origin, a teacher), wishes to structure their children's time. He did not ask his four-year-old son and ten-year-old daughter to read rather than play video games, to have a routine bed time, or to learn new academic skills. He led his life in what Vicki called a "type-Z" fashion, which opposed what she called her "type-A" style of "We need to plan! We need to schedule! We need to be neurotic!" According to his wife, his approach was that "the kids will do whatever," a style that mirrored the type-Z style he used in many aspects of his life.

Blue-collar-origin women and men then did not share white-collar-origin women's belief in organizing their children's time to build their skills. What did white-collar-origin and shared-origin men believe? While a few stressed extracurricular activities and structured home lives, over two-thirds of this group had little to say about their children's time use. Here, their gender likely trumped their class origin in thinking about parenting, as most white-collar-origin men in different- and shared-origin marriages simply said that they followed their wives' lead. Thus, while they were likely to take a managerial approach to their own lives, their gender exempted them from the expectation that they would closely manage their children's time use as well.

Ideas of Strictness

The patterns above situate white-collar-origin and shared-origin women as managers and everyone else as more laissez-faire parents.

However, when it came to strictness, white-collar-origin men sometimes joined white-collar-origin women in preferring to more strictly manage their children's behavior. Enforcing behavioral standards was a managerial action that white-collar-origin men could do while they were with their children, one that left childrearing decisions about what their children did out of their sight to their wives. Blue-collar-origin respondents tended not be as strict, and blue-collar-origin women called upon their white-collar-origin husbands to cut back on their managerial approach to discipline.

White-collar-women continued to believe in strict standards. Rebecca (white-collar-origin, a teacher), for example, did not let things slide because boys will be boys, as her husband did. Her husband, Joe (blue-collar-origin, an accountant), explained: "She may be more strict than I am. When you have two boys, and as a father I remember the days of being a teenager, so I'm a little more understanding when they do something stupid. It's like, you know, they're just boys." Vicki (white-collar-origin, a teacher) also felt more strongly than her husband that their ten-year-old daughter and four-year-old son should abide by stricter standards. She said: "I'm more strict and would be even more so if he would agree more. I'm more strict. But I can't get him to be strict so I have to compromise." She described more quickly punishing behavior that she defined as inappropriate and having a broader definition of what constituted unacceptable behavior.

White-collar-origin men also thought of themselves as strict or were identified as strict by their blue-collar-origin wives. Scott (white-collar-origin, a businessman) named himself as the stricter parent: "I have a hard line on things. I think she's more inclined to lower the bar more quickly whether it's eating healthy food or cleaning up or asking for something nicely. I'm probably more likely to be patient and wait for them to do it the right way." Gabriella (blue-collar-origin) also named Dan (white-collar-origin) as the stricter partner: "Dan's a little more 'You need to do it the right way,' and I'm a little more casual about things. I think that's as far as behavior goes. I have a higher tolerance for misbehavior than Dan does." Katie (blue-collar-origin, a social scientist in the private sector) similarly identified her husband, Ryan (white-collar-origin, a lawyer), as the stricter parent: "Ryan sometimes feels like I am too permissive with them. Sometimes he feels like we need to be a little bit more strict."

Blue-collar-origin women generally tolerated their white-collar-origin husband's strictness until it was shrouded in managerial tones. Direct orders contradicted their desire to let their children grow in a laissez-faire manner, and, as such, they pushed back. Gabriella (blue-collar-origin) said that her only recurring fight with Dan (white-collar-origin) occurred on occasions when he would exclaim to their seven-year-old son: "This is what we need you to do. We need you to do it." Madison (blue-collar-origin) generally thought her husband, Evan (white-collar-origin), was an admirable father but objected when he did not ask their four-year-old daughter if she had a minute and instead ordered her to "stop now and do what I say." Lillian (blue-collar-origin) felt that her husband, Parker (white-collar-origin), was raised by a mother who said: "This is how you do things. Here's the list." She disliked that Parker had followed his mother's managerial lead and would instruct their six-year-old daughter: "You need to do what I say because I say you do it. You don't talk back to me like that."[6]

Blue-collar-origin men also had wives who managed their own time and were generally managerial parents. They, however, were less likely to complain that their wives made strict demands of their children. This may be because of some combination of the following: men may be more accepting of strict standards, or women's greater involvement in parenting communities taught them to couch orders in less managerial language (asking, for example, if their child wants a bath now or in 15 minutes). Either way, blue-collar-origin men complained less about their white-collar-origin wives' strict parenting than blue-collar-origin women did about their white-collar-origin husbands' tendencies toward strictness.

Shared-origin respondents were evenly divided about whether the mother or father was stricter, with several parents suggesting that they used strict standards to help their children succeed. Kent (shared-origin, an engineer), for example, said: "Sometimes I'm a little too hard on my kids. I'm too critical. I just want them to do the right thing."

EXPLANATIONS FOR MANAGERIAL AND LAISSEZ-FAIRE PARENTING

Though they all currently resided in the middle class and wanted what was best for their children, class origin and gender were nevertheless associated with how respondents wanted to raise their sons and daughters. To some degree, respondents' differences paralleled their general sensibilities and were then mediated by gender. They were also, however, related to the types of skills they wanted their children to develop and their ideas of who their children should become. Blue-collar-origin respondents were more likely than those in other groups to want their children to learn from mistakes and learn to persevere through struggle. A laissez-faire approach was much more suited toward this goal, while a managerial approach might prevent children from making mistakes. Taking a hands-off approach therefore did cultivate skills, skills associated with blue-collar upbringings.

Jason (blue-collar-origin, a professor), for example, wanted his 14-year-old daughter to learn to overcome struggles. He felt this emphasis derived from his background:

I think most people in my position feel this. We had to struggle for things. And when I look at my daughter I see she is not struggling for anything. And part of me is happy about that because she still is a smart kid and does better in school than I did at her age. But there's no uphill battle in her life. And that to me is such an important part of my self-narrative. It might be false consciousness. But the fact that she doesn't have that kinda disturbs me. And it makes me think that when she does encounter a real hardship, if she ever encounters that in her life, she's not going to be ready for it.

Blue-collar-origin individuals often face "uphill battles" as they overcome obstacles associated with growing up with fewer resources. Their children's ability to take on uphill battles may help them identify with their children and diminish the ambivalence they sometimes felt about raising their children in more privileged settings. Blue-collar-origin individuals also may be especially likely to see struggles as simply part of life as their fewer childhood resources meant that they were likely to struggle more. A managerial parenting approach was less likely to prepare their children to take on uphill battles and learn to struggle without giving up. A laissez-faire approach could engender these skills—the skills of independence and resilience, skills that blue-collar-origin respondents were more likely to consider important.[7]

Other blue-collar-origin respondents also took a hands-off approach, intent on teaching resiliency and the ability to learn from inevitable hardships. Lillian (blue-collar-origin, a stay-at-home mother) believed in giving her children the freedom to grow because she wanted them to practice learning from their own mistakes. She revealed:

Part of me wants them to fail miserably. To cover my eyes and say, "Okay, I know this is good for you." I do think it's important for them to fail because you learn so much from that. But to fail safely. Not to crash a car into a tree or whatever. Or not to take some psychedelic drug where their minds are out of it for the rest of their lives. But to do something they could learn from, like if they went for a job, and it didn't work out for them . . . because you can learn so much from what didn't work in that situation.

Ben (blue-collar-origin, a sales manager) agreed: "I use the phrase 'encourage failure.' People say, 'Why do you encourage failure?' 'Because I want them to know it's part of life and it's okay. You learn from it, and maybe the next time you do better or you don't.' " Blue-collar-origin respondents may have made a virtue of necessity as they equated struggle with worthwhile characteristics, but they nonetheless wanted to develop their children's ability to learn from mistakes. This approach meant letting mistakes happen, which meant taking a more laissez-faire parenting approach.

Some blue-collar-origin parents may have also preferred a laissez-faire approach because they questioned whether academic achievement and prestigious occupations should be the primary goals for their children. Their parents had not attended college or worked in exalted careers, and they had grown up around many admirable blue-collar people. The idea that their children might also enter blue-collar jobs was not to be dismissed, as it was for some white-collar-origin parents, but was at least ambivalently accepted.

Christie (blue-collar-origin, a social worker), for example, said of parenting: "It just came naturally. It wasn't difficult." She did not think deeply about her parenting strategies, and she limited her children's involvement in organized activities. Her parenting style aligned with her future goals: She did not use organized activities and structured time to cultivate her children's skills because she was not trying to shape her children into academic achievers with prestigious jobs. Rather, she questioned whether a heavy focus on academic achievement was healthy: "My kids are self-motivated to make sure they have an A. Getting a B is not acceptable for them. That makes them almost too competitive." She also would be happy if her children learned a blue- or pink-collar trade: "I think that if they wanted to go vocational . . . if the economy goes too bad, I think that's a gift. Somebody that can cut hair. Somebody that can weld. I'm almost sad that none of them have taken an interest in automotive or something hands-on." Christie's goal was not to have her children become white-collar-professionals. As such, a managerial parenting style was out of place.

Others also did not rule out the possibility that they might be pleased if their children became blue-collar workers. Isabelle (blue-collar-origin, a therapist) explained: "If either one of them decided not to go to college, I might feel a little sad. But then I'm like, 'Oh, but if they wanted to be a farmer then that'd be pretty cool, or a carpenter.'" Madison (blue-collar-origin), the mother of two young children, concurred: "If they chose to go to a community college, that's okay with me . . . They actually give you something you can hold in your hand and say, 'I know how to do this.'" For these blue-collar-origin respondents, strictly monitoring their children's behavior and using organized time to cultivate skills was less necessary as they were not convinced that their children had to become highly educated professionals.

White-collar-origin parents, however, were less likely to equivocate about their children's educational future. Thus, Mia (white-collar-origin) firmly stated: "They will go to college. They will go to college," and Joel (white-collar-origin) called college "nonnegotiable." Mary (white-collar-origin) thought of a bachelor's degree as a minimum: "I would like for them to go to college at least. I'd love for them to get an advanced degree." Nick (white-collar-origin), like others, tried to instill the inevitability of college in his young sons: "They already know it's expected that they'll go to college, get degrees." Shared-origin respondents agreed. Abby, a doctor, said: "College is not an option. The option is what grad school. I want them all to be successful." When asked whether he cared if his children went to college, Brad (shared-origin, a lawyer) also said that he thought college was necessary: "Yeah, I think they should . . . I would pay for it because I wouldn't want 'em to not go just because they didn't want to pay."

White-collar-origin and shared-origin respondents then were firm about their educational aspirations and expectations for their children. They, however, often said that they had few career goals for their children—that whatever they wanted to do was fine. But getting a college degree would likely lead them toward a white-collar professional track and away from a blue-collar track. Thus, many made statements like Alice's: "I don't have career goals for them, not at all really. I think they have to find their own way. I hope they'll go to college, but I don't have specific goals for them." Yet, there was no reason to hope for college if they equally hoped their children entered blue-collar careers. White-collar-origin respondents were raised in families and neighborhoods where college degrees were the norm. They did not hope that their children would then become unlike the people they knew. As such, a managerial parenting style made sense, as preventing mistakes and cultivating an appreciation for organized activities could help their children gain admission to college and become people like them.

PARENTING WITH A PARTNER WITH DIFFERENT BELIEFS

Husbands and wives from different classes often had different ideas about parenting. How they navigated their differences was based on the intersection of class origin, gender, and gender ideology.

Couples who had the most heated differences about parenting were those composed of white-collar-origin women and blue-collar-origin men. However, not all of these couples found their differences problematic. Couples who had the most heated disagreements were those in which the woman expected her husband to be an equal parent and defined equal parenting as managerial parenting. In these cases, fathers felt that their involved but laissez-faire style was underappreciated, and mothers felt that they were doing the majority of the parenting work. Mothers like Leslie then spent years trying to change their husbands' parenting styles, and fathers like Tom spent years resentful that their efforts went unnoticed. These parenting differences tended to exist for years without being resolved.

White-collar-origin women and blue-collar-origin men fought less when the woman was less concerned with equal parenting and therefore did not mind if her partner was less managerial or less involved. These women could make parenting choices independently and did not ask their husbands to change their childrearing approach. Zoey (white-collar-origin) and Austin (blue-collar-origin), for example, did not report arguing about parenting. Because Zoey did not expect Austin to be an equally involved parent, there was little for them to argue about. Zoey took their daughter to a half dozen organized activities, talked to her about becoming a pediatrician, and helped her cultivate a love of learning. Austin completely deferred to Zoey on these issues, believing that because Zoey was more immersed in the parenting community, she was better able to make childrearing decisions. When men deferred to women and women did not expect men to be equal parents, differences in parenting beliefs were rarely experienced as problematic as neither partner accused the other of being a bad parent.

Blue-collar-origin women and white-collar-origin men also tended to resolve their differences with relative ease. Their differences were not as great, as white-collar-origin men were less likely than white-collar-origin women to enter parenthood with a toolkit of managerial strategies or the desire to carefully structure their children's time. In addition to their smaller differences, when white-collar-origin men did want to implement a managerial style, they generally did not force it on their wives. Thus, even though Dan (white-collar-origin) preferred to actively cultivate his son's talents and take a stricter approach to their son's behavior, he did not impose his views on his wife: "We respect each other's views. So we allow the other to approach it the way they want to. But when it's our turn we do it differently." With only one exception, white-collar-origin men did not report initiating disagreements over parenting with their blue-collar-origin wives.

Blue-collar-origin women, for the most part, also respected their husbands' parenting styles. While they disliked it when their husbands became too managerial, they enjoyed that their husbands were involved. They may have been more likely to grow up in homes where men denounced childrearing (though were still involved [Pyke 1996; Shows and Gerstel 2009]) and were then pleased when their husbands spent time with their children. Thus, though Gina (blue-collar-origin) and her husband, Scott (white-collar-origin), had strong disagreements about several aspects of parenting, Gina still named Scott's fatherhood skills as the thing she most admired about him. She explained that he was a good father because "he comes home from work after a long day, and he immediately plays on the floor with the kids. He doesn't say, 'I need a half an hour to watch the news' like a lot of people." Jill (blue-collar-origin) similarly named Eric (white-collar-origin) as an admirable father because "he wants to be part of their lives." Likewise, Isabelle (blue-collar-origin) appreciated Ian (white-collar-origin) because he regularly interacted with their children: "Even though he's very busy, he comes home and is present for the two-and-a-half hours between when he gets home and bedtime." They did not define good fatherhood as equal parenting or managerial parenting but were grateful when their husbands enjoyed a few hours a day with their children. Their husbands also tended to defer to them, so they had few conflicts over parenting.

Finally, shared-origin couples reported having only minor disagreements, often about exactly how much management should take place. Some couples agreed that they needed to set times for their children to do homework but disagreed whether it was okay to take breaks. Some agreed that they wanted to strictly limit their children's television time but disagreed about what the limit should be. Other couples shared a commitment to communicating with their children's teachers but disagreed whether a particular issue warranted a meeting. Overall, however, they got along well, partly because men still tended to defer to their wives, and partly because their general managerial sensibilities were well aligned. Arguments about large philosophical issues regarding what children need were reserved for couples in which white-collar-origin women expected their husbands to be equal parents and when they defined equal parenting as managerial parenting.

CONCLUSION

Leslie's and Tom's parenting differences may have appeared personal to them, but they were, in fact, experienced by many different-origin couples. For the most part, those who shared Leslie's gender and class origin shared her parenting beliefs. They wanted to act as managerial parents. They entered parenthood imagining who their children would be and assumed they would be able to shape their children as they pleased. After their children were born, they continued to try to shape them through organizing their time and setting strict standards. Their goal was to get their children into college.

Leslie and other white-collar-origin mothers' ideas of parenting are often viewed as emblematic of college-educated parents' style, but, in practice, they were primarily preferred by women who grew up in white-collar professional households. These beliefs were not widely shared by many men with white-collar-origins; though these fathers were managerial concerning strictness, they did not manage their children's time. Managerial parenting sensibilities also cannot be conflated with those of college-educated women because college-educated women from blue-collar backgrounds were likely to reject this approach. Men from blue-collar-origin backgrounds, even though they raised children with white-collar-origin women, also did not share their beliefs. Many college-educated parents, then, maintained laissez-faire parenting sensibilities.

Differences in parenting sensibilities reflect different goals. Blue-collar-origin respondents were more likely to feel ambivalent about contributing to their children's class reproduction. Rejecting the idea that they needed to carefully cultivate their children's academic and extracurricular skills may have been a way to reject the idea that their children needed to enter a class that they were not always a part of. Moreover, a laissez-faire approach could encourage their children to learn how to struggle—a skill that, likely due to their experiences, they believed was particularly important. Their laissez-faire style, therefore, should not be viewed as fully discarding the idea that they needed to cultivate their children's skills but as encouraging them to develop skills that are associated with their own past.

These differences had consequences for some couples' satisfaction, which may be associated with the likelihood of later divorce. In general, husbands' and wives' discrepant parenting styles can raise their risk of divorce (Block, Block, and Morrison 1981), and in this study, two of the women who were the least satisfied with their husband's parenting styles did consider terminating their marriages due, in part, to their parenting differences. Divorce has consequences for children as well as couples; children of divorce have lower odds of entering the middle class as adults than those in two-parent families (McLanahan and Sandefur 1994).

Class reproduction could also be furthered because schools reward managerial parenting. Parents' management of their children's time is associated with positive evaluations by teachers and children's greater academic achievement (Bodovski and Farkas 2008; Cheadle and Amato 2010; Dumais, Kessinger, and Ghosh 2012; Roksa and Potter 2011).[8] However, it is not clear if having two parent-managers is necessary for reaping the benefits of this association, or if one parent, especially if the parent is the mother, will suffice. What is clear, however, is that taking the person out of the class did not take the class out of the person, and years of married life did not lead to the assimilation of parenting beliefs.

[8]

FEELING RULES

Lori (white-collar-origin), a serious and confident middle-aged woman from the South, remembered what shocked her most during the first week she spent with Jason's (blue-collar-origin) family. Shortly after meeting his parents, they began to loudly argue in front of her. She wasn't sure what the fight was about, but she knew that neither was backing down, and soon Jason's mother threatened to forgo sex with his father. Lori cowered in the corner as Jason's parents yelled, feeling like her family dog who now cowered as she and her husband fought. She had not seen such publicly displayed emotions before, especially not a display of such unpleasant emotions expressed so intensely. Jason, however, felt that his parents' emotional exchange was quite normal. He remembered that his family commonly expressed what he called "raw emotions"—those that had not yet been mulled over and that were not couched in polite language or soft tones. Emotions were simply expressed as they were felt, and not always in a nice or calm way. In Jason's family, emotions appeared to be relatively unmanaged.

Jason, a short, bright social observer, in turn, found Lori's family's way of dealing with emotions surprising. Jason observed that Lori's family had a ritual that he named the "stomp off." The stomp off occurred in a sequenced manner: After they had considered their feelings, one family member would quickly express their dissatisfaction with the perceived offender, the offender would reply, and then the accuser would stomp out of the room. The stomp off ensured that powerful and unpleasant emotions would be kept mostly out of the public sphere; displaying raw emotions was viewed as crass and unseemly in Lori's patrician family. In Lori's family, emotions were to appear carefully managed. They were processed before displayed, and strong emotions were mostly hidden.

The ritualized family interactions that Jason's and Lori's families practiced—the expression of "raw emotions" and the "stomp off"—taught each partner different "feeling rules." Feeling rules, according to Hochschild (1983), are social guidelines about what individuals should feel and how they should express their feelings in a given situation. Individuals often try to align their feelings with what their feeling rules indicate they *should* feel, and by doing so they teach themselves to actually feel different things. Thus, Jason watched his parents and learned that powerful feelings should be felt as well as expressed. Lori, on the other hand, observed her family rituals and learned that intense emotions should be hidden and not felt. They learned not only to display their feelings in different ways but also to have different feelings.

I refer to Jason's feeling rules as laissez-faire and Lori's as managed. This is not to imply that a laissez-faire set of feeling rules is less socially regulated or that only Lori had to manage her emotions to align with feeling rules. Rather, I call Jason's feeling rules laissez-faire because, while they are learned, they emphasize the *appearance* of freedom from regulation. Emotions appear more unregulated as they are expressed immediately and because a broader and more intense set of emotions are felt and displayed. The style, in short, appears to be unmanaged because it calls for the display of "raw emotions"—those not carefully sifted through, sanitized, or intellectualized. Likewise, I call Lori's emotional style "managed" not because it requires more work to align her emotions with her feeling rules, but because it appears more controlled. Managed feeling rules call for a delay in emotional reactions, the sanitization of intense and disagreeable feelings, and the intellectualization of emotions. Thus, these feeling rules give the *appearance* of being more managed.

This chapter shows that Lori and Jason did not follow unique feeling rules, but ones that reflect the feeling rules of their class. It shows that blue-collar-origin respondents, like Jason, felt they grew up with feeling rules that emphasized a laissez-faire emotional style, while white-collar-origin respondents, like Lori, felt they internalized managerial feeling rules. The chapter also shows that, compared to ideas about money, housework, time, paid work, play, and parenting, respondents believed their emotional sensibilities were somewhat malleable. However, though many respondents tried to change, many said they stayed the same.

Before proceeding, a note about methodology is important to consider. Unlike most of the arguments in the earlier chapters, the arguments in this chapter did not stem from answers to questions about the topic at hand. In other words, the interview protocol did not include any questions about emotions. Rather, feeling rules came up in response to questions about how the respondents were different from their spouse and how their parents were different from their in-laws. That many of the patterns were as strong as those in other chapters suggests the salience of emotional differences to different-origin couples.[1] Shared-origin couples, on the other hand, rarely brought up emotions in their interviews. As such, their experiences are not documented in this chapter.

CLASS AND MEMORIES OF FEELING RULES

Feelings are often experienced as personal and individual but are, in fact, socially patterned (Kemper 1978). On the occasions when feelings are thought to be socially organized, it is popularly assumed that gender divides people into relatively emotional and unemotional camps (Cancian 1987). However, research that examines self-reports of feelings largely finds that the popular conception is mistaken: Gender is not strongly associated with differences in feelings or their expression (Ridgeway and Smith-Lovin 1999; Simon and Nath 2004). Rather, feelings are often aligned with more generic power differences, one of which is a difference in social class (Ridgeway and Smith-Lovin 1999).

Those from different classes often learn different feeling rules. White-collar parents tend to repeatedly ask their children to use a managed emotional style (Kohn 1969; Walkerdine et al. 2001). Rather than punishing their children because of their deviant actions, they punish their children for their deviant emotions. This teaches children that they need to internally and externally regulate and restrain their feelings, often in order to appear kind and composed (Kohn 1969; Hochschild 1983; Walkerdine et al. 2001).[2] They also ask their children to turn their emotional reactions into rational arguments, thereby appearing calm and even-tempered (Walkerdine et al. 2001). Such strategies are important for white-collar parents as they prepare their children for white-collar jobs; these positions tend to require a restricted range of emotional displays and the ability to remain calm on the job (Wingfield 2010). Learning a managed emotional style can then help children become managers or take on other professional positions.

Blue-collar parents, on the other hand, tend to teach their children to use a more laissez-faire style when expressing their emotions. During the time when respondents were growing up, blue-collar workers were less likely to need to turn a feeling into a logical argument in order to get ahead at work. If they worked in factories or other non-service-sector jobs, their performance at work was less likely to be evaluated based on their emotional style. A more restrictive emotional style was then unnecessary for their career success; emotions could be less regulated (Kohn 1969). Furthermore, blue-collar communities tend to find direct and unmediated emotional displays to be signs of authenticity and integrity (Williams 2010). An emotional style that focuses on slow and processed emotional reactions might lead others to question their motives and find them suspect. Fitting into blue-collar communities and reaping the social capital they provide may mean learning to follow more laissez-faire feeling rules.

Aligned with this literature, blue- and white-collar-origin respondents in this study described their parents as abiding by different feeling rules. Those from blue-collar backgrounds tended to describe their parents as expressing emotions as they felt them and expressing a broad range of emotions, while those from white-collar backgrounds tended to describe their parents as expressing a narrower range of emotions and processing them before publicizing them. In other words, those from blue-collar backgrounds typically remembered that their parents expressed their emotions in a laissez-faire manner, while those from white-collar backgrounds recalled that their parents used a managed emotional style.[3]

Such differences were repeatedly raised when respondents answered open-ended questions about the difference between their parents and their in-laws.[4] Differences fell along lines of class origin and did not intersect with gender. In other words, respondents tended not to identify differences between their mothers' and fathers' feeling rules, but instead pinpointed large differences between their mother and mother-in-laws' and father and father-in-laws' feeling rules. In terms of differences between his mother and mother-in-law, Mike (white-collar-origin), for example, identified his mother as displaying managed emotional sensibilities and his mother-in-law as possessing more laissez-faire sensibilities: "My mom is more reserved. Again, less outward emotion. Her mom is the opposite. Her mom is insanely running around, hugging people. Just kind of crazy. Very different there." Andrea (white-collar-origin) believed that her blue-collar mother-in-law expressed a broader range of emotions than her white-collar mother: "Mine is a little more unemotional, a little more even, and his is very up and down." Tom (blue-collar-origin) noticed the same pattern: "My mom was always much more open with her feelings than my mother-in-law is. My mother-in-law is more guarded."

Fathers and father-in-laws were also not described in a uniform way that cohered around gender but were instead portrayed in ways that cohered around class. Again, white-collar fathers were typically described as managing their emotions while blue-collar fathers were depicted as expressing them in a more laissez-faire manner. Brandon (white-collar-origin) described the difference he noticed between how his father and father-in-law displayed their feelings:

Her [blue-collar] dad is wide open emotionally. A wonderful person who just wants you to like him. Very considerate of other people . . . He's just a really nice guy. Very emotional, cries at various things. Cried at my mom's funeral. Cries if he talks about his daughters and his grandson. He'll start to get teary. My father believes showing emotion is a sin. He's just a very closed person.

Isaac (blue-collar-origin) put the differences in emotional sensibilities simply: "[My wife's] father was more into the intellectual component. My father was more into the emotional." Chelsey (white-collar-origin) also noticed that one father was more emotionally expressive than the other. She focused on just one emotion, anger, and noticed the difference in their fathers' likelihood of expressing it: "His dad had a bad temper, and [my husband] got into a physical fight with his dad at one point. I mean [my father and father-in-law] are completely different in every way. My dad is calm, quiet, patient, never raises his voice, never loses his temper."

There was not only a divide in the emotions that were expressed but also in the likelihood that respondents discussed personal and emotional topics with their families. Blue-collar-origin respondents were more likely to describe growing up with feeling rules that allowed them to discuss emotional topics with their parents. Madison (blue-collar-origin), for example, said that she grew up discussing everything with her parents but that her in-laws put restrictions on emotional topics: "They don't talk about love or money or relationships and sex, and that is a big problem for me now." She emphasized her point by recalling two incidents when her husband was a teenager. Her father- and mother-in-law, a doctor and a nurse, left a pamphlet about HIV on her husband's bed rather than discussing the emotional topic of sex with him. Additionally, when their teenage daughter ran away from home with her boyfriend, Madison asked her in-laws if their daughter loved her boyfriend. Their response was that they did not know and would not dare ask their daughter such an intimate and emotional question. For many respondents, this norm extended to less severe circumstances. When asked about their parents' first impressions of their spouses, few white-collar-origin respondents were able to answer the question, saying that they did not discuss personal matters with their parents. Most blue-collar-origin respondents, in comparison, relayed their parents' reactions.[5]

Those from white-collar and blue-collar backgrounds then remembered growing up with different feeling rules. White-collar-origin spouses felt their parents' feeling rules called for managed emotional sensibilities, while blue-collar-origin spouses felt their parents' feeling rules called for laissez-faire emotional sensibilities. The next section shows that, to a certain degree, respondents' emotional sensibilities mirrored the ones they attributed to their parents. After countless emotional exchanges in years of marriage, a class divide still existed in respondents' perceptions of their default reactions in how to express their emotions.

FEELING RULES IN THE PRESENT

The divide respondents observed between their parents and in-laws was the same one that they experienced in their marriages. Blue-collar-origin respondents commonly depicted themselves as more likely to display their emotions and to do so before mulling over them, while white-collar-origin respondents were more likely to say that they were less emotional and that they weighed their emotions before expressing them.[6] This class divide was not mediated by gender; though no questions asked about emotional sensibilities, nine white-collar-origin women and ten white-collar-origin men were named as less likely than their partner to feel strong emotions and display them quickly. In contrast, only two blue-collar-origin partners, both men, were identified the same way. These differences existed despite that those with white-collar-origins said that they initially felt attracted to their partners because of their more laissez-faire emotional style.

Respondents tended to feel that their emotional reactions were better aligned with their parents' rather than their partners'.

Elliott, the son of a tool-and-die worker, noted that he tends to react emotionally to events, while his wife, Alice (white-collar-origin), responds with less emotion:

> If we have an argument, I'm very much emotional. She has a very analytical mind, and she always wins the argument because she can analyze the situation and bring it down to bare bones, where I'm purely emotional ... It's hard for me to zone in on the analytical side. "Well, this is what I feel." "Well, why do you feel that way?" "I don't know. I just feel this way."

Elliott described himself as "purely emotional" and his wife as "analytical" and less emotional. Elliott observed that this pattern paralleled the way they grew up: "Her mom can be emotional, too, but not to the same degree as my family. I mean there's some analytical there, too ... Alice gets very frustrated with my mom because you can't have a disagreement with my mom because she's emotional—the analytical side never works." Elliott believed he mirrored the more laissez-faire feeling rules of his mother, while Alice mirrored the more managed feeling rules of her mother.

Mike (white-collar-origin) grew up with parents who were more likely to restrain their emotions than display them, an emotional style that he deeply disliked. Yet even though he wanted to express more emotions, after 25 years of marriage, he still found it difficult. His wife, Christie (blue-collar-origin), called their emotional styles the biggest difference between them: "How are we most different? Probably in the way that we express feelings and deal with feelings. And that's probably rooted in our families . . . He's still learning, still trying." Similarly, asked about how they were most different, Anneka (white-collar-origin), like other respondents, discussed emotional sensibilities. She explained: "When something upsets him, he reacts very emotionally . . . My knee-jerk reaction to things is that I shut up. I go underground, back off, think about the situation and then come back and react to it." In other words, Anneka felt she usually used a managerial emotional style while her husband, William, often took a more laissez-faire approach. These differences were representative of those that different-origin couples experienced. Emotional sensibilities cohered around class origin despite that each respondent experienced countless emotional encounters with their spouse.

Anger, Conflict, and Affection

Some of respondents' broad emotional differences played out in terms of specific emotional expressions. Though no questions were asked about emotions, about a third of couples mentioned experiencing a specific emotional difference: Blue-collar-origin respondents were more comfortable expressing anger and engaging in conflict, while white-collar-origin respondents were more likely to shy away from anger and conflict. This pattern was not moderated by gender, as blue-collar-origin men *and* women were perceived to have shorter tempers, while white-collar-origin men and women were thought to be more even tempered.[7]

For example, Sidney (blue-collar-origin), a bubbly and outgoing stay-at-home mother, reflected that her husband, Joel (white-collar-origin) was less likely to show anger: "He's so level headed, he barely gets upset. It's mostly me." She continued, illustrating their difference:

> I just get real quick to anger; I don't have a lot of patience. Like today I couldn't find the remote control, and I knew my [six-year-old] son was the last person to have it, so I got furious.

I was so angry because I'd made lunch and wanted to sit down and just eat and watch a show and to me it was a huge deal. Joel came downstairs and asked, "What's the big deal?" I was just like, "He never should have had it though!"

Others described similar differences. Chelsey (white-collar-origin) felt her husband, Nathan (blue-collar-origin), was much more likely to show his anger and to do so before processing it: "Nathan gets very angry . . . He'll yell and swear. I mean that's a big difference too." Bethany (white-collar-origin) mentioned the same difference, though it did not bother her as much: "I am very, very calm and easygoing. And he definitely has more of a temper. Not in a bad way, but he has more ups and downs, and I am definitely very stable."

While they were more likely to rise to anger quickly—a sensibility aligned with laissez-faire feeling rules that allow for stronger emotions that are more immediately expressed—blue-collar-origin partners also tended to be the spouse who initiated conflict resolution. Their more emotional childhood culture may have prepared them for more heated disagreements as well as for finding resolutions to these disagreements. White-collar-origin individuals also tended not to be privy to others' arguing and did not feel as comfortable with conflict or conflict resolution. Zoey (white-collar-origin) put it plainly, "I'm an avoider, a conflict avoider." Jason (blue-collar-origin) stated, "She avoids conflict a bit more than I do." Gordon (white-collar-origin) concurred, "I want to really avoid confrontation" but then added:

It just wasn't acceptable to her, and understandably, that I didn't want to deal with anything. I learned that you have to get things worked out. It's almost like I didn't have to learn that because she demanded that. We used to laugh that people say, "Never let the sun go down on your arguments." Pfft, there wasn't—it was like it's got to be done now. I mean, they never festered. They never go on. We have a problem, a conflict, it's dealt with until it's no longer a problem. It's not, "We'll talk about it later," and it comes up again later. So it's not like I had to learn that. It was forced upon me.

Isabelle (blue-collar-origin) also had to teach Ian (white-collar-origin) that conflict did not need to be avoided at all costs; they could disagree without the relationship falling apart:

He would be very afraid of disappointing me or having opinions. If he's fairly neutral about something he's like, "Oh, why would I have an opinion?" And I'm like, "I want you to have an opinion!" So learning to express his feelings more. To just be able to say, "I don't like that," or, "I'm upset about this," or, "I'm nervous" without it feeling like he was going to ruin me or something would be bad.

In addition to initiating conflict and conflict resolution, blue-collar-origin respondents were also more likely to report working on adding public displays of affection to their relationships. Blue-collar-origin respondents were more acclimated to expressing emotions in public and wanted to express their love publicly as well.[8] This took effort on their part, as their partners' feeling rules suggested that affection should be expressed in private more than in public. George (blue-collar-origin, a scientist), for example, repeatedly tried to initiate more public displays of affection. He recounted that it took several years for his wife, Norah, to feel comfortable with such displays: "We didn't have public displays of affection and things like that. And that was something that I was fond of . . . We talked about it often enough and are affectionate enough in private, but it was nice when we could hug and kiss and hold hands [in public]." Anneka (white-collar-origin) also said that it was her blue-collar-origin husband, William, who initiated public displays of affection: "I am a lot more openly affectionate than I would have been otherwise, because William is really openly affectionate, and he's just not embarrassed at all about just saying 'I love you' or holding hands or dancing. He's not funny about any of that." Jenny, a quiet daughter of an electrician, confessed that she also wanted more public romance: "Sometimes I wish we could be more openly affectionate."

Blue-collar-origin partners then recounted taking charge of some of the emotional aspects of their marriage, both initiating conflict and conflict resolution, as well as working to institute a norm of public displays of affection. The feeling rules of their past were often ones that normalized the display of anger, conflict, love, and the discussion of emotional topics; such feelings and discussions of feelings were then not threatening or uncomfortable to them but normal parts of relationships. Their feeling rules, in other words, prepared them to be the emotional leader in these aspects of the relationship, as they expressed emotions more freely and asked that their partner do the same. Those from white-collar backgrounds were less comfortable with the expression of emotions and were more likely to avoid highly charged emotional situations.

CHANGE

Marriage tends to be a site where feelings are confessed, processed, and mulled over. Both white- and blue-collar respondents tended to want emotionally intimate relationships but they carried different ways of expressing their feelings into their marriage. Yet, unlike other sensibilities, respondents felt open to adopting their partners' style of expression. Compared to any other sensibility, respondents more often felt that their own emotional sensibilities changed.

Even the respondents above who described emotional sensibilities that were different than their spouse still discussed some change. George's wife eventually became more willing to engage in public displays of affection, and Anneka (white-collar-origin) learned to say "I love you" in public. Gordon (white-collar-origin) learned to engage in more emotional conflict, and Ian (white-collar-origin) learned to express more emotions about his relationship. Three more widely named changes also occurred. First, some tried to change the amount they drew upon their emotions in making decisions. Second, white-collar-origin respondents, especially women, learned to express more disagreeable feelings. And, third, respondents reported general shifts from a managed to laissez-faire sensibility or vice versa.

Emotions can be used to inform decisions or they can be bracketed as irrelevant. When differences in the use of emotions were raised, it was blue-collar-origin partners who wanted to consider them in making decisions while white-collar-origin respondents tended to ignore them. Some white-collar-origin respondents learned, however, to consider their emotions in making decisions. Ben, the outgoing son of an electrical line man and a manager himself, reported that he had some success in convincing his wife, Mary, that emotions were useful in making decisions. He repeatedly mentioned that Mary had a 4.0 GPA and graduated at the top of her law school class, but that the skills that led her to do well in school led her astray in making daily decisions. Book learning and endless research did not prepare her to make decisions; his gut served as a more able compass. Several times he remarked that Mary believed he lived a "charmed life." He explained what living a charmed life meant:

Good things happen. For instance, we were going to buy a new car and I looked online and I did my diligence and I found a car that I thought, "Wow, that's a good deal for that price. It seems like it's got a good background." And we went. She's not like that. She would have to study a bazillion [different cars] and then after she's got all of this paper, she'll say, "How do we make the decision?" There's not a book that gives you an answer to that. You've just got to go with your gut. So she says, "You have a really good gut!"

Ben used his "gut," or his learned emotional reactions, as a source of knowledge. Mary, the daughter of a professor, had not been taught that emotions can be a source of information or a way to help make decisions. Her family and class culture told her that she needed to make decisions through endless research and objective decisions. Though she did not adopt this style, Mary gained a new respect for using her gut to make decisions—she learned that it could lead to a "charmed life." Like Mary, Ian, the son of a lawyer and a professor himself, learned from his spouse to consider emotions as providing useful information: "I think she has helped me by modeling somebody who very extremely makes most of her decisions from her gut, from her intuition." Some white-collar-origin respondents then developed a new respect for integrating emotions into decision making.

Some blue-collar-origin respondents also said they learned to respect the idea of using less emotion in decision making. Jill (blue-collar-origin, a politician) explained what her white-collar-origin husband, Eric, taught her:

[He's taught me] how to look at things from a different perspective and sit back and not react so quickly. He'll pull me back before I want to make a rash decision, an emotional decision. He'll say, "Let's look at this for a minute first." I don't always like to hear his ideas but he offers them and I hear them. He does help me sit back and analyze the situation a little better.

Danielle, who grew up in a blue-collar family, also felt she learned to make decisions more slowly and without as much emotion. She relayed what she learned from her husband: "To be more patient. Have a little slower burner, not as a high of a flame; the idea that you can turn the burner on really high, you can cook it really fast, but you can singe. If you have a lower burner it can take longer but you probably do a better job. So I think I've learned not to jump in as quickly." Blue-collar-origin respondents may have been particularly open to hearing that they should remove some of their emotions from their decision making as white-collar institutions tend to reward calm and reasoned arguments over emotional ones (Lareau and Calarco 2012; Wingfield 2010). Similarly, white-collar-origin respondents may have been open to hearing that they should give more weight to their emotions given that ideas related to psychotherapy have infiltrated widespread notions about how to live an informed and satisfying life (Illouz 2008).

Respondents reported that another change in emotional styles occurred—learning to express more disagreeable feelings. This was a change that about half of white-collar-origin women but only a few of respondents in other groups said they made. White-collar-origin women often grow up learning that they are not supposed to express disagreeable feelings but instead appear easygoing, nice, and deferential (Brown 2003; Walkerdine et al. 2001). Men of all classes are not as often taught that disagreeable feelings should not be expressed. In fact, their anger and displeasure can be viewed as a sign of confidence and competence (Miller 1983). Men with blue-collar-origins are particularly unlikely to keep their disagreeable feelings quiet, as expressing feelings, even negative feelings, is more aligned with blue-collar feeling rules (Williams 2010). These differences in feeling rules position blue-collar-origin men as equipped to encourage their white-collar-origin wives to relinquish their idea that they must always be agreeable.

White-collar-origin women tended to be grateful that their husbands helped them learn to express disagreeable feelings. They often found such an ability empowering. Mia (white-collar-origin, a stay-at-home mother), for example, was pleased that she learned from her husband, Kevin (blue-collar-origin, a graduate student), to express disagreeable feelings. She explained: "Kevin doesn't mind other people being uncomfortable. That's not a problem for him. He'll tell it like it is, and I get that from Kevin now." Mia offered an example of how she no longer restrains her emotions when they are not pleasant. She said that when asked if her son can spend the night at the home of one of his friends whom she dislikes, she now firmly tells his parents: "Nope, that's just not something we're going to do at this time." If pushed, she directly explains, "I don't like the way that you run your household." She attributes her new expression of disagreeable feelings to her husband: "I would have never done that before Kevin. No, I would have been like, 'Oh, we're busy every week for the rest of our lives.' Now I would just lay it on the line."

Alice (white-collar-origin) felt she also learned from her husband that she did not need to repress her disagreeable emotions to the extent that she had in the past. She explained that her ability to express not-nice feelings came not from her training as a lawyer but from her blue-collar-origin husband, Elliott: "I've learned a lot about standing up for myself a little bit more . . . I'm used to letting things slide by me and not making waves. And I'm not saying to randomly make waves. I think I'm still kind of a peacekeeper at heart; I don't really love conflict or anything. But he's allowed me to know that you can stand up for something without being obnoxious." Alice's account mirrored those of many white-collar-origin women; though she still preferred to express agreeable feelings, she learned from her blue-collar-origin husband to express disagreeable ones on occasion.

Finally, in equal numbers, men and women from both classes said they changed their more general emotional styles—using a more or less managed emotional style. For example, William, the son of a sawmill repairman and an operations analyst himself, said he made a rather large change in his emotional reactions. He admired his wife's emotional style—a less emotional style—and wanted to emulate it:

> She doesn't run fully on emotion. And that's commendable. It's changed the way that I think about things and the way that I react to statements . . . I'm an emotional person. I could get angry. But not so much anymore. I used to wear my, you know, I used to let my emotions get me. I couldn't control them very well . . . Now I want to make sure before I run my mouth off that I've thought it through long enough to say, "One, is it worth saying? And two, am I even making a good argument here?" So usually if I think about it for longer than ten minutes, I come to the realization that I should just really go on about my business because I shouldn't have been upset about it to begin with.

William believed he used to have a laissez-faire emotional style—he felt emotions deeply and expressed them immediately. He felt that he adapted to more managed feeling rules, however, as he learned to think about his emotions before verbalizing them. He attributed this change to living with his white-collar-origin wife, Anneka: "It's very hard being married to someone who studies and reads as much as she does. Because if you don't go into something with facts, then you're usually going to end up wrong. So I have tended over the years to listen a little bit more and to hesitate a little bit longer before I go to mouthing off."

Just as William observed and strived to follow his wife's feeling rules, so too did Elliott. He explained: "I'm not nearly as emotional with stuff. I have gotten a little bit more analytical, like when I go back and say, 'Okay, step back, take a breath, and try to figure it out.'" He still felt more emotional than his wife, Alice, and still had trouble articulating why he felt the way he did, but he also believed he developed the ability to take a more removed stance.

Lori (white-collar-origin) also perceived that she had taken on her husband's feeling rules. She explained that her new emotional sensibilities had been difficult to internalize but the change had been worthwhile. She said: "We're not necessarily emotionally honest where I'm from. So I had to learn to, instead of just being angry and resentful, to just ask for the things I need and to make it explicit. And so I did. It just took me a long time to get there." She attributed these changes to her husband, Jason, who did not stomp off, as her family did, but expressed raw emotions as they argued. Lori said: "I was always shocked that we would have these arguments where I thought he was clearly in the wrong, and he would defend himself. He would make me fight. And it was really hard for me to learn how to argue like that. But I did . . . I'm much more emotionally honest . . . I fight. I really will argue and get down in the mud." Lori also attributed the ability to talk about more emotional topics to her marriage to Jason, an experience that she greatly enjoyed: "We just talk all the time. We talk constantly. And there's nothing we don't talk about. So to me that's just wonderful. I was not raised in a house where people did that."

However, while respondents felt their emotional sensibilities changed, they still often felt their default styles had not been entirely reset. Alice, for example, learned to express disagreeable feelings but still preferred to be agreeable. William learned to think about his emotions before reacting, but his wife, Anneka, still called this difference the biggest one between them. Elliott became slower to react emotionally to events but still did so more than his wife. Additionally, implied in that William, Elliott, and Lori changed their emotional styles to be more in line with their partners' sensibilities was that their partners' sensibilities adjusted less. Changes then did not result in spouses believing that their emotional sensibilities were indistinguishable.

CONCLUSION

Emotions seem personal and marital conflicts seem unique. However, the sum of respondents' statements indicated that their emotions were not shaped only by individual factors. Rather, respondents who grew up with blue-collar parents felt they internalized rules that called for feeling and expressing emotions intensely and quickly. Those with white-collar parents, in contrast, felt that they internalized rules that called for feeling and expressing emotions calmly and slowly. More than any other sensibility, respondents learned to appreciate their partners' different feeling rules and tried to emulate them. Most, however, at least partly defaulted to their own styles while still appreciating their partner's.

If respondents' perceptions are accurate and emotional sensibilities changed more than other sensibilities, this may be because some convergence on this topic could facilitate couples' ability to deal with other differences. They could feel heard and respected when they disagreed as their discontent would not be disregarded if it was expressed in a laissez-faire or managerial manner.

Appreciation for or change in emotional sensibilities may then have allowed other differences to fester without causing dissolution.

Feeling rules are also important to couples not only because they are related to how the couple communicates but also because feeling rules matter for class reproduction. Schools and professional workplaces often reward those who follow managed feeling rules. Students and workers are expected to discuss their differences calmly, to process their emotions before expressing them, and to use rational arguments more than emotions (Lareau and Calarco 2012; Wingfield 2010). These standards favor those who have managed feeling rules—those that are often from white-collar backgrounds.

That respondents are white may have made such rules less obvious to them. Blacks, especially black men, are often aware that a laissez-faire emotional style will lead them to be negatively judged. In workplaces, they tend to temper their anger in order to avoid being stereotyped as an angry or scary black man (Wingfield 2010). Whites from blue-collar backgrounds may be less aware of these norms as stereotypes of emotional whites are less salient. Nevertheless, repeated displays of "raw emotion" may have less obvious but still real consequences for upwardly mobile whites as they engage in the workplace or advocate for their children at school.[9] Thus, even though white-collar-origin respondents tended to admire aspects of their blue-collar-origin partners' emotional sensibilities, using their own emotional sensibilities may help them win what they want at work and as advocates for their children at school.[10] Though respondents from each class valued their partners' emotional sensibilities, these sensibilities are not equally rewarded in institutions that help allocate class positions.

[9]

CONCLUSION

The first time that Lori drove up to her future husband's childhood home, she thought, "Oh my God, what am I doing?" She made herself park her car, but she continued to wonder if she was, metaphorically, in the right place. Her boyfriend's father looked up from tinkering with a car in the garage and greeted her in casual clothes that struck her as underwear. She then entered the three-bedroom house where her future husband, Jason, grew up with his four brothers. Maneuvering around a maze of cribs that were set up for the daycare Jason's mother ran out of the house, she moved through the house, careful not to knock over the stacks of clothes piled high on the couches. Soon Jason's brothers came home and "kept asking me things like, 'Is it true you're a millionaire?' Which I was like, 'No! I'm not a millionaire!' 'Is it true that your family has three houses?' 'Yes, they do have three houses.'" Lori stayed for a week, and although Jason's family stopped peppering her with questions about her family's wealth, she never felt at home. She did not like the tacky furniture, the cramped space, the processed food, or the way Jason's brother mocked her formal dinner table etiquette. She did not like that Jason's family did not venture outside their home, that their mannerisms were rough, or that Jason's parents argued about sex in front of her. Her family was so different.

When Jason, accompanied by Lori, first drove up to his future wife's home, the family's yardman greeted them at the gate: "Oh Miss Lori! Is this your beau?" They drove up the winding driveway, and the family's live-in nurse and cook let them inside. Jason exclaimed, as he did repeatedly that weekend, "This isn't normal!" as he was introduced to the lifestyle that was normal to his wife. He was awed by the size of their multiple homes, intimidated by the norm of putting his napkin in his lap, and felt that he "didn't really know how to eat." He made a social gaffe when his soon-to-be father-in-law asked if he would like to go on a night sail: "And I thought, 'Well is it like we're going to go to Walmart or something for a special discount late at night?'" After returning from their sojourn on the sea, Jason's father-in-law asked him to tie up the boat. Not wanting to admit that he did not know what knots were used to dock a boat, Jason gave it his best try and then stayed awake all night worrying that his fiancée's family's boat had drifted out to sea. During the entire weekend Jason felt anxious and on guard. He too wondered if he was in the right place.

Lori and Jason now feel certain that they are in the right place because they are with each other. They have been married for a quarter of a century, and both report living happily together. But their long and happy marriage does not mean that their differences have disappeared. Lori remembered being initially attracted to Jason because of his emotional honesty, a sensibility that she felt she adopted, but not to the same degree as her husband. Jason originally felt drawn to Lori because of her achiever identity. Twenty-five years later, he still marvels at the intelligent and eloquent way she speaks in public, how she creates new programs at work, and how she builds networks with ease. And, just as they did not fully adopt the sensibilities that they admired in the other, they also did not adopt the ones that they initially disliked. The first time Lori visited Jason at his family's home, she became frustrated with his family's disinclination to leave the house. A quarter century later, she still struggled to get him out of the house, on a boat, or to feel comfortable at a dinner party. Similarly, years after first meeting her family, Jason still felt put off by his in-laws' genteel mannerisms and found that taking care of upscale amenities was beyond him. Their experiences in their respective class origins were etched into their sensibilities. Their marriage required navigating differences that were rooted in their unequal pasts.

This chapter summarizes the findings of this book and draws out their implications. It reviews the theories of cultural complements and patterned sensibilities before moving to the lessons the couples' stories tell.

CULTURAL COMPLEMENTS

Cultural differences that are associated with class differences are more often viewed as a source of segregation and derision than a source of appreciation (Bettie 2003; Bourdieu 1984; Illouz 1997; Johnson and Lawler 2005; Kalmijn 1994; Lamont 1992, 2000). This book has shown, however, that they can be both. Respondents in different-origin marriages tended to tell stories indicating that they appealed to each other because each had internalized a sensibility that the other desired but that was difficult to acquire in the class milieu of their youth. Their class differences then correlated with cultural differences, ones that respondents felt operated as magnets that pulled the two individuals together.[1]

That respondents remembered their complementary differences—ones that, unbeknownst to them, were associated with their class origin—as being a source of appeal refutes several myths. The myth that class and love are disconnected was severed, as class differences were central to the stories individuals in different-origin marriages told about why they fell in love with their spouse. Similarly, the myth that class *origin* does not matter when adults share a level of education was also defeated as individuals' class origin lived on in their sensibilities and was associated with why respondents said they loved their partners. And, most importantly, the myth that cultural differences associated with class differences are uniformly divisive was deflated. While class differences are often divisive, they may also be one reason why two individuals born into different classes remember making public vows to each other.

CLASS AND SENSIBILITIES

Most respondents saw their lives as free from the influences of social class. But the stories they told of how they preferred to live their life and how their partner preferred to live theirs told otherwise. Lining up the ways 32 blue-collar-origin and 32 white-collar-origin individuals recounted going about their lives revealed patterns of which no individual respondent was aware. The analysis uncovered that blue-collar-origin and white-collar-origin partners maintained disparate sensibilities.[2] Upwardly mobile respondents with blue-collar roots tended to want to go with the flow and live in the moment. They wanted to enjoy the resources they had without thinking too much about them. They favored spending without thinking and using time without scheduling. They enjoyed letting their career paths and the household division of labor unfold as well as letting their children grow without intensive parental interventions. Life, to those with blue-collar-origins, was best lived free from self-imposed constraints.[3]

Those whom they vowed to have and to hold favored a different approach. Those born into professional white-collar families typically wanted to manage their lives. They wanted to organize, supervise, plan, and control their resources. They preferred to research purchases and stick to a budget, strategize about their career trajectory, and manage their cultural capital accumulation in their leisure time. They enjoyed planning their down time, organizing their children's time use, and weighing their emotions before expressing them. They preferred their lives to be orderly, predictable, and managed. Their sensibilities oriented them to tirelessly invest in their futures, unlike their partners, whose sensibilities were oriented more to enjoying the resources they had and trusting that the future would work out.[4] These differences are summarized in Table 9.1.

Table 9.1 reveals the systematic nature of managerial and laissez-faire sensibilities. These sensibilities are likely a product of the patterned ways that individuals learned to respond to the amount of resources they had as children. Those born into blue-collar families often lived with economic insecurity and in families that possessed little authority. Needing to quickly and flexibly respond to unforeseeable events and others' orders, they likely learned that going with the flow and making decisions spontaneously best allowed them to adapt to events outside their control. Though they gained additional resources as part of their upward mobility, they had little reason to try to change their sensibilities. Their sensibilities were useful early in their life, and they had not prevented their mobility.

In contrast, respondents born to white-collar-professional parents grew up with fewer unforeseeable events, a more secure family safety net, and in families that possessed more authority. Their stability allowed them to organize and plan, their surplus resources offered them more choices, and their authority allowed them more freedom from others' demands upon their resources. They could then focus on using their resources to create new ones, rather than going with the flow. Managerial sensibilities, in short, may have been the result of having more resources to manage.

Table 9.1. THE CONTENT OF RESPONDENTS' STATED SENSIBILITIES

	Blue-Collar-Origin Laissez-Faire Sensibilities	White-Collar-Origin Managerial Sensibilities
Money	Spend without thinking	Spend after thinking, researching, and budgeting
	Spend to live for the day	Save to live for tomorrow
Paid work	Watch for new opportunities	Actively create new opportunities
Play	Let weekends unfold at home	Organize leisure to accumulate cultural capital
Housework	Allow the division of labor to unfold (women only)	Organize, monitor, and evaluate the division of labor (women only)
Time	Go with the flow	Plan
Parenting	Let children take charge of their time	Organize children's time (women only)
	Take a permissive approach to children's behaviors	Set strict rules regarding children's behaviors
Emotions	Express a wide range of emotions spontaneously	Express a narrow range of emotions after processing them

Whatever the exact source of respondents' sensibilities, they marked the hidden ways that class origin lived on through upward mobility for the blue-collar-origin respondents and through years of marriage for both sets of respondents.[5] They show that many Americans' perception that class is divorced from intimate experiences is incorrect and that scholars should not assume that the effects of social class on sensibilities are erased by shared educational and occupational experiences. The systematic nature of respondents' sensibilities also shows that class origin does not simply rear its head in areas most connected to the economic aspects of class—money and work—but neatly packages individuals' conceptions of the best ways to go about their lives more generally. To a certain extent, laissez-faire and managerial sensibilities provide the framework through which those born into different classes make sense of their roles as spouses, parents, consumers, and workers.

The existence of systematic sensibilities that span multiple domains has several implications, the first being the need to consider the all-too-often neglected importance of adults' class origin. Sociologists know that the class individuals are raised in provides the environment where they have their first dates and first kisses, their first exposure to ideas of what it means to be a good husband, wife, father, or mother. It is where they learn how to use money, allocate time, attend to work, and express emotions. Intuitively, it makes sense that these early experiences shape adults' later ideas of how to go about their daily lives. But as achievement has overshadowed ascription in the modern era, sociologists have too often forgotten that the importance of achievement does not negate the importance of class ascription. Achievement moderates the effects of class origin on life chances, lifestyle, and life decisions, but it does not nullify it. Even for those who share an education and a set of resources, class origin still operates, though not out in the open. It is still influential, but more in sorting sensibilities than (homogamously) sorting suitors.[6]

The manner in which class origin lives on—in internalized managerial and laissez-faire sensibilities—may have unique implications, ones that are different than the implications of class-based tastes. Sensibilities, in comparison to tastes, are unlikely to be easily known from observing someone's body. Unlike tastes, they are not apparent through fashion or physical comportment; they do not show up in hairstyles or body art. In addition, sensibilities are less likely than tastes to become apparent upon first meeting. Two individuals on a date are likely to discuss their taste for food, movies, or sports, but they are unlikely to discuss whether they prefer to spend money without thinking or carefully budget it, whether they plan their career trajectory or keep their eyes open for new opportunities. In addition, tastes are classified as "classy" and "classless" whereas sensibilities are less overtly linked to class. These features of sensibilities—their lower visibility, the longer amount of time they take to discern, and their hidden link to class—may mean that they only sort people slowly. And, if obverse sensibilities are initially found to be complementary, sensibilities may not only sort individuals in a slow manner, but in a limited manner as well.[7] This is in contrast to tastes, in which mismatches between high and low tastes or omnivore and univore ones can deter relationships from even beginning (Gorman 2000; Johnson and Lawler 2005).

Respondents, however, did not report a constant view of their partners' sensibilities. While different sensibilities could be appealing at first, they felt that over time they became differences to deal with. Such differences, however, were not always divisive, and here again the features of sensibilities, as opposed to tastes, may matter in how they are negotiated. Differences in sensibilities are less containable than tastes, as instead of affecting preferences for objects and activities they affect more general strategies for using resources and going about daily life. But, at the same time, they are also less moralized. At least in personal relationships, planning is not clearly ranked above spontaneity; restraining emotions is not always viewed as superior to immediately expressing them; organizing the household division of labor is not clearly viewed as better than letting it unfold. Compared to tastes for high or low culture, many activities or a few, sensibilities do not exist in a clear moral hierarchy.[8] That managerial and laissez-faire sensibilities carry a relative lack of moral weight may allow greater neutrality in dealing with differences. Compared to other ways that class organizes personal relationships, this one may be relatively benign.

In institutions as opposed to interpersonal relationships, however, managerial and laissez-faire sensibilities may operate differently and have more severe consequences. Within institutions, class sensibilities are less likely hidden as they may be the source of gatekeepers' initial inquiries. Teachers reward planning, restraining emotions, and charting career trajectories; employers ask about ways of approaching work. Managerial and laissez-faire sensibilities may then matter in who gains entry into some institutions and who advances in them. If white-collar-origin individuals' sensibilities are expected and normalized, they will receive more rewards, even if institutions do not intend to favor individuals born into one class above the other. The consequences of sensibilities may then vary by setting. In personal relationships they may do little to sort people or create divides, while in schools and workplaces they may both sort individuals and opportunities. That upwardly mobile individuals acquired the credentials of their partners may then not provide them with all of the same life chances.

THE LIMITS OF SOCIAL CLASS

The class each partner was born into had a profound impact on how each reported approaching their lives and their marriage. No respondent was better characterized by sensibilities more associated with the other class; no couple was characterized by a blue-collar-origin spouse who preferred a managerial approach and a white-collar-origin spouse who favored a laissez-faire one.[9] However, the findings do not capture every respondent, every aspect of respondents' lives, or every marriage. Of the seven differences described in previous chapters—money, work, play, housework, time, parenting, and emotions—most couples spoke of a managerial/laissez-faire difference in four to five domains. On occasion, a blue-collar-origin respondent would favor a managerial approach in one or two domains, or a white-collar-origin respondent would prefer a laissez-faire approach in one or two areas. Moreover, for a small number of couples, the managerial/laissez-faire distinction was not salient. One couple did not describe having any differences that fell along these lines, and two couples described these differences only in one domain.[10] That said, there are reasons that extend beyond the data at hand to believe that managerial and laissez-faire sensibilities generally characterize college-educated white-collar-origin and blue-collar-origin spouses' sensibilities. In general, these sensibilities are taught to children by their parents. White-collar parents are known for managing their money, children, and emotions, whereas blue-collar parents report going with the flow on many more issues (Cooper 2014; Lareau 2003). It makes sense that children internalize and replicate the sensibilities that their parents and communities conveyed.

Factors other than class were also at play. In domains that are heavily marked by gender, such as housework and parenting, gender intersected with class to shape sensibilities. Though women's sensibilities were still divided according to their class origin, men's were less so. In these domains, men professed to follow their wives' lead or to have few ideas at all. In addition, gender ideology intersected with class origin as it shaped how wives and husbands evaluated their partners' sensibilities.

The respondents also differed on dimensions outside of class and gender. Several couples differed in their demeanor—one was reserved whereas the other was more extroverted. In each couple, one person might enjoy hunting, running, painting, or martial arts while the other did not. Sometimes one partner had mental health issues while the other did not, or one had substance abuse problems and the other did not. Importantly, many of the couples also said they had a lot in common. They shared commitments to their family, values about how to treat others, senses of humor, and some tastes. Some couples felt united by their religion, others by their hobbies. All also shared a race and most shared a college degree—commonalities that were rarely named but that were surely important.

The shared educational level and race of respondents were also important in that they, along with sexuality and citizenship status, limit the generality of the findings. Couples with other demographic traits may not be represented by the findings as class may play out differently for groups with different experiences, socialization, networks, and resources. Class mattered in the way described for highly educated, white Americans in different-sex marriages in which neither partner was substantially downwardly mobile. For now, it is unknown if the same sensibilities and marital dynamics would play out in the same ways for other groups.

WHY IT MATTERS

If ignorance is bliss, it may be preferable to believe that each individual has unique sensibilities, and each couple is free from the class influences of their pasts. But, if the goal is to increase the well-being of couples or to alleviate inequality, then blissful ignorance will not do.

Lessons for Individuals in Different-Origin Marriages

This book has demonstrated that each partner in a different-origin couple tends to have different sensibilities. This means that for these relationships to work each partner must commit to dealing with difference. Successfully doing so involves two strategies. First, those in the happiest marriages did not try to remake their partner in their own image. Such attempts not only failed, but they also made both spouses unhappy in the process. One partner would be unhappy that the other did not change; the other that they were not accepted as they are. Second, for many, living in a different-origin marriage meant living with conflicts that may never be resolved. In the best cases, they respected and admired their partner's approach or at least thought it was reasonable. In other cases, respondents in happy marriages learned to say things like, "I've come to accept it, but it's definitely not what I would do on my own."[11] Continually arguing over their differences was both unproductive and futile. Figuring out how to live with differences allowed couples to be happier.

Living in a different-origin marriage, however, was about not only tolerating differences but about also sincerely loving one's spouse. Most of the respondents in this book reported being very happy in their marriage. Several talked of being in a "classic love story" and being unable to imagine marrying anyone beside their spouse. Some lit up when talking about their spouse and still gushed over how lucky they were to have found their partner. Only three couples said they discussed the possibility of divorce. Two of these had dealt with major changes—job losses—that made their different sensibilities especially salient.[12] Those who lived with more stability generally found a way to navigate their differences in a way that worked for them.[13] Different-origin couples should then not feel overly discouraged by their differences; the majority of the respondents I talked to reported deeply loving their spouse and their life together.

Lessons about Upward Mobility

There are two primary ways that scholars think about the connection between sensibilities and upward mobility: as preventing mobility and as facilitating it. One subset of scholars who see sensibilities as preventing mobility ascribe to the culture of poverty perspective. Often attributed to Oscar Lewis (1961, 1966), this perspective posits that the poor have values and sensibilities that are distinct from the middle class. These values and sensibilities originally stem from structural conditions but outlast them. This becomes problematic as, according to the culture of poverty thesis, the sensibilities of the poor that are different than those of the middle class lock them in poverty. Cultural assimilation is a prerequisite to mobility.[14]

Another group of scholars assumes that upwardly mobile individuals have different sensibilities than those born into the middle class. Rather than casting these differences as problematic, they see them as associated with upward mobility. According to this assumption, upward mobility is difficult. Given that they have achieved such a difficult feat, upwardly mobile people must be particularly hardworking, motivated, savvy, organized, and disciplined. Class reproduction, by contrast, is less difficult. Middle-class children who become middle-class adults are not necessarily lazy or unmotivated, but they are not as exceptional as their upwardly mobile counterparts. Most data sets, however, do not include measures of hard work, motivation, savvy, or organization; the assumption that upwardly mobile individuals are especially high on these traits is not tested.[15]

Findings from this study cast doubt on both perspectives. The culture of poverty thesis predicts that the poor's cultural differences prevent their mobility. In this study, respondents born into poor and working-class families had systematic and pervasive differences from the middle-class, but these differences did not prevent their mobility.[16] At the same time, the upwardly mobile individuals in this sample were not especially driven to succeed, organized, or savvy in regards to education or work. In fact, compared to their white-collar-origin counterparts, they reported more difficulties navigating college, less interest in advancing at work, and less organization regarding their use of time and money. Though they were perhaps more driven and organized than their peers who remained in blue-collar jobs, they would not count themselves as exceptionally so.[17] It is likely that cultural sensibilities do deter or facilitate mobility, but, at least for this sample, not in two of the ways often assumed.[18]

Lessons about Inequality

The sensibilities that institutions tend to reward are managerial ones (Lareau and Calarco 2012; Lizardo 2013; Rivera 2015; Wingfield 2010). This book shows that the sensibilities that help individuals pass their privileges down to their children and stay ahead are not family resources but individual resources. Despite their coaching and encouragement, white-collar-origin respondents struggled to help their blue-collar-origin partners access the managerial sensibilities that would help them succeed in middle-class institutions. Jason, for example, did not follow Lori's lead by showing more agency at work or networking over dinner with his colleagues. Isabelle did not internalize Ian's "entitlement lessons." Jack admitted that Caroline got more done at work because of her planning sensibilities but did not adopt them himself. Potentially helpful sensibilities were not often transferred from one spouse to the other.

Class inequality then often produces sensibilities, and the nexus between sensibilities and institutions can reproduce class inequality.

That white-collar-origin partners had sensibilities that were more likely to be valued by middle-class institutions could generate inequalities within relationships, such as putting white-collar-origin partners' careers first. But, given that blue-collar-origin respondents were often happy to have a less prestigious career, this inequality, assuming the couple remained married, may not be the biggest one. Rather, inequalities between different-origin and shared-origin couples may be bigger. College-educated couples composed of two individuals born into professional white-collar families may have more advantages in navigating workplaces and their children's schools than those in which one partner is upwardly mobile.[19] On top of these additional cultural resources, shared-origin couples are, of course, also more likely to have two sets of parents who provide greater financial resources and deeper safety nets (Schoeni and Ross 2005).[20] Assortative mating by class destination is on the rise and is a major source of inequality amongst Americans and their children (Fernández and Rogerson 2001; Mare 1991; Schwartz and Mare 2005; Schwartz 2010; see Breen and Salazar 2011 as well as Rosenfeld 2008 for opposing views). Assortative mating by class origin may also be a major source of inequality within couples who share their class destinations.

The observed relationships between sensibilities and class inequality, however, also suggest some counterforces that may work to alleviate inequality. The nonassimilation of upwardly mobile respondents may make it harder for them to succeed at work and advocate for their children, but it may help those who come after them. Their presence injects new sensibilities into middle-class spaces. This slows cultural closure as not all individuals who share a social space share an exclusive set of sensibilities. A diverse array of sensibilities, in turn, can help future upwardly mobile individuals succeed as they are more likely to encounter others who share or who have been exposed to their sensibilities. Though institutions may still favor managerial sensibilities, a culturally diverse middle-class is more favorable for those striving for upward mobility than a culturally homogeneous one.

The class sensibilities of this generation may also shape those of the next as it shapes parents' socialization of their children. Adults raised in different classes not only tend to parent their children in different styles—styles that schools unequally reward (Bettie 2003; Dumais, Kessinger, and Ghosh 2012)—but they also expose their children to different ideas about how to use resources and attend to their daily lives. In this way, the children's grandparents' resources are indirectly related to the sensibilities that children are exposed to at home. One implication of this is clear—children whose parents are from different class origins are then not exposed to a unified set of sensibilities but conflicting ones. The meaning of this implication, however, is unclear as it is unknown what sensibilities children of different-origin couples develop or how they deploy them.

Finally, respondents remind us that the maintenance of their class position is simply not everyone's goal. Some upwardly mobile respondents felt ambivalent about turning their children into those with middle-class sensibilities and middle-class jobs. Many found joy in the class they came from and did not think that their children's potential downward mobility was something to fear.

Lessons for Policymakers

The personal lives of different-origin couples have public policy implications. Specifically, what did *not* happen in different-origin marriages is relevant for policymakers. Cultural osmosis—the idea that immersion in a setting will lead individuals to soak up the sensibilities of their new surroundings—rarely happened in different-origin marriages. It did not happen despite that respondents spent an average of 13 years together. It did not happen despite that individuals entered their relationships voluntarily, that husbands and wives typically were each other's strongest tie, or that their interactions were frequent.

Policies and programs, however, are sometimes designed with the assumption that cultural osmosis will occur. For example, the grand experiment, Moving to Opportunity (MTO), randomly assigned a group of low-income families to live in higher income neighborhoods. One of the assumptions behind this program was that low-income people would be immersed in a higher income neighborhood and would soak up the sensibilities of their new neighbors. Not surprisingly, given that cultural osmosis did not occur in different-origin marriages—relationships that involve much more frequent and intense interaction—it also did not occur when lower income individuals lived amongst higher income neighbors (Popkin, Harris, and Cunningham 2002). Sensibilities did not travel from one neighbor to another through sheer proximity.

Recently, social commentator Charles Murray (2012) called for another program that assumed that cultural osmosis occurs among adults. Murray believes that the working class has lost the American values of marriage, civic responsibility, religion, and hard work. He sees the elite as possessing these values but criticizes them for not pushing their values on others. His advice for stemming the class divide: convince the elite to preach what they practice. *New York Times* columnist David Brooks (2012) takes Murray's call one step further by proposing a national program that would compel young adults from the upper and lower classes to live together for a short period of time. This shared space, he thinks, would allow elites to effectively preach what they practice and model their behavior. The result, he assumes, is that the working class would absorb the values and sensibilities held by the elite.

Putting aside the elitism of these approaches, that cultural osmosis was largely absent in marriages casts doubt on the effectiveness of any policy that is predicated upon the idea that lower class adults will soak up the sensibilities of those in a higher class. As cultural osmosis did not occur in marriage, it is unlikely to occur in shorter term, less intimate interactions between adults who may or may not respect one another. If sharing a home, bank account, college degree, friendship network, and children does not produce cultural osmosis, sharing a year or two in a program is unlikely to as well.[21] Simply hearing the ideas of distant others is especially unlikely to produce a change in values or sensibilities.

Of course, it is possible that it is marriage itself that is ill-suited to the transfer of sensibilities and cultural capital. Marriages, most importantly, are between adults—those whose sensibilities are already firmly rooted. Marriages are also presumed to be between equals; no partner has a position of authority by which to demand cultural changes. There is also not a formal curriculum by which one tries to change the other. In fact, in some marriages, the opposite is true. One idea about marriage is that spouses should accept each other as they are, not ask for change. The lack of a hierarchy, formal curriculum, or idea that asking for change is appropriate may deter cultural osmosis. It is then possible that sensibilities are more easily soaked up in adult relationships outside of marriage. Policymakers, however, should remain skeptical. Even within an institution where two are said to become one, each partner maintained separate sensibilities, ones influenced by the power of the class of their past.[22]

Appendix A

Data and Methods

Sociology professors sometimes tell their American students that their marriages will be arranged. This can produce shock amongst students as Americans think of themselves as free to choose their spouses. What these professors mean is that while parents no longer choose their children's spouses by weighing their class background, many people marry the same type of person that their parents would have picked had they considered their in-laws' assets. Social forces now do the arranging rather than parents.

With this in mind, I had doubts about whether I could recruit enough individuals in different-origin marriages to make this study possible. Worried, I veered from the sample I found ideal to make a sample that would be more feasible to recruit. This meant that while I had initially hoped to find couples who had been married about the same number of years and who were around the same age, I settled for a sample in which couples could be married for any number of years and be of any age provided that they had a child together who was at least four years old. I also would have preferred a sample that was diverse by race, educational attainment, sexuality, and marital status, but instead chose a group that was populous in my geographic region—those who were white, highly educated, and in different-sex marriages. While it would not have been difficult to find some respondents outside of these groups, I worried that having a minority of respondents in other groups would introduce variation that I could not explain in a small sample.

Of course, these decisions about who to include in the sample still left a sociological elephant in the room; I had not decided how to define or operationalize class. Class is a notoriously nebulous concept, one that escapes easy definitions. Sociologists wage heated debates about if class is categorical or continuous, how many classes there are, where the line is between one class and another, and if culture is a product or cause of class conditions or both (Bourdieu 1985; Lareau and Conley 2008; Marx in Tucker 1978; Weber in Grusky 1994; Willis 1977; Wright 1985; Zweig 2000). Trying to resolve these debates or please all stripes of class scholars is impossible; I settled on a definition that has wide, but not universal, agreement. I think of classes as large groups of people who share similar amounts of occupational prestige, educational attainment, income, wealth, and debt; I measured class using the first two categories. I view culture as stemming from one's class (economic) position but also creating a loop to reproduce economic differences. I think of culture therefore as separate from class but closely related to it. People's class is not defined by their culture, but their culture is often an indicator of their class.

In this study, I use the categories of white- and blue-collar to operationalize individuals' class origin. White-collar-origin respondents are those that had fathers with bachelor's or advanced degrees and who worked in professional or managerial jobs. Blue-collar-origin respondents are those that had fathers with at most a high school diploma and who tended to work with their hands (though, of course, their jobs also often required mental work). White-collar occupations included doctors, lawyers, engineers, accountants, professors, and teachers, while blue-collar occupations included factory workers, truck drivers, electricians, mechanics, police officers, farmers, and repairmen. I divided the sample into white- and blue-collar for practical rather than theoretical purposes. Recruiting was facilitated by simple class categories, as potential respondents were aware of their fathers' educational attainment and work history. White- and blue-collar categories were also useful for analyzing the data: In a small sample it was practical to divide respondents into a small number of groups.

There are two main disadvantages of the white-collar/blue-collar categories. The first is that it reproduces patriarchal ideas of class by defining participants' class origin by their fathers' but not their mothers' class position. I made the decision to define class by fathers' occupation and education as I knew that at the time when respondents were growing up fathers were more likely than mothers to be the primary breadwinners and because housewives are difficult to classify (Fischer and Hout 2006). As it turned out, in terms of educational attainment, most respondents' parents had matching levels of educational attainment: 29 of the 32 blue-collar-origin respondents' mothers did not have a bachelor's degree, while 26 of the 32 mothers of white-collar-origin respondents had a bachelor's degree and all but one had attended at least some college. Father's class position therefore was usually an adequate proxy for both parents' class position.

The other potential problem with the white-collar/blue-collar categories is that they contain considerable variation. White-collar-origin respondents included, for example, the son of a teacher, the daughter of a university president, and the granddaughter of a wealthy Fortune 500 company founder.

Blue-collar-origin respondents included those whose working fathers struggled to feed 10 children to those whose fathers earned a sizeable income in a unionized factory. I examined if those who recalled growing up with more or less resources than those whose fathers had similar levels of education had sensibilities that differed from others with blue- or white-collar roots. This was not the case. Though the categories of blue- and white-collar were broad, they still captured respondents' sensibilities.

I made one other decision about operationalizing class. I recruited respondents based on their father's class position, not their own. As such, I ended up with 82 college graduates and 2 respondents who had begun but not completed college. I could have decided to analyze only the 30 couples in which each spouse had a bachelor's degree, but I decided to keep the remaining two couples in the sample instead. I did this because each respondent who lacked a bachelor's degree had nonetheless undergone a substantial amount of college—one was a semester shy of a bachelor's degree while the other completed two years of college. This allowed for some socialization through higher education to occur. Furthermore, keeping them in the sample enabled me to peer across another class line—educational attainment—and to see if the patterns still held. Some "messiness" in the sample seemed acceptable as it reflects the messiness of the real world.

In addition to the different-origin marriages, I also recruited a sample of shared-origin couples. These were couples in which each partner and their father had graduated from a four-year college and worked in a white-collar job or as a stay-at-home parent. This group allowed me to understand if the reasons why white-collar-origin partners felt they "married down" were different than those given by respondents who married laterally. It also permitted me to understand if the white-collar-origin respondents took on some of their upwardly mobile partners' sensibilities or if their sensibilities were not related to the class origin of their spouse. In a world that had endless resources, I would have also interviewed several other comparison groups: Couples in which each partner grew up in and remained in a blue-collar milieu, different-origin couples in which one partner was downwardly mobile, couples that were different-origin but disbanded, cross-class couples by their destination as well as their origin, and couples that had mismatching class destinations but shared class origins. These groups would all give me analytical purchase on other types of arguments. Unfortunately, those arguments will need to be made at another time.

In the end, I came away with a sample that included 32 different-origin couples and 10 shared-origin couples. I conducted 84 interviews as I interviewed spouses separately in each of the 42 couples. Fifteen couples involved a woman "marrying up" by class origin while 17 couples were composed of men doing the same. At the time of the interview, all but two respondents graduated from college, and all but five worked in a professional or managerial job or as a stay-at-home parent. In other words, nearly all respondents ended up in white-collar positions or as stay-at-home parents, but half of those in different-origin marriages did not begin there.

Respondents were also middle-aged (a median age of 41) and most had been married over a decade (the median years of marriage was 13 for different-origin couples) (see Table A.1). All but one participant had all of their children after marrying, and only two respondents had been previously married. Again, all were white, heterosexual, married, and United States citizens.

Table A.1 RESPONDENTS' DEMOGRAPHIC CHARACTERISTICS

Respondents' Demographic Characteristics	Respondents with Blue-Collar Origins in Different-Origin Marriages	Respondents with White-Collar Origins in Different-Origin Marriages	Respondents in Shared-Origin Marriages
Highest Level of Education			
High school	0	0	0
Some college	2	0	0
Bachelor's degree	16	12	10
Advanced degree	14	20	10
Current Occupation			
Professional managerial	15	22	14
Middle class	3	0	0
Blue- or lower-white-collar	3	2	0
Graduate student	1	1	3
Stay-at-home-parent	8	6	3
Unemployed	2	1	0

(*Continued*)

Table A.1 (CONTINUED)

Respondents' Demographic Characteristics	Respondents with Blue-Collar Origins in Different-Origin Marriages	Respondents with White-Collar Origins in Different-Origin Marriages	Respondents in Shared-Origin Marriages
Median age	42	41	40
Median years married	13	13	14
Number previously married	2	0	0
Modal number of children	2	2	2
Median age of oldest child	8	8	12.5

Notes: Professional managerial occupations refer to positions that offer authority and autonomy, including lawyers, doctors, engineers, teachers, scientists, managers, computer programmers, and elected politicians. Middle-class positions were operationalized as having less authority or autonomy, for example a physicians' assistant and a project manager for others' research projects. Blue-collar and lower-white-collar positions included one secretary and bus driver/office worker, a filing clerk, a lab assistant, and a stock attendant at a store. One unemployed respondent was recently encouraged to retire from a teaching job while the other was laid off from a sales job during the recession.

Recruiting the Sample

Though the sample was designed, in part, to facilitate recruiting, my first efforts at finding interviewees failed. I posted fliers in buildings and on listservs, only to be met with an empty in-box. Finally, one woman called me. She told me that she would do the study if she was paid, but otherwise her life as a hockey mom made her too busy to be altruistic. I got the hint and reallocated some of my transcription funds to pay participants.

Now, offering $50 per couple, I found my in-box flooded with interest. I sent fliers that announced a study about marriage, family, and "economic backgrounds" to every parenting listserv, school, parent-teacher organization, Meet-Up group, and activity-based club I could find in a small midwestern city and its surrounding rural areas. The kindness of strangers also facilitated recruitment; without my knowledge someone posted a flier about the study in a high school newsletter and a church bulletin. Parenting listservs, parent-teacher organizations, and fliers posted on preschool bulletin boards proved to have the highest payoffs, though some respondents heard about the study through their church dispatches and social clubs. In the end, all different-origin respondents were recruited through listservs, social clubs, and organizations located in and serving middle-class neighborhoods. They were thus among groups likely to feel comfortable in the middle class—those most likely to have middle-class(-origin) sensibilities.

Recruiting shared-origin couples turned out to be more difficult than recruiting different-origin couples. This came as a surprise, as I had assumed that shared-origin couples were more common and therefore easier to find. I recruited them only after I had interviewed all but a few of the different-origin couples and turned to the listservs and groups that had yielded the most different-origin participants. By this time, I felt that I had worn out my welcome—these listservs had sometimes posted three announcements recruiting different-origin couples— and I was more reluctant to ask them to send my shared-origin announcement multiple times. Maybe because of my hesitancy in posting repeatedly, shared-origin couples' belief that they represent the norm and have little of interest to say, or shared-origin couples' possibly better financial position, it was more difficult to recruit these couples. For the shared-origin group, I turned to interviewing one couple who were friends of a friend and one couple who attended synagogue with my mother's friends. While the interviews with my friend's friends went well, the interviews with my mother's friends' friends did not. They clearly had signed up for the study as a favor to their friend and had little interest in answering my questions with more than a perfunctory reply.

After the e-mails were sent out, I began the screening process with the potential respondents. I often felt nervous about patronizing potential respondents by asking them to confirm information that was clearly on the flyer, and sometimes felt too shy to ask them if they were white or had children. I should have done so, however, as I ended up meeting one couple who did not have children and another couple in which both partners were black. I went ahead with the interviews in both cases—they hinted that they needed the money, and I figured their interviews would still be informative. I ended up including the childless couple as there was no reason to exclude them other than from the parenting section. I did not include the black couple in the study, though their interviews were strikingly similar to the others' with the exception that they were both especially class aware. After recruiting the couples, I began the interviews.

The Interviews

The interview had several sections (see Appendix C). I first asked respondents to tell me the story of how they met. I asked about their first impressions of their partner and why they wanted to marry them. I asked about their parents' and friends' first impressions. I also asked them to tell me about their wedding.

The next section of the interview focused on how respondents were alike or different. Based on my reading of the literature, I came up with a list of topics where I thought class origin might matter in marriage. I asked respondents to tell me if they were mostly similar or mostly different to their partner, and how so. I probed for information about what criteria they used to judge similarities or differences; this is the basis of much of Chapters 4—8. I also asked open-ended questions about general similarities, differences, and changes. These questions helped me gather data on how the couples were alike or different in ways that I could not predict. The sections on planning and emotions come from these general questions about difference. In addition, I asked about childrearing, their childhood, and their ideas about social class. The latter was saved for the end of the interview in case questions on this topic were contentious. For some respondents, as discussed below, they were.

In nearly every case, I interviewed the husband and wife separately. I did this so that I would not get couples' stories but individuals' stories. I thought that each partner might have different understandings of the same events, and indeed this was sometimes the case. Rarely did spouses' answers conflict with their partners', but one spouse often emphasized different details than their partner or added additional information. I also interviewed wives and husbands separately in case they were in unhappy marriages or would not reveal some information in front of their partners. In interviewing partners separately, I promised each respondent that I would not report anything to their spouse. During the course of the interviews, I also tried to assure them of the confidentiality of the interviews. The second partner to be interviewed inevitably would ask something along the lines of: "Have you already heard this story?" I would tell them that I could not answer what I had or had not heard, and in any case I was interested in their interpretation of the story.

Due to the couples' time constraints, I did conduct the husband's and wife's parenting section together for two couples. This produced a different set of data than the data from individual interviews; each partner seemed deeply interested in what the other would say and seemed to be performing partly for the other. They seemed to also want to help each other come to an agreement on answers, as if there was one "true" answer that they were working together to produce. While no data is "pure," the data produced here was qualitatively different than the data from individual interviews. Here I had the opportunity to see how the couple interacted together, but I lost their individual accounts of their lives. Data from these dual interviews do not appear in the parenting chapter.

It is also worth noting that while I conducted at least part of every interview with just one partner at a time, there were several instances when the other partner would briefly overhear part of the other's interview. I asked the respondent to choose where we met, and a few respondents asked if it was acceptable to conduct the interview at home when their partner was also home and watching their children. Knowing that the only way for some people to be able to participate was if I could accommodate their schedules, I agreed. I requested that we conduct the interview in a room where their partner was out of hearing distance; I also alerted them that I planned on promising them confidentiality but it was theirs to waive. Most of the time they found a private space for us to chat, though there were several times when a partner would briefly walk through the interview room. This posed some challenges, as I was afraid that a respondent would be less honest if their partner could hear the interview. While it is likely that some respondents concealed some of their thoughts when their partner could listen in, I was repeatedly surprised by what respondents would say in front of their partners. A few respondents said strikingly negative things about their spouses even though it was possible that their partners could listen to our conversation. Only once did a partner interrupt the flow of the interview. In this case she wanted to make sure that I understood that her husband's comments were a subtle jab at her. Having a partner in hearing distance thus helped me acquire some data while probably preventing me from acquiring other data. For most of the couples, eavesdropping was not an issue as their partner was not in hearing distance.

The timing of the interview of each spouse may have also shaped the findings. I conducted several of the interviews with the husbands and wives back-to-back. This had the advantage of making sure that the first member of the couple did not tell the second member about the interview and possibly influence their answers. However, as respondents were busy professionals, I did not require that interviews be at consecutive times. I do not believe this was a problem, first because many respondents said that they were waiting until they both completed the interviews to compare notes, and second, because respondents' answers were unlikely to change enough to alter the findings substantially.

Regardless of the timing of the interviews, respondents tended to be fairly open about their marriage. Interviews lasted a median of one hour and forty-five minutes, and even the above conditions, signed consent forms, and an audio-recorder seemed not to deter many from telling the details of their lives. I was often surprised at the end of the interviews when respondents profusely thanked me for the opportunity to talk about their marriages and families. Many equated the interview to a therapy session, including the one respondent who worked as a therapist. For many this seemed a positive thing—they said they were happy I made them think about their marriages and family decisions in ways they had not before, or they were happy to have a chance to reflect on such a routine but important part of their lives. Others seemed less thrilled that their interviews resembled therapy sessions. They said that they had revealed more than they intended and seemed worried about the potential consequences. Of course, not all interviews resembled therapy sessions. Some respondents stuck to short answers about the facts of their lives. In most of these cases, their partners' gregariousness partly made up for their relative closure, and I was still able to get some sense of each partner's sensibilities.

Respondents' level of talkativeness may have resulted from their own agendas. Some had clearly come prepared to tell me the story of a happy marriage in times of high divorce rates. Others seemed to come for "girl talk." I distinctly remember one woman plopping down on her couch in a way that made me think that she was approaching the interview as a teen girl might approach a sleepover with an intimate friend. Still others said they signed up for the $50, out of a sense of obligation to help the university, or because they saw themselves in the flyer and felt compelled to join. A small subset also seemed to have been dragged into the study by their partners who felt more desire to participate than they did.

Analysis

I analyzed the interviews using a combination of strategies derived from the extended case method (Burawoy 1998) and grounded theory (Strauss and Corbin 1998). The first, the extended case study, is an approach that acknowledges that researchers are immersed in a sea of theories. Rather than asking them to temporarily disregard these theories, it asks the researcher to consider and expand them. Using the extended case method often involves selecting a case that cannot be explained by the existing theory or analyzing an existing theory in light of a new group. In each case, the goal is to revise the theory, if necessary, to fit the new situation. In choosing to study the reasons individuals from different class backgrounds gave about why they were drawn to each other, I chose a group whose attraction could not be easily explained by cultural matching theory. In studying adults who shared their class destination but not their class origin, I chose a group that two theories—cultural reproduction theory and cultural mobility theory—offer opposing expectations regarding respondents' sensibilities and tastes. As the extended case method calls for, these samples allowed me to extend existing theories on social class and relationships and social class and sensibilities.

Qualitative research is also useful not only to extend theories but also to discover them. In these cases, researchers use aspects of grounded theory to analyze what concepts emerge from the data. I followed this approach in two ways: By analyzing respondents' ideas of time and emotions—topics I did not ask about—and by examining the organizing principles of sensibilities. In each case, the themes that emerged from the data were not ones that I had begun the study intending to analyze.

Both grounded theory and the extended case method ask the researcher to use inductive coding. I did this for each section of the interview. Here, I wrote multiple memos documenting possible emerging patterns. I then used open coding to capture these themes and also coded other themes that emerged from multiple readings of the transcripts. After this was complete, I used selective coding to refine the open codes. For the portions of the study in which I was looking to extend existing theories, I used deductive coding in addition to inductive coding. Here, I examined if existing theories fit my data. For each type of coding, I checked for disconfirming data and to ensure that each piece of data fit each code.

After each type of coding was complete, I constructed tables to understand how often each type of data was associated with each type of person. These tables were organized so that each column represented a specific group by class origin and gender (blue-collar-origin women, blue-collar-origin men, etc.) and each row delineated a belief. I then filled in each cell with the appropriate respondents' identifiers (e.g., R15F for Respondent in Couple 15, female). These filled-in tables allowed me to visualize the class and gender patterns for each theme, as some cells were quite full while others were empty.

Even with the tables, the interpretation of the differences between different-origin and shared-origin couples was not always straightforward. That the questions were open-ended meant that those in different-origin and shared-origin relationships did not always talk about the same themes. Partners were asked to compare themselves to their spouses on a variety of broad domains; that each interviewee's reference was a person with a particular classed history meant that those with different partners sometimes brought up different categories of answers. For example, I asked the question: "How are you and your spouse different?" Respondents in different-origin marriages often brought up their varied ways of expressing feelings; respondents in shared-origin marriages rarely did the same. This means that I have little data on how those in shared-origin marriages express their feelings. It is possible that the lack of data is in some ways data in itself—it may indicate that shared-origin couples had more similar ways of expressing their emotions. However, I cannot say for sure that this is the case. In these cases, I include information of different-origin, but not shared-origin, couples.

Finally, the analysis is limited to those groups included in the sample. I did not interview any couples who disbanded before marrying or who divorced after wedding. This means I may have filtered out the couples in which class differences caused them to end their relationships early on as well as the couples who married then found their class differences too much to handle. The analysis does not include anyone who was considerably downwardly mobile, leaving it an open question as to whether sensibilities are differentially likely to change for upwardly and downwardly mobile individuals. The analysis also cannot be extended to different racial groups, those in interracial marriages, or those not in heterosexual marriages, as each group may have semi-independent marriage markets, sensibilities, and understandings of class (Banks 2011; Hochschild 1995). The analysis, in short, is only applicable for whites whose marriage consists of one upwardly mobile partner and one partner who has spent their entire life in the middle class.

Reflexivity

The contours of the interviews were not just influenced by who the respondents are but who I am as well. Before the project began, I considered how my class, gender, and age might influence the interviews.

CLASS SENSIBILITIES

I worried about how respondents would see my class position and how this might influence my ability to quickly build rapport. I grew up with two parents with terminal degrees and professional jobs; my father works as a law professor while my mother writes grants for a university. I had spent time in a variety of class milieus—living in an upper-middle-class suburb of Cleveland, a working-class rural community in northwestern Ohio, and attending a college with many elites. I felt that these experiences allowed me to build rapport with those from a variety of class backgrounds, but that my position at as a graduate student at the University of Michigan loudly signaled the class that I was entering, if not the one I was from.

I thought about how I should perform my class during the interviews. As someone who had already studied social class, I doubted that parts of my presentation of self would be easy to change. I had internalized the "niceness" and soft-spoken sensibilities that often defines white middle-class women (Brown 2003), the natural use of "proper" grammar that is typical of the upper-middle class, and the body type associated with women from my class. I thought about what to wear—something I could change—but thought it best to dress in casual business attire for all the interviews.

Deciding that the combination of my sensibilities, appearance, and status as a graduate student would not allow me to significantly alter the performance of my class, I instead tried to be aware of how reactions to me were classed. The primary way that I noticed class mattering in the interviews was that several of the blue-collar-origin men seemed to have false beliefs about the purpose of the study. At the end of the interview, some asked me what the study was *really* about after I had told them a vague but true premise of the study. They seemed to think I was tricking them. I'm not sure if this was distrust of me as a classed person or because some studies—perhaps especially psychology studies—do tell subjects that the study has one premise when it really has another. Other blue-collar-origin men seemed to think the study was designed to help me in my own relationships. They would offer general advice about marriage, telling me things to do and things to avoid. One blue-collar-origin man also noted that he was thinking of going back to school in sociology to become a therapist like me. He did not realize that a sociology degree would not lead into a career as a therapist, either for me or for him.

The combination of my class upbringing with blue-collar-origin men's class upbringing also occasionally clashed during the final stages of the interview. Here I asked whether they ever thought about class, if they believed class mattered in their marriage, if they had advice for others in different-origin marriages, what class they grew up in, and what class they are in now. Sometimes interviews that had been going perfectly well took an emotional turn during these questions. Several blue-collar-origin men became angry, and some who had not previously cursed in the interview started swearing. One became teary. Some angrily told me that they knew that the purpose of my study was to show that class mattered. As it does not matter, they said, the study was inherently flawed.

My reaction to their reactions was to listen and to try to be reassuring. If they were upset that the study was looking for class differences, I assured them that I was interested in similarities as well. I also suggested that differences were not necessarily problematic and that I had not seen any evidence that different-origin marriages were especially likely to end in divorce.[1] I sometimes went further, saying that sociology studies assumed that these marriages are rare, and so I just wanted to understand how couples got together and how they worked out. I tried to assure them that my goal was not to show that different-origin marriages were doomed to fail.[2] I doubt that any of these reassurances were effective; by this point these respondents seemed distrustful of me and angered by the fact that I had brought up class at all.

The anger and sadness that some respondents expressed when discussing social class reveals that "hidden injuries of class" (Sennett and Cobb 1972) can occur during the interview process. Simply talking about class seemed upsetting for some. This might be because they desperately wanted class to not matter, but my questions suggested that it might. Respondents may have also become upset because of the language they used when talking about class. William, for example, described his wife as coming from a "pretty good background" and noted that her great-grandparents "did really good for themselves." He noted that his background was different than his wife's "pretty good" background. By implication, then, his would have been "pretty bad." This type of language, used commonly throughout our society, leaves blue-collar people in a defensive position. If respondents perceived my upper-middle-class background and future, they then may have felt especially defensive around me.

This process raises the question about if and how it would be possible to construct an interview about class that does not risk invoking hidden injuries of class. Given the way that American society thinks about class—the myths of the lazy and undeserving poor and the hardworking and morally superior middle class—I'm not sure that this is possible. If that is right, then a debate might be needed as to when it is appropriate to interview people about class and when it is not.

That said, it is also worth considering that my class upbringing might have led me to misread if hidden injuries of class occurred. As Chapter 8 showed, those raised in white-collar families tend to show less emotion than those raised in blue-collar families. Perhaps my own class background led me to read too much into what to me were sudden and expressive displays of emotions. After William's interview, for example, I felt sure that his wife would cancel her interview. But, to my great surprise, she showed up and seemed happy to be there. It is also worth keeping in mind that the majority of blue-collar-origin men did not seem disturbed by my line of questioning and that no blue-collar-origin women seemed equally upset. I do not know why some reacted more strongly than others. And, while I can make educated guesses about why men were more upset than women in talking about class, I did not push the subject and do not know for sure.

My class background, as well as creating distance between myself and some respondents, also held some advantages. It likely put some respondents at ease as white-collar-origin interviewees may have imagined that I shared a background with them. My past was also helpful in that my experience living in three different class milieus made me feel that I could fairly accurately know a person's class background by spending a few minutes with them. As an informal and unscientific test of the lasting influence of class, I arrived at the interview without looking at my notes about which respondent was from which class (although sometimes, of course, I remembered without checking my notes), and then I would guess the class background of the respondent before the interview began. I used cues from the way they talked, their general mannerisms, and their bodily disposition. In all but a few cases (all blue-collar-origin women), I felt that I could easily and accurately identify respondents' class backgrounds. While this information is not "scientific" and this study examines sensibilities rather than speech styles or the way individuals hold themselves, it still added to my impressions that it is difficult to take the class out of the person after taking the person out of the class.

Finally, I have never been in a significant different-origin relationship. As the topic was not personal, I did not feel that I began with any insights into what it was like to live with and love a partner from another class.

AGE AND GENDER

I also thought about how my age and gender might shape the interviews. I worried that as I look much younger than I am and given my gender as a woman, respondents might perceive me as unprofessional. If this did matter, it was only apparent to me a few times when respondents interrupted the flow of the interview to ask how old I was. They underestimated my age; finding out that I was in my mid-20s seemed to set them at ease. Others asked what the project was for, and when I replied that it was part of my dissertation research, they seemed to think that my status as a graduate student justified my presence and probing questions.

Gender also mattered in instances in which I felt unsafe. In these cases, being alone with respondents in their homes under what first seemed to me suspicious circumstances made me uncomfortable and caused me to try to rush through parts of the interviews. Those two interviewees, however, were both very talkative, so my efforts to rush through the interview failed. It also turned out that they were unnecessary as I was safe throughout the time I spent with them.

Though I would have felt more comfortable going to strangers' homes if I was a man, my gender may have been an asset in other ways. Cultural norms suggest that it is women, rather than men, who often ask personal questions and who are available to listen to personal confessions. White and short women fit the image of individuals others open up to, and these characteristics might have also facilitated respondents' comfort with me. I did not notice any differences about whether men or women were more talkative or open. Overall, those who agreed to interviews were likely those who felt comfortable talking about marriage and family, and most respondents were, indeed, quite talkative.

Appendix B

Respondents' Demographic Characteristics and Meeting Places

Table B.1 RESPONDENTS' CLASS CHARACTERISTICS

Pseudonym	BC/ WC[a]	Respondent's Occupation	Respondent's Education	Father's Occupation	Father's Education	Mother's Occupation	Mother's Education
Different-Origin Couples							
Jill	BC	politician	MA	stenographer	HS	financial planner	HS
Eric	WC	businessman	MA	doctor	MD	office manager	BA
Rebecca	WC	teacher	BA	engineer	BA	secretary	SC

(Continued)

Table B.1 (CONTINUED)

Pseudonym	BC/ WC[a]	Respondent's Occupation	Respondent's Education	Father's Occupation	Father's Education	Mother's Occupation	Mother's Education
Joe	BC	accountant	BA	factory	8th grade	farm, factory	HS
Christie	BC	social worker	BA	maintenance worker	GED	SAHM[b] then secretary	HS
Mike	WC	small-business owner	BA	professor	PhD	SAHM	MA
Rachel	BC	lab assistant	BA	police officer	HS	SAHM	GED
Gordon	WC	teacher	BA	accountant	MBA	SAHM	BA
Sue	BC	physician's assistant	MA	farmer	8th grade	nurse	SC[d]
Nick	WC	SAHF[c]	BA	engineer	BA	SAHM	BA
Jenny	BC	SAHM	BA	electrician	HS	SAHM	HS
Matt	WC	product manager	MBA	teacher	MA	SAHM	BA
Chelsey	WC	teacher	MA	vice president of a company	PhD	SAHM	BA

Nathan	BC	unemployed, formerly in sales	BA	millwright	8th grade	SAHM then secretary	HS
Amelia	WC	social worker	MSW	university president	PhD	SAHM	MA
Isaac	BC	teacher	BA	factory worker	4th grade	SAHM	HS
Danielle	BC	preschool teacher	MSW	chemical worker	11th grade	SAHM then clerk	HS
Jim	WC	office worker	BA	scientist	PhD	SAHM	BA
Alice	WC	lawyer	JD	doctor	MD	SAHM	SC
Elliott	BC	SAHF	SC	tool and die	HS	SAHM	HS
Caroline	WC	scientist	PhD	engineer	PhD	bookkeeper	BA
Jack	BC	engineer	MA	factory worker	HS	SAHM then secretary	HS
Evelyn	BC	project manager	BA	factory worker	HS	factory worker	HS

(Continued)

Table B.1 (CONTINUED)

Pseudonym	BC/WC[a]	Respondent's Occupation	Respondent's Education	Father's Occupation	Father's Education	Mother's Occupation	Mother's Education
Colton	WC	SAHF	BA	engineer	BA	art gallery attendant	BA
Anneka	WC	PhD student	MA	engineer	PhD	math teacher	MA
William	BC	operations analyst	BA	sawmill repairman	HS	salesperson	< HS
Vicki	WC	teacher	MA	upper-level manager	BA	vice president of hospitals	MBA
John	BC	SAHF, part-time restaurant manager	SC	heating and cooling	GED	factory	HS
Lori	WC	professor	PhD	preacher	PhD	SAHM	BA
Jason	BC	professor	PhD	bus driver and preacher	HS	day care worker	HS
Zoey	WC	SAHM	BA	engineer	MS	seamstress	6th grade

Name	Class	Occupation	Education	Occupation	Education	Occupation	Education
Austin	BC	lawyer	JD	police officer and waiter	HS	SAHM then cleaner	HS
Alexa	WC	computer scientist	PhD	engineer	BA	accountant	BA
Aaron	BC	retired teacher	BA	factory worker	10th grade	SAHM	10th grade
Lillian	BC	SAHM	BA	machinist	GED	SAHM	HS
Parker	WC	graphic designer manager	BFA	lawyer	JD	nurse	HS
Mia	WC	SAHM	MA	vice president of a university	MA	retail worker	BA
Kevin	BC	graduate student	MA	auto worker	HS	HR at retail store	HS
Gabriella	BC	librarian	MA	military, warehouse worker	GED	secretary	Associates
Dan	WC	financial analyst	MBA	engineer	BA	art gallery attendant	MFA

(Continued)

225

Table B.1 (CONTINUED)

Pseudonym	BC/ WC[a]	Respondent's Occupation	Respondent's Education	Father's Occupation	Father's Education	Mother's Occupation	Mother's Education
Katie	BC	social scientist	MA	steel worker	HS	several pink-collar jobs	HS
Ryan	WC	lawyer	JD	college president	PhD	nurse	RN
Leslie	WC	office worker	BA	manager	MBA	SAHM	BA
Tom	BC	programmer	BA	security guard	HS	nurse	Associates
Andrea	WC	SAHM	BS	engineer	BS	SAHM	BA
Adam	BC	manager	MBA, MA	electrician	GED	SAHM	HS
Gina	BC	SAHM	MA	metal worker	HS	SAHM	BA
Scott	WC	director of business	BA	scientist	PhD	principal	MA
Sidney	BC	SAHM	BA	steel worker	HS	secretary then SAHM	HS

Joel	WC	sales manager	MBA	engineer	BS	teacher then SAHM	BA
Mary	WC	SAHM	JD	professor	PhD	teacher	MA
Ben	BC	director of sales	MBA	electrician	HS	SAHM then nurse	RN
Ann	BC	school cook	MA	farmer	HS	SAHM	MA
Brandon	WC	unemployed	BA	accountant	BA	SAHM	BA
Isabelle	BC	therapist	MA	farmer	HS	bartender	< HS
Ian	WC	professor	PhD	lawyer	JD	therapist	MSW
Bethany	WC	doctor	MD	bank manager	BA	secretary	SC
Bob	BC	SAHF	BS	truck driver	HS	SAHM then librarian	HS
Norah	WC	SAHM	PhD	scientist	MD	SAHM then teacher	BA

(Continued)

Table B.1 (CONTINUED)

Pseudonym	BC/WC[a]	Respondent's Occupation	Respondent's Education	Father's Occupation	Father's Education	Mother's Occupation	Mother's Education
George	BC	scientist	BS	factory worker	HS	SAHM and nurse	Associates
Madison	BC	SAHM	BA	security guard	HS	engineer, sales	Associates
Evan	WC	software engineer	BA	doctor	MD	SAHM then nurse	BA
Anita	WC	marketing	MA	dentist	MA	nurse, teacher	MA
Todd	BC	retail	BA	navy	HS	accountant	HS
Shared-Origin Couples							
Hannah	WC	SAHM, grant writer	BA	dentist	MA	SAHM	BA
Bryce	WC	medical resident	MD	professor	PhD, JD	SAHM	MA
Leah	WC	SAHM, writer	BA	media producer	BA	SAHM	Associates

Luke	WC	IT worker	MA	engineer	BA	medical clerk	BA
Adrienne	WC	graduate student	BA	agent	BA	teacher, banker	MA, MBA
Paul	WC	journalist	BA	professor	JD	scientist	MS
Abby	WC	doctor	MD	doctor	MD	nurse	MA
Sam	WC	doctor	MD	doctor	MD	teacher	BA
Amy	WC	graduate student	MA	university president	PhD	teacher	MA
Shawn	WC	investor/manager	BA	business owner	MA	teacher, business owner	MA
Rose	WC	SAHM	BA	lawyer	JD	human relations	JD
Phil	WC	architect	MA	doctor	MD	professor	PhD
Alisha	WC	educational therapist	MA	minister	JD	social worker	MSW

(Continued)

Table B.1 (CONTINUED)

Pseudonym	BC/ WC[a]	Respondent's Occupation	Respondent's Education	Father's Occupation	Father's Education	Mother's Occupation	Mother's Education
Brad	WC	lawyer	JD	lawyer	JD	SAHM	BA
Carlie	WC	engineer	BA	engineer	BA	SAHM	BA
Clint	WC	engineer	BA	engineer	BA	SAHM	BA
Diana	WC	preschool teacher	BA	engineer	BA	teacher	BA
Ted	WC	educator	MA	professor	PhD	teacher	MA
Jen	WC	SAHM, artist	MA	business owner, farmer	BA	teacher, farmer	MA
Kent	WC	engineer	BA	professor	MA	teacher	BA

Notes: Women are listed first in each couple. The respondent listed below each woman is her husband.

[a] BC = blue-collar, WC = white-collar.

[b] SAHM = stay-at-home mother.

[c] SAHF = stay-at-home father.

[d] SC = some college.

Table B.2 RESPONDENTS' FAMILY CHARACTERISTICS

Pseudonym	BC/WC[a]	Age[b]	Years Married	Number of Children	Age 1st Child	Gender 1st Child	Age 2nd Child	Gender 2nd Child	Age 3rd Child	Gender 3rd Child	Age 4th Child	Gender 4th Child
Different-Origin Couples												
Jill	BC	42	17	2	14	G[c]	12	B[d]				
Eric	WC	43	17	2	14	G	12	B				
Rebecca	WC	44	21	2	18	B	16	B				
Joe	BC	48	21	2	18	B	16	B				
Christie	BC	45	25	3	21	B	20	B	17	G		
Mike	WC	46	25	3	21	B	20	B	17	G		
Rachel	BC	55	27	2	23	G	21	G				
Gordon	WC	52	27	2	23	G	21	B				
Sue	BC	46	11	3	10	B	8	B	4	B		
Nick	WC	41	11	3	10	B	8	B	4	B		

(Continued)

Table B.2 (CONTINUED)

Pseudonym	BC/WC[a]	Age[b]	Years Married	Number of Children	Age 1st Child	Gender 1st Child	Age 2nd Child	Gender 2nd Child	Age 3rd Child	Gender 3rd Child	Age 4th Child	Gender 4th Child
Jenny	BC	42	20	3	14	G	10	B	10	B		
Matt	WC	46	20	3	14	G	10	B	10	B		
Chelsey	WC	46	23	2	19	G	17	G				
Nathan	BC	55	23	2	19	G	17	G				
Amelia	WC	57	19	1	17	G						
Isaac	BC	58	19	1	17	G						
Danielle	BC	56	27	4	36	G	26	B	24	G	12	B
Jim	WC	53	27	3	26	B	24	G	12	B		
Alice	WC	39	10	2	8	G	6	G				
Elliott	BC	39	10	2	8	G	6	G				
Caroline	WC	37	18	3	11	B	8	B	6	B		
Jack	BC	37	18	3	11	B	8	B	6	B		

Evelyn	BC	40	19	2	17	B	14	B		
Colton	WC	40	19	2	17	B	14	B		
Anneka	WC	31	8	2	6	G	4	G		
William	BC	37	8	2	6	G	4	G		
Vicki	WC	42	13	2	10	G	4	B		
John	BC	42	13	2	10	G	4	B		
Lori	WC	47	25	1	14	G	1	B		
Jason	BC	48	25	1	14	G	1	B		
Zoey	WC	43	13	2	4	G	1	B		
Austin	BC	44	13	2	4	G	1	B		
Alexa	WC	44	17	3	13	B	10	B	8	B
Aaron	BC	63	17	3	13	B	10	B	8	B
Lillian	BC	45	14	2	6	G	1	B		
Parker	WC	39	14	2	6	G	1	B		

(Continued)

Table B.2 (CONTINUED)

Pseudonym	BC/WC[a]	Age[b]	Years Married	Number of Children	Age 1st Child	Gender 1st Child	Age 2nd Child	Gender 2nd Child	Age 3rd Child	Gender 3rd Child	Age 4th Child	Gender 4th Child
Mia	WC	40	10	2	6	B	3	G				
Kevin	BC	40	10	2	6	B	3	G				
Gabriella	BC	—	8	1	7	B						
Dan	WC	—	8	1	7	B						
Katie	BC	36	12	2	5	G	2	G				
Ryan	WC	36	12	2	5	G	2	G				
Leslie	WC	40	20	2	11	G	7	G				
Tom	BC	48	20	2	11	G	7	G				
Andrea	WC	—	12	3	9	B	7	G	5	G		
Adam	BC	—	12	3	9	B	7	G	5	G		
Gina	BC	—	9	2	6	B	3	G				
Scott	WC	—	9	2	6	B	3	G				

Name									
Sidney	BC	29	11	3	6	B	5	G	1	G
Joel	WC	32	11	3	6	B	5	G	1	G
Mary	WC	39	13	2	6	G	4	G		
Ben	BC	39	13	2	6	G	4	G		
Ann	BC	39	10	0	6					
Brandon	WC	43	10	0	6					
Isabelle	BC	39	10	2	5	B	3	B		
Ian	WC	39	10	2	5	B	3	B		
Bethany	WC	38	10	2	7	G	0.3	B		
Bob	BC	38	10	2	7	G	0.3	B		
Norah	WC	38	8	1	4	G				
George	BC	38	8	1	4	G				
Madison	BC	33	12	2	6	B	4	G		
Evan	WC	33	12	2	6	B	4	G		
Anita	WC	41	6	2	5	B	3	B		

(Continued)

Table B.2 (CONTINUED)

Pseudonym	BC/WC[a]	Age[b]	Years Married	Number of Children	Age 1st Child	Gender 1st Child	Age 2nd Child	Gender 2nd Child	Age 3rd Child	Gender 3rd Child	Age 4th Child	Gender 4th Child
Todd	BC	45	6	2	5	B	3	B				

Shared-Origin Couples

Hannah	WC	31	8	2	6	G	3	G				
Bryce	WC	29	8	2	6	G	3	G				
Leah	WC	38	13	3	9	B	6	B	1	G		
Luke	WC	33	13	3	9	B	6	B	1	G		
Adrienne	WC	45	3[c]	2	9	B	5	B				
Paul	WC		3	2	9	B	5	B				
Abby	WC	48	23	6	20	G	18	G			15	G
Sam	WC	48	23	6	20							
Amy	WC	39	14	2	11	B	9	G				
Shawn	WC	40	14	2	11	B	9	G				

Rose	WC	37	13	3	13	B	6	B	2	G
Phil	WC	37	13	3	13	B	6	B	2	G
Alisha	WC	38	14	2	12	B	10	B		
Brad	WC	42	14	2	12	B	10	B		
Carlie	WC	36	18	2	13	G	9	B		
Clint	WC	37	18	2	13	G	9	B		
Diana	WC	50	23	2	19	G	14	B		
Ted	WC	50	23	2	19	G	14	B		
Jen	WC	41	17	2	14	B	11	G		
Kent	WC	46	17	2	14	B	11	G		

Notes: Women are listed first in each couple. The respondent listed below each woman is her husband.

[a] BC = blue-collar; WC = white-collar.

[b] Age: Age was not asked about but could often be inferred through information in the interview (i.e., knowledge of age at marriage and years married). When age could be inferred plus or minus two years it was included.

[c] G = girl.

[d] B = boy.

[e] 3 = This couple has only been married for 3 years but were together for 22 years prior to marrying.

Table B.3 MEETING PLACES

Meeting Place	Total Number of Respondents in Different-Origin Marriages Meeting in this Place	Total Number of Respondents in Shared-Origin Marriages Meeting in this Place
Junior high or high school	7*	1
College**	11	10
Graduate school	1	2
Work during college	2	0
Work after college	15	3
Religious institution	4	0
Friends or family	10	2
Bar	4	2
Leisure activity	6	0
Online	2	0
Other	2	0

Notes:

*Odd numbers exist because half a couple (one person) was in one category, while the other partner was in another. For instance, one couple met when she was in high school and he was at work as her teacher.

**The category of "college" includes all meetings that happened in college, including those which happened at a bar or through friends.

Appendix C

Interview Questionnaire

Matching Mechanisms

- Will you tell me the story of how you met your partner?
  - First impressions?
  - Reason for first attraction?
- Before you met your spouse, what characteristics were you looking for in a partner?
  - Was there anything in someone you dated in the past that you were trying to get away from?
- What made you think this was someone you wanted to marry?
- What did your friends and family first think about your partner? What do they think now?

Engagement and Wedding

- Tell me about the wedding planning.
- Tell me about the wedding.
- Tell me about some of the decisions you and your partner first made as a married couple.

Life Together

- How are you and your partner most alike? Most different?
- How do you think being in this relationship has changed you?
- How do you think being in this relationship has changed your partner?

- What compromises do you feel like you've made in your relationship?
- Do you think you and your partner are mostly alike or mostly differently when it comes to your ideas about the following? Please explain your answer.
  - Gift giving?
  - Holiday rituals?
  - How to spend money on yourself? On your kids? On your family as a whole?
  - The types of food you like to eat?
  - How your home should look?
  - Your politics?
  - Ideas about work?
  - Things to do on the weekend?
  - How to spend vacations?
  - Other people to spend time with?
- What do you admire about your partner?
- All couples disagree about some things. What types of things do you and your partner disagree about?
  - How do you resolve these disputes?
- What types of things have you learned from your partner?
- What types of things do you think your partner has learned from you?
- Who do you think has changed more?
- On a scale of 1–10, how satisfied are you with your marriage?
- If you could change one thing about your marriage, what would it be?

In-Laws

- Tell me about your in-laws.
  - What were your first impressions?
  - Do they have any customs that you aren't (or weren't initially) used to?
  - How are your moms alike? Different? Your dads?
  - How has your relationship with them evolved over time?

Parenting

- Tell me about your children.
- What personality traits do you appreciate in your children?
- What personality traits do you think your children get from you?
  - From your spouse?
- What kind of activities does your child do?

- How did you decide on these?
- Are there any activities your child has ever wanted to do that you've not allowed?
- What type of elementary and high school do you want your child to go to?
  - How did you decide on this?
- Do you have a career goal for your child?
  - How would you feel about them doing your father's job?
  - Your father-in-law's job?
- What are some life lessons you hope your child learns?
- How do your ideas of how to parent compare to your partners' ideas?
  - Can you tell me about a time when you and your partner disagreed about what or how to teach your child?
  - How did you work out the differences?
- What is the most important thing you can do as a parent to make sure your child turns into the adult you would like them to be?
- Has your child ever befriended someone you disapprove of?
  - What did you not like about this person?
  - What did you do when your child was hanging out with that person?
- Has your child ever dated someone you disapproved of?
  - What did you not like about this person?
  - Can you tell me about someone your child has dated that you've really liked?
- What could be the biggest thing your child could do to rebel?
- Since your child was born, how have your ideas about parenting changed?

Life before Your Relationship

- Tell me about the family you were born into.
- Is there anything about your childhood that stands out to you as being particularly formative?
- Describe the neighborhood(s) you grew up in.
- How was your family similar to other families in the neighborhood?
  - Different?
- What were some of the activities you did outside of school while growing up?
- What did you want to be when you grew up?
- Tell me about what school was like for you.
  - What type of elementary school did you go to? High school?
- Did you go to college? What was it like?
  - How did you pick your major?
- What values did your parents instill in you?
- Do you disagree with any of your parents' values?

- If so, which ones?
- Do you feel more similar or different than your parents?

Direct Questions about Class (mostly for different-origin couples)

- When did you first realize that you and your partner were from different class backgrounds? What made you think so?
- Before agreeing to this interview, did you think much about being from a different class background than your partner?
- Before you met your partner, did you have many friends from a different class background?
- Before you met your partner, did you date people mostly from your partner's class background?
  - Did you also date people from your own class background?
- What did your grandparents do?
- What class would you say you grew up in? Why?
- What class would you say you're in now? Why?
- Is there any advice you'd give to those who marry someone from a different class background?
- Looking back on it, is there a time when you remember learning of your family's class position?
  - How did you find out/figure it out?
- Many people who are upwardly or downwardly mobile say they never fully feel comfortable in their new position. They sometimes describe this as experiencing permanent culture shock, or that they're straddling two worlds. Did you feel this way at one time?
  - Do you still feel this way?

Demographic Questions

- What was your father's job when you were growing up?
- What was your mother's job when you were growing up?
- What was your parents' marital status?
  - If they were divorced, how old were you when the divorce took place?
  - Which parent did you live with?
  - If they divorced, did your parents remarry? What was their occupation and highest level of education?
- What was your father's highest level of education?
- What was your mother's high level of education?
- Did your parents own a home?

- What is your own occupation?
- What are some of your previous occupations?
- What is your highest level of education?
  - [If respondent went to college] Where did you go to college?
- What is your religion?
- How long have you been married?
- Were you married to anyone before this person?
  - What was his/her occupation?
  - What was his/her highest educational level?
  - What did his/her father do?
  - What was his/her father's highest educational level?
  - Why did you get divorced?
- Where is the last vacation you went on?
  - Did you take vacations when growing up?
- What are some of the places you went to?
  - Where is your favorite place you've ever been on vacation?

Reflections

- Is there anything else you think I should know about your background or your marriage?
- How do you feel about the interview?
- Do you have any questions for me?

NOTES

Preface

1. This person is Dwight Lang—one of my favorite people with whom to talk about class. I thank him for his candor in telling me about his surprise that I was so interested in studying class.
2. The suburb where I was raised, Shaker Heights, is mentioned in Charles Murray's (2012) book as a place where people with class privilege have historically resided.
3. Murray, Charles. 2012. *Coming Apart: The State of White America 1960–2010.* New York: Crown Forum.
4. Bourdieu (1984); Kozol (1992); Lareau (2003); Reardon and Bischoff (2011).
5. Morin, Rich. 2012. "Rising Share of Americans See Conflict Between Rich and Poor." *Pew Research: Social and Demographic Trends.* Washington DC.

Chapter 1

1. This myth is perpetuated by many films and novels that portray cross-class couples as struggling against the odds to be together before living happily ever after.
2. "Cultural mobility" is the name given to the theory that predicts that when upwardly mobile individuals acquire new resources, networks, and socialization experiences, they adopt the sensibilities that are dominant in middle-class settings. This perspective does not deny that class origin is one primary source of sensibilities but suggests that by adulthood its influence

has been overshadowed by resources and experiences associated with adults' new class position. Erickson (1996:224) summarizes this view: "As [adults] move they continue to learn; the early influence of family of origin is just one influence among many and not so powerful overall as later effects of education and adult social networks."

Some readings of Swidler's (1986) toolkit theory yield similar implications. Lizardo and Strand (2010:208) summarize the implications of toolkit theory for thinking about cultural mobility:

> [Swidler's] toolkit theory presumes that actors are only relatively "lightly" touched by their socialization history, being provided only with a loosely structured set of skills, heuristics, routines and shallow habits that allow them to best navigate (and select) which strategies of actions go best with which externalized institutional structure at a given moment.

Toolkit theory, like cultural mobility theory, then also suggests that class origin would have little to do with the cultural aspects of marriages between two highly educated adults as individuals are only "lightly touched" by their childhood class experiences. Given their time together and similar positionality as adults, spouses would likely learn to use the same cultural tools. In contrast to these two theoretical perspectives, *The Power of the Past* argues that individuals are heavily influenced by the class of their past, even when they have long been immersed in middle-class settings and have middle-class resources. This finding is better aligned with Bourdieu's views of the habitus than a toolkit model of culture.

3. Bourdieu (1998:10) takes this perspective when he writes: "People located at the top of the space have little chance of marrying people located at the bottom, first because they have little chance of physically meeting them, secondly because, if they do accidentally meet them on some occasion, they will not get on together, will not understand each other, will not appeal to one another." In short, he sees individuals' tastes and sensibilities as tightly linked to class position and as nearly insurmountable obstacles to cross-class relationship formation.

Another myth that *The Power of the Past* dispels is that of the death of class. Scholars in this tradition argue that class has lost its influence on social life and identities. They argue that several other axes (for example, gender, race, and age) divide broad classes into fragments, that people have increasingly individualized identities, and that class has lost its association with lifestyles (Beck 2000; Kingston 2000; Pakulski and Waters 1996). I do not explicitly argue against the death-of-class position in this book, but the findings make it clear that class (origin) is still tightly linked to lifestyles and sensibilities.

4. This number excludes days spent together before marriage.

5. In 1991, Kalmijn noted that homogamy by class origin was weak and declining. In 2003, Blossfeld and Timm found that there is no direct relationship between parents' education and the education of individuals' spouses. In 2013, Charles, Hurst, and Killewald found that some forms of different-origin marriages are not unusual. They documented that 19 percent of men whose parents have less than $1,000 of wealth marry women whose parents have over $100,000 of wealth. On the other hand, rates of homogamy by adulthood class position, not childhood class position, are increasing (Schwartz and Mare 2005).

6. Bourdieu (1980, 1984), a French social theorist, wrote that individuals internalize different sensibilities in their different childhood class positions and that these sensibilities are slow to change even when individuals leave their original class position. He called these durable and transposable sensibilities and tastes "the habitus." The findings in this book support his notion that this part of the habitus is slow to change. While the findings cannot reveal if the habitus changes at all, the book does demonstrate that the sensibilities of the upwardly mobile do not match those of their partners who were born into a different class.

Other social scientists have also suggested that the habitus is relatively durable through mobility but the research design of these studies has made their findings inconclusive. Several studies have found that college students with working-class roots have sensibilities that differ from those born into the middle class (for example, Aries and Seider 2005; Armstrong and Hamilton 2013; Granfield 1991; Hurst 2007; Ostrove 2003; Stuber 2011). However, upwardly mobile college students are experiencing their first few years in a middle-class setting, and sensibilities may change only after spending more years in the middle-class and acquiring more resources. Other autobiographical portraits and journalistic accounts also suggest sensibilities are hard to change (for example, Dews and Law 1995; Lubrano 2004; Ryan and Sackrey 1984; Tokarczyk and Fay 1993) but those who choose to write about their experiences are also those likely to feel most out of place in their new class. This makes it difficult to know how sensibilities change for a wider group. In *The Power of the Past*, I did not select those new to the middle-class or those who were especially likely to feel out of place. The findings then provide more conclusive evidence that the habitus exerts a lasting influence.

It should also be noted that not all studies reach the conclusion that the habitus is durable. Others find that education, work, resources, and networks can substantially change individuals' habitus (Chin and Phillips 2004; DiMaggio 1982; Erickson 1996; Lacy 2007).

7. I use "sensibilities" as a nontechnical way to refer to the dispositions that are part of the habitus. It does not include tastes, which are also part of the habitus.

8. Of course, this book is not the first to discuss class and sensibilities. Lillian Rubin (1976) and Mirra Komarovsky (1962), for example, did the same without calling them such. Bourdieu wrote in detail about the relationship between class and sensibilities. As noted, however, this book is the first to consider how sensibilities systematically span several domains of daily life for the upwardly mobile as compared to the stable middle class. What is new is the focus on upward mobility and the new social organization of sensibilities.

9. This paragraph is based on *theories* of how sensibilities matter within institutions. A mismatch between the culture of an individual and an institution is generally thought to penalize the individual. To my knowledge, however, no *empirical* study has looked at how organizations reward the sensibilities of the upwardly mobile as compared to those who spent their entire lives in the middle class. The closest has been Stuber's (2005) study, which found that upwardly mobile workers framed their ability to understand two class cultures as helping them accomplish their job. It does not, however, report on what their bosses, colleagues, or clients thought.

10. In contrast, there are at least three organizational schemes that describe the relationship between class and tastes. Bourdieu (1984) described two of them. First, he wrote that those from higher classes enjoy high culture while those from lower classes enjoy low culture. This is also described as aesthetic and vulgar tastes. Second, those from higher classes enjoy items that distance themselves from necessity. They may, for example, enjoy lobster, a food that is expensive but not terribly filling—a food that shows that they do not eat for subsistence alone. Those from the lower classes, by contrast, enjoy items that make a virtue out of necessity. They develop a taste for the items they can afford. Finally, Peterson and Kern (1996) suggested that tastes are not only organized by their content but also by the array of items that individuals enjoy. Those from higher classes are "cultural omnivores," consuming a wide variety of culture. Those from the lower classes, according to this framework, are "cultural univores," consuming a narrower range of items. While these three schemes describe class and tastes, none are easily applicable to sensibilities. There is not a clear sense of what sensibilities are high and low, aesthetic or vulgar. And while individuals may appreciate a small or large number of objects and activities, individuals tend to have more limited set of default preferences for going about their daily lives.

The existing organizational system that most closely maps onto sensibilities is that of making a virtue of necessity or distancing oneself from necessity. However, it is often difficult, a priori, to determine which sensibilities fit into which category. For example, Bourdieu (1984) wrote that the tendency to save money makes a virtue of necessity, as the working class must carefully save their money in order to survive. However, we could also argue that saving distances oneself from necessity, as it shows that one does not need to spend every penny in order to survive. The categories are not clearly defined. In addition, none of the categorization schemes describe the sensibilities of the upwardly mobile compared to the stable middle class. For all these reasons, a new organizational scheme is needed—one that captures sensibilities, clearly demarcates differences between categories, and captures the upwardly mobile.

11. For example, Lareau (2003) connects parenting sensibilities to adulthood class position. Others link class to sensibilities within individual domains such as education (Bettie 2003; Willis 1977), leisure (Holt 1997; Graham 1999), sub-cultural styles (Bourgois 1996; Wilkins 2008), and language styles (Hart and Risley 1995; Lareau 2003). Some also look at family interaction styles and adulthood class position (Hansen 2005; Rubin 1976, 1994) but do not fully consider how class *origin* is related to familial interactions. My use of sensibilities, however, is, of course, heavily indebted to Bourdieu's concept of dispositions within the habitus.

12. The findings about class origin pertain only to how it plays out amongst highly educated white adults.

13. Sensibilities are preferred ways of attending to daily life. I do not have observational data and cannot comment on the extent to which preferences were enacted. However, each member of the couple talked about their own and their partner's sensibilities as agreed upon, consistent, acted upon, and even fought over. They told stories that illustrated tight connections between their sensibilities and their actions, and their spouses often corroborated their stories. My best guess is that sensibilities—while preferences—were generally consistent with behaviors.

14. I thank Rick Rodems for suggesting the term "laissez-faire."

15. This binary resembles Annette Lareau's (2003) conception of concerted cultivation and the accomplishment of natural growth but extends it to sensibilities beyond parenting. Those who preferred a managerial style, like those who prefer concerted cultivation, view many aspects of their lives as requiring monitoring, planning, and work. Those who favored a laissez-faire style, like those who favor the accomplishment of natural growth, think that things are best when they are left to be.

   It should also be noted that although the class designations of respondents' pasts are wide, they mapped on well to the managerial and laissez-faire categories. Respondents who grew up in poverty and those who grew up in stable working-class families, for example, both tended to prefer laissez-faire sensibilities. Likewise, respondents who grew up in the middle class and those who grew up in the upper class (though this only included two respondents) both tended to say they took a managerial approach to daily life.

16. Binary categorization systems have a long history in social science, dating back to the work of Emile Durkheim, Levi Strauss, and Mary Douglas.

17. Some researchers also examine each spouse's class position separately. Most of these studies, however, examine what class individuals identify with based upon the occupation, earnings, and education of each spouse. This study differs by examining how class plays out within marriage, regardless of which class each partner believes him or herself to be in.

18. The range of ages was from 29 to 63 years old, with the majority of spouses in their 30s and 40s.

19. The range of years married varied from 3 (for a couple who had been together for over 20 years but had only recently legally married) to 27 years. Couples also varied considerably in how long they had been together before deciding to marry. Some had known each other for a few months at the time they decided to marry, while others had known each other for decades.

20. The recruitment fliers asked for couples in which each spouse was from a different "economic background." Recruiting respondents on this criterion did not mean that the sample was especially primed to discuss class or their differences. In fact, as Chapter 2 shows, few respondents thought much about class at all, and even fewer thought that their differences from their spouse were associated with their class origin.

21. In two cases, the parenting section of the interview was conducted with the husband and wife together while the remainder of the interview was conducted with the husband and wife apart. This was done for couples who were short on time.

Chapter 2

1. By class awareness I mean an understanding that class is related to sensibilities and life chances. I do not mean an awareness that class exists.

2. Sociologists would call this "sex" rather than "gender" but lay people may not make this distinction.

3. Even the Occupy Movement has not helped Americans think about nuanced class differences. By differentiating the bottom 99 percent from the top 1 percent they mask the substantial variation in lifestyle and life chances within the 99 percent.

4. Divides between genders and races, however, can also be fuzzy.

5. In contrast, some parents were likely able to read their daughter-in-law's or son-in-law's class origin more quickly. Elliott (blue-collar origin) remembered: "Her mom was a little bit cold to me . . . She kind of said—not in so many words—that I wasn't quite good enough for Alice . . . I was very angry. But I absolutely understood it. I think as a parent you want your kids to have a better life than you." Similarly, Vicki said of her mother: "She looks down on John's parents and in a sense looks down on John. Like I married some

working-class person." Ryan (white-collar origin) also reported that his father-in-law was skeptical about his daughter marrying Ryan. Using language that implies class without naming it, Ryan explained: "He was very different from me, and I was definitely not what he pictured for his daughter." Asked what his father-in-law pictured, Ryan said: "Someone Italian first, and not a religion major . . . He was kind of a guy's guy and could fix things. I am not."

6. The fourth respondent was Isabelle (blue-collar origin), who realized that Ian (white-collar origin) was from a more privileged background when she observed that he was still financially dependent on his parents. Though still in college, she was financially independent. She felt that his dependence signaled his class position.

7. By contrast, those in interracial marriages seem to have more varied beliefs about how race matters in their relationship. Some see it as a meaningless category (similar to how respondents in this section see class); others see it primarily as a difference that is relevant to those outside of their marriage, and others find race to be highly salient within their relationships (Bystydzienski 2011; Steinbugler 2012).

8. By contrast, interracial marriages may be more likely to increase awareness of how race matters than different-origin marriages are to increase understanding of how class matters. Whites, in particular, may become more aware of racism through their experiences with their partner of a different race (Yancey and Lewis Jr. 2009).

9. The respondents who talked of what they learned in college made it sound like this was not a selection effect. In other words, they did not select social science majors because they were aware of class. Rather, they learned about class after being social science majors.

10. Interestingly, Jason predicted that in her interview Lori would deny being part of the upper class. Indeed, she did, saying she came from an upper-middle-class family. Thus, although Jason helped her understand her privilege, she vacillated when asked to classify it. She could identify her class background differently depending on whether she was referring only to her parents' resources or if she included those she had access to through her grandparents.

Chapter 3

1. Vicki's father had grown up in poverty before becoming a successful lawyer. Vicki, however, had little contact with him. Her parents divorced when she was a toddler, and Vicki and her father rarely spoke to each other. He therefore had little impact on her understandings of social class.

2. Cultural matching theory is associated with Bourdieu's (1984) book, *Distinction*.

3. Cultural mobility theory (DiMaggio 1982) suggests that the couples likely had many cultural commonalities given their shared class position as adults. The stories the respondents told as well as the evidence presented in subsequent chapters shows that while some cultural mobility may have occurred, many cultural differences between each member of different-origin couples still remained.

4. It was not women from both class origins who felt drawn to their partners because of their sense of stability. Only one white-collar-origin woman said that she felt drawn to her blue-collar-origin husband because of his stability. This woman, Mary, grew up with a mother who she said was an alcoholic and had bipolar disorder, and parents who often considered divorce. No woman in a shared-origin relationships said that her husband's stability was a factor in why she was drawn to him.

5. What is important here is that blue-collar-origin respondents identified their partners as achievers, not that their partner identified the same way.

Ease and status at achieving are not precisely sensibilities. For consistency in writing, I refer to them as such.

6. William's quote shows that the predictions of cultural matching theory are not entirely absent from respondents' stories; cultural differences were sometimes remembered as a deterrent. The theory, however, cannot tell us why respondents believed that their spouse was appealing despite these deterrents.

7. Wharton and Thorne (1997) found that middle-class-stable daughters, compared to working-class-stable and upwardly mobile daughters, are least likely to report an intimate connection to their mothers. This finding is consistent with the finding here that middle-class-stable respondents report less familial intimacy than upwardly mobile respondents.

8. Bourdieu (1988) calls the condition that occurs when the internalized dispositions of the habitus become out-of-sync with the changing logic of a field "hysteresis." This is what I am describing concerning white-collar-origin respondents' experiences with emotional expressivity.

9. Lori indicated that at the time when they met she was unaware of class and would not have attributed Jason's emotional honesty to his childhood class position. She is now exceptionally aware of class and makes the connection retrospectively.

10. The data do not allow me to determine why respondents in different-origin marriages disliked some of their own sensibilities while respondents in shared-origin marriages did not.

11. It is not just class differences that can seem at first attractive and later unappealing. Felmlee (1998) finds that this phenomenon occurs more broadly.

Chapter 4

1. She later obtained her GED and then her bachelor's degree.
2. The focus here on managerial and laissez-faire financial sensibilities departs from the more common scholarly focuses on couples and money—focuses on how husbands and wives access money, assign authority over financial decisions, and make sense of different pots of money, or how the poor use their money (for example, Barr and Blank 2009; Himmelweit et al. 2013; Kenney 2006; Pahl 1994; Zelizer 1989).
3. Of all the findings in this study, this one surprised me the most. I had thought that blue-collar-origin respondents would carefully manage their money as I assumed they needed to do so to get by. However, in this study, ten blue-collar-origin respondents reported being "unconscious" about money whereas only two white-collar-origin respondents (Ian and Parker) did the same.
4. In a follow-up question I asked Isabelle who would take their money. A debt collector was her answer.
5. This quote comes from an e-mail Chelsey sent me after the interview.
6. Leslie's example also reflects that making decisions about children is often left to women. However, the dynamic Leslie described did not only refer to decisions about how to spend money on their children but also to all aspects of their financial lives.
7. Contrary to other studies, the main divide in financial sensibilities was not along gender lines. Gender may be less important in this study than in previous ones because this study focuses on sensibilities rather than on the allocation of money within couples or the power to make financial decisions.
8. Saving and spending are relative terms, and respondents compared themselves to their spouse when making these comparisons. It is therefore difficult to tell if those like Todd would consider themselves laissez-faire spenders if their comparison was to a spouse who replicated his or her parents' financial position and spent in a more managerial manner.
9. The other was Zoey, a white-collar-origin woman who had not yet replicated her parents' financial situation. For a time, she spent without managing her money as she continued to buy the clothes and food that she had in the past. In her 20s, her salary as a manager in a large corporation sustained her financial habits. She then married Austin, a blue-collar-origin man who lacked a college-degree when they met, and she quit her job to support his career. Her former spending habits were then out-of-sync with their financial situation. She slowly learned to cut back on the amount she spent and to manage her money more carefully.

Chapter 5

1. Vicki identifies as a feminist. She does not believe that she should not be so wrapped up in work because she is a woman; she believes that no one should be so consumed by work. For a period of their marriage, John did not work for pay as he stayed home to raise their children. Despite Vicki's mother's idea that men should be breadwinners, Vicki admired that John left the paid labor force to take care of their children.

2. Kohn (1969) first wrote that parents' job characteristics shape how they socialize their children. He thought that parents taught their children the sensibilities that would help them succeed in the type of work they did, thereby reproducing their social class. The types of sensibilities Kohn focused on, however, were different. He examined attributes like self-direction and conformity. This study, instead, examines the meaning of work, ways to approach careers, and workers' preferred balance between work and family.

3. Vicki's father was a successful lawyer. However, her parents divorced when she was a toddler, and she has since had minimal contact with her father.

4. It is possible that being white also was associated with white-collar-origin respondents' ideas that work was a place where they felt rewarded. At work, they were unlikely to face blocked opportunities due to their race or interpersonal prejudice from colleagues and bosses. Non-whites with white-collar origins may not find work as validating.

5. The findings in this chapter, in other words, imply that individuals' occupational socialization is filtered through and limited by the socialization they received about work from their parents. Others have similarly found that intrinsic and extrinsic orientations toward work are related to individuals' class origin (Johnson and Mortimer 2011).

6. In some ways, these findings echo Hochschild's (1997) finding that middle-class workers find work to be like home. In this case, they find it a source of play and good feeling.

7. Respondents' perceived difference in drive is striking when considering who the blue-collar-origin respondents are. These are individuals who beat the odds and were upwardly mobile; these are individuals who were usually the first in their family to attend college. One might have assumed that those who achieved so much success felt especially driven. This was not the case.

8. Some scholars believe that companies purposefully encourage workers to tie their identity to their job as a form of social control (Kunda 1992). If this is the case, blue-collar-origin workers appear to be less influenced by this form of control than their white-collar-origin counterparts.

9. Blue-collar-origin respondents were more likely to grow up with parents who worked hourly, not salaried, jobs. Hourly work may provide more clear

cut-offs between work and home. Salaried jobs, by contrast, tend to have less clearly defined work hours, allowing for more work-to-home spillover. In addition, blue-collar-origin respondents were more likely to have parents whose work could not be done outside a physical location away from the home—for example, a factory or a retail store. This physical divide would make it impossible for some blue-collar workers to work at home, creating more rigid boundaries between the two.

10. Leslie explained that their difference was not in their level of satisfaction with their jobs—they were both happy with their current positions. Rather, she perceived their difference to be about the desire to climb a career ladder. She believed that adults should be ambitious about their careers and regularly look for new opportunities. Her husband was happy staying in one job; he did not have the idea that career advancement was necessary.

11. Anita, probably correctly, attributes their difference both to different ideas of what is desirable and different knowledge of how to find new work and advance at work.

12. There were two white-collar-origin men (Jim and Brandon) and two white-collar-origin women who said that their blue-collar-origin spouses were more driven and took more agentic approaches to work. Interestingly, Jim and Brandon have elaborate stories that explain their lack of agency concerning work, while the women's lesser agency is taken as normal and not in need of an explanation.

13. These findings as well as others in this chapter showcase the need to move beyond gender in examining work/family balance. In addition to gender, class origin must also be considered.

14. Men may have been less likely than women to help their spouse with their career as it is not seen as unusual if women are less invested in or successful at work.

15. Men may also be more likely to see a college degree as tied to a paycheck because of the ideology of men as breadwinners. Men may also be more likely to drop out of college to pursue extrinsically rewarding careers because their job options without a college degree may be better than women's (Dwyer, Hodson, and McCloud 2013).

16. Following orders is often a skill learned by the children of blue-collar workers (Kohn 1969).

17. Jason is not alone in feeling that his academic colleagues would look down on his class origins. Working-class-origin academics have written poignantly about their anxiety of being judged because of their class origin (for example, Dews and Law 1995; Ryan and Sackrey 1984; Tokarczyk and Fay 1993).

18. Even young adults with college-educated parents tend to have ideas of jobs that are misaligned with reality (Schneider and Stevenson 1999).

19. The shared-origin women framed their decision to opt out of full-time work as a choice in response to unfulfilling careers. It is possible that when they became mothers they were pushed out of their jobs as well (Stone 2008).

20. These respondents' idea that they could leave the full-time labor force may also relate to their whiteness. On average, white men earn more than black and Hispanic men (Hamilton, Austin, and Darity Jr. 2011), making it more feasible for married white women to leave the full-time labor force than married women of other races. In addition, college-educated white women have lower divorce rates than black college-educated women (Banks 2011). They may then be less worried about divorce and more willing to leave the full-time labor force.

21. Four white-collar-origin men joined 16 blue-collar-origin respondents in preferring to relax in their leisure time. No white-collar-origin women said the same. It is possible that gender intersects with class origin here. Women generally have less leisure time than men (Sayer 2005). It is possible that they made a virtue of necessity and preferred to be busier in what they consider their leisure time.

22. The univore/omnivore thesis has received some pushback, with critics claiming that there are several types of omnivores and univores (see Bennett and Silva 2011). However, the broad categories did capture the patterns in the data used for this study. In small samples, with an interview guide that used open-ended question and covered a variety of topics, providing more specific subgroups is difficult at best.

    Readers should also note the distinction here between sensibilities and tastes. Sensibilities are general approaches to leisure time—to actively manage it or to see what comes, to be busy or relaxed, to enjoy leisure in different combinations of being inside and outside the home. Tastes are for specific objects or events—for basketball versus ice skating or action movies versus documentaries.

23. Others have also found that college-educated upwardly mobile and college-educated nonmobile individuals tend to have different collections of tastes (van Eijck 1999).

    Petev (2013) similarly found that those from the lower classes (the parents of blue-collar-origin respondents) are disproportionally likely to be what he calls "homebodies"—those involved in little social contact in their leisure time. What social contact they have tends to be with family.

24. Lareau (2003) also found that middle-class children reported being bored after small amounts of unorganized time.

25. Others find that spouses' leisure participation becomes more similar over time (see, for example, Upright 2004). *The Power of the Past* cannot comment on change over time that is caused by marriage other than to note that spouses who had been married for relatively short and long periods of time

were not noticeably different. The book instead makes the point that while change may have happened, it did not result in merged leisure sensibilities.

26. On average, blue-collar children watch more television than white-collar children (Bianchi and Robinson 1997). Such differences may carry over into adulthood.

27. It was only white-collar-origin *women* who complained about their spouses' television watching habits. This finding may reflect the intersection of gender and class origin. Blue-collar children tend to watch more television than white-collar children, and men tend to spend more time on leisure than women (Bianchi and Robinson 1997; Sayer 2005).

28. In addition, white-collar-origin respondents' omnivore tastes may be useful in expanding their networks of weak and strong ties (Lizardo 2006).

29. The phrase "look for" is important. Gendered opportunity structures shape what jobs men and women are able to actually obtain.

30. As the example of Scott and Gina shows, such beliefs *can* be put into a hierarchy even though both sets of sensibilities are widely valued.

Chapter 6

1. There are often discontinuities between their beliefs and what they do. Some authors have found that blue-collar families tend to have a more equitable division of labor while preferring a gendered division of labor, while professional white-collar families profess a greater belief in gender equality but practice a more gendered division of labor (Hochschild 2003; Pyke 1996; Shows and Gerstel 2009).

2. The others believed there was an even split.

3. Interview questions did not ask about time; it was spontaneously raised in response to questions about how the respondent was different than his/her spouse. The data is slightly more mixed than in other categories. Sixteen couples agreed that the white-collar-origin spouse planned more, whereas five couples said that the blue-collar-origin partner planned more (this includes couples in which only one partner raised the topic of planning). Of the five couples in which the blue-collar-origin partner was said to plan more, four were women. It is possible that when blue-collar-origin individuals plan more than their white-collar-origin spouse, it is likely that the former is a woman.

4. Decades ago, O'Rand and Ellis (1974) also found that college students from different class backgrounds had different notions of time. They also concluded that middle-class institutions favor greater planning and that the upwardly mobile are then disadvantaged.

Chapter 7

1. The data, of course, are taken only from married parents who reside with their children. Nearly all the children in this study were the couple's biological children. The findings may not extend to single, cohabiting, nonresidential, adoptive, and stepparents.

2. Lareau and Weininger (2008) do point out that the work of concerted cultivation often falls to women. However, in broader discussions of concerted cultivation, it is sometimes portrayed as relating to class alone rather than to class and gender.

3. Others have argued that parenting sensibilities are tied only to parents' current resources (Chin and Phillips 2004). My findings do not support this view but instead indicate that parenting sensibilities are also tied to the financial and cultural resources of their parents.

4. Additionally, blue-collar-origin parents were less likely to believe that their children were as malleable. Some talked of not having any expectations of parenting before their children were born because they would need to wait and see who their children were before knowing how to parent them.

5. Using a nationally representative and longitudinal data set, Roksa and Potter (2011) similarly found that college-educated women with blue-collar-origins used slightly different amounts of concerted cultivation than did college-educated women from professional, white-collar backgrounds. They did not, however, examine the beliefs behind mothers' parenting practice but instead looked, in part, at whether they enrolled their child in at least one organized activity.

6. As Weininger and Lareau (2009) point out, even though middle-class parents wish to instill their children with a sense of direction, they tend to undermine this goal by giving their children orders. Working-class parents, who often wish to instill their children with a sense of conformity, instead tend to give their children more freedom to choose their own direction.

7. Kusserow (2004) also points out that parents without a college degree tend to allow their children to make more mistakes in order to help them learn to persevere. Respondents may be following the lead of their parents.

8. Positive evaluations by teachers, however, is correlated with aspects of parents' managerial styles primarily for white students (Dumais, Kessinger, and Ghosh 2012).

Chapter 8

1. Although no questions asked about feeling rules or emotions, the topic came up repeatedly. Nineteen white-collar-origin respondents described themselves as abiding by managerial feeling rules, compared to two

blue-collar-origin respondents. Conversely, sixteen blue-collar-origin respondents described having laissez-faire feeling rules, compared to two white-collar-origin respondents. The remainder of respondents did not give enough information about their emotions to classify them.

2. Hochschild (1983:158) also notes that middle-class parents teach their children to manage their emotions. She writes that in middle-class families: "Feelings are meant to be managed—monitored, sanctioned, and controlled. Thus when Timmy spills ink on the new rug, he will be punished less for damaging the rug than for doing it in anger. His transgression lies in not managing his anger." She adds: "It seems, then, that middle-class children are more likely to be asked to shape their feelings according to the rules they are made aware of. At the very least, they learn that it is important to know how to manage feelings" (1983:158).

3. A large strand of the research on emotions focuses on the proportion of positive and negative emotions felt by members of different social classes and social statuses (for example, Kemper 1978; Lovaglia and Houser 1996; Turner 2010). Respondents' accounts show that the differences that resonate with them are not the amount of positive and negative emotions each felt but instead the range, intensity, and immediacy by which emotions are expressed.

4. It is important to consider that respondents recalled the feeling rules their parents exhibited within the family setting. Had those outside the family been asked about respondents' parents' feeling rules, they may have given different answers.

5. Studies repeatedly find that white-collar families talk with each other more than blue-collar families (Hart and Risley 1995; Heath 1983; Lareau 2003). These studies, however, focus on word count more than the content of the words. The stories respondents in this study told suggest that blue-collar families may talk about more personal topics—relationships, love, and money—while white-collar families may talk more about logistics and achievement.

6. The dichotomy between emotional and rational has been criticized by scholars (for example, Illouz 2010). Nevertheless, it is one that respondents used.

7. Some scholars have argued that people raised in white-collar positions learn to hide their anger in order to maintain standards of professionalism (Hochschild 1983; Stearns and Stearns 1986). When they do express anger, it is likely to be outside the home and not addressed at family members (Collett and Lizardo 2010). The findings here are consistent both with the idea that white-collar-origin adults were socialized to manage their anger and that they tend not to express anger at home. However, others studies contradict these findings to some extent (Gibson and Schroeder 2002; Lively 2000; Ridgeway and Johnson 1990).

8. The difference in the number of blue- and white-collar-origin respondents who mentioned initiating affection was not particularly strong: five

blue-collar-origin respondents raised this theme compared to no white-collar-origin respondents. The difference is noted in the text as it arose despite that no questions were asked about it, making it a meaningful theme.

9. Lareau and Calarco (2012) find that school administrators reacted more favorably to parents who expressed their concerns in the calm and rational manner that characterizes managed emotional sensibilities.

10. What emotional sensibilities their children develop may also matter for class reproduction. Cahill (1999) finds that emotions channel individuals into and out of some types of work.

Chapter 9

1. Cultural complements were not the only source of couples' attraction. They were, however, a primary one.

2. Similarly, although racial intermarriages were once thought to create assimilation, researchers now find that interracial marriages do not result in merged attitudes or sensibilities (Song 2009; Steinbugler 2012).

3. A future study should untangle whether laissez-faire sensibilities are associated only with upwardly mobile individuals with blue-collar roots or also nonmobile individuals with blue-collar roots.

4. How one interprets the findings in regards to cultural reproduction theory and cultural mobility theory depends on where one draws the line between them. If cultural mobility is considered to require full assimilation into a new class, then we can conclude that it did not occur. If, on the other hand, cultural mobility refers to having some sensibilities that are different than those gained through classed childhood socialization, then it is likely that this occurred.

5. In other words, managerial and laissez-faire sensibilities map the content of the habitus for college-educated individuals with white- and blue-collar roots.

6. Homogamy here refers to class origin, not class destination.

7. Of course, when respondents share their level of educational attainment, they may also overlook more cultural mismatches. Chapter 3, however, shows that mismatches are not always overlooked but are noticed and remembered as a source of appeal.

8. Those in the lower classes tend to dispute these hierarchies (Lamont 2000) while also internalizing them (Skeggs 1997).

9. When presenting this work, two audience members have told me that they are blue-collar-origin individuals with managerial sensibilities and that their white-collar-origin spouses have laissez-faire sensibilities. It is likely, then,

that these couples exist. They did not exist, however, among the 32 couples in the sample and are unlikely to be common.

10. It is possible that they had experienced managerial/laissez-faire differences but did not think to raise them during the interviews.

11. This quote is from Evan (white-collar-origin) when talking about his wife's, Madison, (blue-collar-origin) laissez-faire approach to money.

12. These two couples were Chelsey and Nathan and Alexa and Aaron. In the former, Nathan lost his job but still wanted to spend money without worry, wait to see if new work came to him rather than actively seeking it out, relax at home in his leisure time, and stay in the large house that symbolized his class position. Chelsey found these approaches intolerable given his job loss. In the second case, Aaron left his job after being told he had to teach students on a lower academic track or quit. Alexa then went from part-time work to full-time work. She expected Aaron to take a managerial approach to parenting and housework as she attended to paid work. He did not, which greatly upset Alexa.

13. Couples who are in happy marriages may be more likely to sign up for a study on marriage, therefore biasing the sample toward couples in happy relationships. Nevertheless, it is meaningful that given all the differences that these couples navigated, most reported being highly satisfied with their unions.

14. The culture of poverty argument is heavily criticized by academics but lives on in the popular imagination.

15. This assumption is discussed in Brand and Xie (2010), Mare (1980), Musick, Brand, and Davis (2012), and Torche (2011).

16. The sensibilities and values named by Lewis (1961, 1966) both overlap with and are distinct from laissez-faire sensibilities. Lewis, for example, believed that a more short-term time horizon marked the poor as different from the middle class and prevented their mobility. Other aspects of the culture of poverty thesis, however, are quite different than laissez-faire sensibilities such as the propensity to have single-mother households.

17. The sample in this study is not perfectly suited to address this argument. The sample suffers from selection bias. The white-collar-origin respondents tended to say that they selected their spouse because of their ability to disconnect from work. Upwardly mobile individuals not married to white-collar-origin spouses may then be more driven. Nonetheless, the findings from this study offer an improvement over using no data, which is often the case when making the assumption that upwardly mobile people are positively selected on their drive and discipline. To offer one more example of how upwardly mobile individuals are not necessarily especially driven, one blue-collar-origin respondent said he wanted to write a book called "How to

Live a Productive Life While Remaining Largely on Your Back or Relaxing with a Friend."

18. Another way that sensibilities may matter is through mismatch theory (Bourdieu and Passeron 1977). This theory suggests that the match between individuals' sensibilities and those expected by institutions is what leads to getting ahead; a mismatch is what leads to failed mobility attempts. This theory has been used throughout the book. However, it also cannot explain how blue-collar-origin respondents became college-educated professionals.

19. The argument that differences in blue- and white-collar-origin respondents' sensibilities may create inequality as individuals interact with workplaces runs counter to Torche's (2011) findings that college graduates are on an equal playing field regardless of their class origin. At the same time, Torche finds that college-educated men born into the bottom third of the income distribution earn only 83 percent of what college-educated men from more advantaged backgrounds earn. She calls this gap "non-negligible but limited" (p. 794) though its size is not terribly different than the gender pay gap—a gap often described as important. On the other hand, Torche finds that class origin is strongly associated with advanced-degree holders' pay. For both bachelor's degree holders and advanced degree holders, sensibilities may be one sorting mechanism in who gets what rewards.

20. Schoeni and Ross (2005) find that between the time when they are 18 and 34 years old, the children of parents in the lowest two income quartiles receive an average of $25,000 of financial support from their parents, while the children of parents in the highest income quartile receive an average of nearly $71,000 over the same period. Thus, the consolidation of resources (or lack thereof) occasioned by marriages between individuals who share their class background potentially creates substantial disparities between couples. If parents give at the same rate no matter who their child marries, then couples composed of two adults from the highest income quartile will receive about $92,000 more than couples in which each partner is from the lowest quartile. Couples that cross class quartiles would receive an amount in the middle. Their marriage then disperses parents' financial support rather than concentrating it.

21. Murray's and Brooks' approaches also assume that if the working class learns new values the country will benefit and inequality will be alleviated. These assumptions, in themselves, are misguided.

22. This main finding—that highly educated, white adults' sensibilities are strongly connected to their class origin—raises questions about how sensibilities do change. One possibility is that a generational change in sensibilities happens when children are raised in a new class. The children of upwardly mobile adults may adopt the sensibilities associated with their class of birth—ones that are quite different than their blue-collar-origin parent

and blue-collar grandparents. If sensibilities are products of early class conditions, then it seems likely that the class individuals are born into—to a far greater extent than the class their parents' were born into—will shape sensibilities. A study that examines the children of different-origin parents is needed to test this hypothesis.

Appendix A

1. This is true. I looked for studies about divorce rates for different-origin and shared-origin couples but could not find any.
2. In fact, despite what many respondents assumed, my interest was never in marital satisfaction. Instead, I am more interested in how sensibilities vary by class origin.

REFERENCES

Aries, Elizabeth and Maynard Seider. 2005. "The Interactive Relationship between Class Identity and the College Experience: The Case of Lower Income Students." *Qualitative Sociology* 28(4):419–443.

Armstrong, Elizabeth and Laura Hamilton. 2013. *Paying for the Party: How College Maintains Inequality.* Cambridge, MA: Harvard University Press.

Arum, Richard, Josipa Roksa, and Michelle Budig. 2008. "The Romance of College Attendance: Higher Education Stratification and Mate Selection." *Research in Social Stratification and Mobility* 26(2):107–121.

Aschaffenburg, Karen and Ineke Maas. 1997. "Cultural and Educational Careers: The Dynamics of Social Reproduction." *American Sociological Review* 62(4):573–587.

Autor, David, Lawrence Katz, and Melissa Kearney. 2008. "Trends in U.S. Wage Inequality: Revising the Revisionists." *The Review of Economics and Statistics* 90(2):300–323.

Banks, Ralph. 2011. *Is Marriage for White People? How the African American Marriage Decline Affects Everyone.* New York: Penguin.

Barr, Michael and Rebecca Blank. 2009. *Insufficient Funds: Savings, Assets, Credit, and Banking among Low- and Moderate-Income Households.* New York: Russell Sage.

Beasley, Maya. 2011. *Opting Out: Losing the Potential of America's Young Black Elite.* Chicago: University of Chicago Press.

Beck, Ulrich. 2000. *Brave New World of Work.* Malden, MA: Blackwell.

Bennett, Tony and Elizabeth Silva. 2011. "Introduction: Cultural Capital—Histories, Limits, Prospects." *Poetics* 39(6):427–443.

Bettie, Julie. 2003. *Women without Class: Girls, Race, and Identity.* Berkeley: University of California Press.

Bianchi, Suzanne and John Robinson. 1997. "What Did You Do Today? Children's Use of Time, Family Composition, and the Acquisition of Social Capital." *Journal of Marriage and Family* 59(2):332–344.

Bielby, William and Denise Bielby. 1992. "I Will Follow Him: Family Ties, Gender Role Beliefs, and Reluctance to Relocate for a Better Job." *American Journal of Sociology* 97(5):1241–1267.

Blair-Loy, Mary, 2003. *Competing Devotions: Career and Family among Women Executives.* Cambridge, MA: Harvard University Press.

Block, Jeanne, Jack Block, and Andrea Morrison. 1981. "Parental Agreement-Disagreement on Child-Rearing Orientations and Gender-Related Personality Correlates in Children." *Child Development* 52(3):965–974.

Blossfeld, Hans-Peter and Andreas Timm. 2003. *Who Marries Whom? Educational Systems as Marriage Markets in Modern Societies.* Dordrecht, The Netherlands: Kluwer Academic Publishers.

Blossfeld, Hans-Peter. 2009. "Educational Assortative Marriage in Comparative Perspective." *Annual Review of Sociology* 35:513–530.

Bodovski, Katerina and George Farkas. 2008. "'Concerted Cultivation' and Unequal Achievement in Elementary School." *Social Science Research* 37(3):903–919.

Bonilla-Silva, Eduardo. 2003. *Racism without Racists: Color-Blind Racism and the Persistence of Racial Inequality in the United States.* New York: Rowman and Littlefield Publishers.

Bottero, Wendy. 2005. *Stratification: Social Division and Inequality.* New York: Routledge.

Bourdieu, Pierre. 1980. *The Logic of Practice.* Cambridge, MA: Polity Press.

Bourdieu, Pierre. 1984. *Distinction: A Social Critique of the Judgment of Taste.* Cambridge, MA: Harvard University Press.

Bourdieu, Pierre. 1985. "The Social Space and the Genesis of Groups." *Theory & Society* 14(6):723–744.

Bourdieu, Pierre. 1988. *Homo Academicus.* Palo Alto, CA: Stanford University Press.

Bourdieu, Pierre. 1998. *Practical Reason: On the Theory of Action.* Cambridge, MA: Polity Press.

Bourdieu, Pierre. 2000. *The Weight of the World: Social Suffering in Contemporary Society.* Palo Alto, CA: Stanford University Press.

Bourdieu, Pierre. [2002] 2008. *The Bachelors' Ball.* Malden, MA: Polity Press.

Bourdieu, Pierre and Jean-Claude Passeron. 1977. *Reproduction in Education, Society, and Culture.* New York: Sage.

Bourgois, Philippe. 1996. *In Search of Respect: Selling Crack in El Barrio.* New York: Cambridge University Press.

Bozick, Robert, Karl Alexander, Doris Entwisle, Susan Dauber, and Kerri Kerr. 2010. "Framing the Future: Revisiting the Place of Educational Expectations in Status Attainment." *Social Forces* 88(5):2027–2052.

Brand, Jennie and Yu Xie. 2010. "Who Benefits Most from College? Evidence for Negative Selection in Heterogeneous Economic Returns to Higher Education." *American Sociological Review* 75(2):273–302.

Breen, Richard and Leire Salazar. 2011. "Educational Assortative Mating and Earnings Inequality in the United States." *American Journal of Sociology* 117(3):808–843.

Brines, Julie. 1994. "Economic Dependency, Gender, and the Division of Labor at Home." *American Journal of Sociology* 100(3):652–688.

Brooks, David. 2012. "The Great Divorce." *New York Times*, January 30. Retrieved January 30, 2012 (http://www.nytimes.com/2012/01/31/opinion/brooks-the-great-divorce.html?_r=1&emc=eta1).

Brown, Lyn. 2003. *Girlfighting: Betrayal and Rejection among Girls.* New York: New York University Press.

Bryson, Bethany. 1996. "'Anything but Heavy Metal': Symbolic Exclusion and Musical Dislike." *American Sociological Review* 61(5):844–899.

Buchmann, Claudia and Thomas DiPrete. 2006. "The Growing Female Advantage in College Completion: The Role of Family Background and Academic Achievement." *American Sociological Review* 71(4):515–541.

Burawoy, Michael. 1998. "The Extended Case Method." *Sociological Theory* 16(1):4–33.

Burton, Linda and Belinda Tucker. 2009. "Romantic Unions in an Era of Uncertainty: A Post-Moynihan Perspective on African American Women and Marriage." *The Annals of the American Academy of Political and Social Science* 621:132–148.

Bystydzienski, Jill. 2011. *Intercultural Couples: Crossing Boundaries, Negotiating Differences.* New York: New York University Press.

Cahill, Spencer. 1999. "Emotional Capital and Professional Socialization: The Case of Mortuary Science Students (And Me)." *Social Psychology Quarterly* 62(2):101–116.

Calarco, Jessica. 2011. "'I Need Help!' Social Class and Children's Help-Seeking in Elementary School." *American Sociological Review* 76(6):862–882.

Cancian, Francesca. 1987. *Love in America: Gender and Self Development.* New York: Cambridge University Press.

Carlson, Marcia and Paula England, eds. 2011. *Social Class and Changing Families in an Unequal America.* Palo Alto, CA: Stanford University Press.

Charles, Kerwin, Erik Hurst, and Alexandra Killewald. 2013. "Marital Sorting and Parental Wealth." *Demography* 50(1):51–70.

Chauncey, George. 1995. *Gay New York: Gender, Urban Culture, and the Making of the Gay Male World, 1890–1940.* New York: Basic Books.

Cheadle, Jacob and Paul Amato. 2010. "A Quantitative Assessment of Lareau's Qualitative Conclusions about Class, Race, and Parenting." *Journal of Family Issues* 32(5):1–28.

Cherlin, Andrew. 2004. "The Deinstitutionalization of American Marriage." *Journal of Marriage of Family* 66(4):848–861.

Cherlin, Andrew. 2009. *The Marriage Go-Round: The State of Marriage and the Family in America Today.* New York: Alford Knopf.

Chin, Tiffani and Meredith Phillips. 2004. "Social Reproduction and Childrearing Practices: Social Class, Children's Agency, and the Summer Activity Gap." *Sociology of Education* 77(3):185–210.

Collett, Jessica and Omar Lizardo. 2010. "Occupational Status and the Experience of Anger." *Social Forces* 88(5):2079–2104.

Coltrane, Scott. 1996. *Family Man: Fatherhood, Housework, and Gender Equity.* New York: Oxford University Press.

Coltrane, Scott. 2004. "Elite Careers and Family Commitment: It's (Still) About Gender." *Annals of the American Academy of Political and Social Science* 596:214–220.

Conger, Rand, Katherine Conger, and Monica Martin. 2010. "Socioeconomic Status, Family Process, and Individuals Development." *Journal of Marriage and Family* 72(3):685–704.

Conley, Dalton. 2001. "Capital for College: Parental Assets and Educational Attainment." *Sociology of Education* 74(1):59–73.

Coontz, Stephanie. 2005. *Marriage, a History: From Obedience to Intimacy, or How Love Conquered Marriage.* New York: Viking.

Coontz, Stephanie. 2011. *A Strange Stirring: The Feminine Mystique and American Women at the Dawn of the 1960s.* New York: Basic Books.

Cooper, Marianne. 2014. *Cut Adrift: Families in Insecure Times.* Berkeley, CA: University of California Press.

Corcoran, Mary. 1995. "Rags to Rags: Poverty and Mobility in the United States." *Annual Review of Sociology* 2:237–267.

Cunningham, Mick. 2001. "Parental Influences on the Gendered Division of Housework." *American Sociological Review* 66(2):184–203.

Davis, Kingsley. 1941. "Intermarriage in Caste Societies." *American Anthropologist* 43:376–395.

DeMott, Benjamin. 1992. *The Imperial Middle: Why Americans Can't Think Straight About Class.* New Haven, CT: Yale University Press.

Deutsch, Francine and Susan Saxon. 1998. "Traditional Ideologies, Nontraditional Lives." *Sex Roles* 38(5–6):331–362.

DeVault, Marjorie. 1999. "Comfort and Struggle: Emotion Work in Family Life." *Annals of the American Academy of Political and Social Sciences* 561:52–63.

Dews, Barney and Carolyn Law. 1995. *This Fine Place So Far from Home.* Philadelphia: Temple University Press.

DiMaggio, Paul. 1982. "Cultural Capital and School Success: The Impact of Status-Culture Participation on the Grades of U.S. High-School Students." *American Sociological Review* 47(2):189–201.

DiMaggio, Paul and John Mohr. 1985. "Cultural Capital, Educational Attainment, and Marital Selection." *American Journal of Sociology* 90(6):1231–1261.

Dumais, Susan, Richard Kessinger, and Bonny Ghosh. 2012. "Concerted Cultivation and Teachers' Evaluation of Students: Exploring the Intersection of Race and Parents' Educational Attainment." *Sociological Perspectives* 55(1):17–42.

Duncan, Greg and Richard Murnane. 2011. *Whither Opportunity? Rising Inequality, Schools, and Children's Life Chances.* New York: Russell Sage.

Dwyer, Rachel, Randy Hodson, and Laura McCloud. 2013. "Gender, Debt, and Dropping out of College." *Gender & Society* 27(1):30–55.

Edin, Kathryn and Maria Kefalas. 2005. *Promises I Can Keep: Why Poor Women Put Motherhood before Marriage.* Berkeley: University of California Press.

Elder, Glen, Jr. 1969. "Appearance and Education in Marriage Mobility." *American Sociological Review* 34(4):519–533.

England, Paula, Elizabeth McClintock, and Emily Shafer. 2011. "Birth Control Use and Early, Unintended Births: Evidence for a Class Gradient." Pp. 21–49 in *Social Class and Changing Families in an Unequal America*, edited by Marci Carlson and Paula England. Palo Alto, CA: Stanford University Press.

Erickson, Bonnie. 1996. "Culture, Class, and Connections." *American Journal of Sociology* 102(1):217–251.

Felmlee, Diane. 1998. "'Be Careful What You Wish For. . .': A Quantitative and Qualitative Investigation of 'Fatal Attractions.'" *Personal Relationships* 5(3):235–253.

Fernández, Raquel and Richard Rogerson. 2001. "Sorting and Long-Run Inequality." *Quarterly Journal of Economics* 116(4):1305–1341.

Finch, Janet. 1989. *Family Obligations and Social Change.* Cambridge, MA: Polity Press.

Fischer, Claude and Michael Hout. 2006. *Century of Difference: How America Changed in the Last One Hundred Years.* New York: Russell Sage.

Gerson, Kathleen. 2010. *The Unfinished Revolution: How a New Generation Is Reshaping Family, Work, and Gender in America.* New York: Oxford University Press.

Gibson, Donald and Scott Schroeder. 2002. "Grinning, Frowning, and Emotionlessness: Agent Perceptions of Power and Their Effect on Felt and Displayed Emotions in Influence Attempts." Pp. 184–211 in *Managing Emotions in the Workplace*, edited by Neal Ashkanasy, Wilfred Zerbe, and Charmine Hartel. Armonk, NY: M. E. Sharpe.

Goldrick-Rab, Sara. 2006. "Following Their Every Move: An Investigation of Social Class Differences in College Pathways." *Sociology of Education* 79(1):61–79.

Goldthorpe, John. 1983. "Women and Class Analysis: In Defense of Conventional View." *Sociology* 17(4):465–488.

Gorman, Thomas. 2000. "Cross Class Perceptions of Social Class." *Sociological Spectrum* 20(1):93–120.

Goyette, Kimberly. 2008. "College for Some to College for All: Social Background, Occupational Expectations and Educational Expectations over Time." *Social Science Research* 37(2):461–484.

Graham, Lawrence Otis. 1999. *Our Kind of People: Inside America's Black Upper Class*. New York: Harper Collins Perennial.

Granfield, Robert. 1991. "Making It By Faking It: Working-Class Students in an Elite Academic Environment." *Journal of Contemporary Ethnography* 20(3):331–351.

Gupta, Sanjiv. 2006. "Her Money, Her Time: Women's Earnings and Their Housework Hours." *Social Science Research* 35(4):975–999.

Gupta, Sanjiv. 2007. "Autonomy, Dependence, or Display? The Relationship between Married Women's Earnings and Housework." *Journal of Marriage and Family* 69(2):399–417.

Gupta, Sanjiv, Liana Sayer, and Phillip Cohen. 2009. "Earnings and the Stratification of Unpaid Time among U.S. Women." *Social Indicators Research* 93(1):153–157.

Hamilton, Darrick, Algernon Austin, and William Darity Jr. 2011. "Whiter Jobs, Higher Wages: Occupational Segregation and the Lower Wages of Black Men." *Economic Policy Institute*. Briefing Paper No. 288.

Hansen, Karen. 2005. *Not-so-Nuclear Families: Class, Gender, and Networks of Care*. New Brunswick, NJ: Rutgers University Press.

Hart, Betty and Todd Risley. 1995. *Meaningful Differences in the Everyday Experiences of Young American Children*. Baltimore, MD: Paul H. Brookes Publishing Co.

Hays, Sharon. 1996. *The Cultural Contradictions of Motherhood*. New Haven, CT: Yale University Press.

Hazelrigg, Lawrence and Joseph Lopreato. 1972. "Heterogamy, Inter-Class Mobility and Socio-Political Attitudes in Italy." *American Sociological Review* 37(3):264–277.

Heath, Shirley Brice. 1983. *Ways with Words: Language, Life, and Work in Communities and Classrooms*. New York: Cambridge University Press.

Himmelweit, Susan, Cristina Santos, Almudena Sevilla, and Catherine Sofer. 2013. "Sharing of Resources within the Family and the Economics of Household Decision Making." *Journal of Marriage and Family* 75(3):625–639.

Hochschild, Arlie. 1983. *The Managed Heart: Commercialization of Human Feeling*. Berkeley: University of California Press.

Hochschild, Arlie. [1989] 2003. *The Second Shift*. New York: Penguin Books.

Hochschild, Arlie. 1997. *The Time Bind: When Work Becomes Home and Home Becomes Work.* New York: Henry Holt and Company.

Hochschild, Jennifer. 1995. *Facing Up to the American Dream: Race, Class, and the Soul of the Nation.* Princeton, NJ: Princeton University Press.

Hoff, Erika, Brett Laursen, and Twila Tardif. 2002. "Socioeconomic Status and Parenting." Pp. 231–253 in *Handbook of Parenting*, Vol. 2, edited by Marc Bornstein. Mahwah, NJ: Lawrence Erlbaum Associates.

Holt, Douglas. 1997. "Distinction in America? Recovering Bourdieu's Theory of Tastes from Its Critics." *Poetics* 25(3):93–120.

Hurst, Allison. 2007. "Telling Tales of Oppression and Dysfunction: Narratives of Class Identity Reformation." *Qualitative Sociology Review* 3(2):82–104.

Illouz, Eva. 1997. *Consuming the Romantic Utopia: Love and the Cultural Contradictions of Capitalism.* Berkeley: University of California Press.

Illouz, Eva. 2008. *Saving the Modern Soul: Therapy, Emotions, and the Culture of Self-Help.* Berkeley: University of California Press.

Illouz, Eva. 2010. "Love and Its Discontents: Irony, Reason, Romance." *The Hedgehog Review* 12(1):18–32.

Jacobs, Jerry and Kathleen Gerson. 2004. *The Time Divide.* Cambridge, MA: Harvard University Press.

Johnson, Monica Kirkpatrick and Jean Mortimer. 2011. "Origins and Outcomes of Judgments about Work." *Social Forces* 89(4):1239–1260.

Johnson, Paul and Steph Lawler. 2005. "Coming Home to Love and Class." *Sociological Research Online* 10(3).

Kalmijn, Matthijs. 1991. "Status Homogamy in the United States." *American Journal of Sociology* 97(2):496–523.

Kalmijn, Matthijs. 1994. "Assortative Mating by Cultural and Economic Occupational Status." *American Journal of Sociology* 100(2):422–452.

Kalmijn, Matthijs. 1998. "Intermarriage and Homogamy: Causes, Patterns, Trends." *Annual Review of Sociology* 24:395–421.

Kemper, Theodore. 1978. *A Social Interactional Theory of Emotions.* New York: Wiley.

Kendall, Diana. 2011. *Framing Class: Media Representations of Wealth and Poverty in America.* Lanham, MD: Rowman and Littlefield Publishers.

Kenney, Catherine. 2006. "The Power of the Purse: Allocative Systems and Inequality in Couple Households." *Gender & Society* 20(3):354–381.

Kennedy, Elizabeth and Madeline Davis. 1993. *Boots of Leather, Slippers of Gold: The History of a Lesbian Community.* New York: Routledge.

Killewald, Alexandra and Margaret Gough. 2010. "Money Isn't Everything: Wives' Earnings and Housework Time." *Social Science Research* 39(6):987–1003.

Kimmel, Michael. 2006. *Manhood in America: A Cultural History.* New York: Oxford University Press.

Kingston, Paul. 2000. *The Classless Society*. Stanford, CA: Stanford University Press.

Kohn, Melvin. 1969. *Class and Conformity: A Study in Values*. Homewood, IL: Dorsey Press.

Komarovsky, Mirra. 1962. *Blue Collar Marriage*. New Haven, CT: Yale University Press.

Kornrich, Sabino and Frank Furstenberg. 2012. "Investing in Children: Changes in Parental Spending on Children, 19722000." *Demography* 50(1):1–23.

Kozol, Jonathon. 1992. *Savage Inequalities: Children in America's Schools*. New York: Harper Perennial.

Kunda, Gideon. 1992. *Engineering Culture: Control and Commitment in a High-Tech Corporation*. Philadelphia: Temple University Press.

Kusserow, Adrie. 2004. *American Individualisms: Child Rearing and Social Class*. New York: Palgrave MacMillan.

Lachance-Grzela, Mylene and Genevieve Bouchard. 2010. "Why Do Women Do the Lion's Share of the Housework? A Decade of Research." *Sex Roles* 63(11–12):767–780.

Lacy, Karyn. 2007. *Blue-Chip Black: Race, Class, and Status in the New Black Middle Class*. Berkeley: University of California Press.

Lamont, Michele. 1992. *Money, Morals, and Manners: The Culture of the French and American Upper-Middle-Class*. Chicago: University of Chicago Press.

Lamont, Michele. 2000. *The Dignity of Working Men: Morality and the Boundaries of Race, Class, and Immigration*. Cambridge, MA: Harvard University Press.

Lareau, Annette. 2000. "My Wife Can Tell Me Who I Know: Methodological and Conceptual Problems in Studying Fathers." *Qualitative Sociology* 23(4):407–433.

Lareau, Annette. 2003. *Unequal Childhoods: Class, Race, and Family Life*. Berkeley: University of California Press.

Lareau, Annette. 2011. *Unequal Childhoods, Class, Race, and Family Life*. 2nd ed. Berkeley: University of California Press.

Lareau, Annette and Jessica Calarco. 2012. "Class, Cultural Capital, and Institutions: The Case of Families and Schools." Pp. 61–86 in *Facing Social Class: Social Psychology of Social Class*, edited by Susan Fiske and Hazel Markus. New York: Russell Sage.

Lareau, Annette and Dalton Conley, eds. 2008. *Social Class: How Does It Work?* New York: Russell Sage.

Lareau, Annette and Elliot Weininger. 2008. "Time, Work, and Family Life: Reconceptualizing Gendered Time Patterns through the Case of Children's Organized Activities." *Sociological Forum* 23(3):419–454.

Leiulfsrud, Hakon and Alison Woodward. 1989. "Cross-Class Encounters of a Close Kind: Class Awareness and Politics in Swedish Families." *Acta Sociologica* 32(1):75–93.

Lewis Friedland, Dhavan Shah, Nam-Jin Lee, Mark Rademacher, Lucy Atkinson and Thomas Hove. 2007. "Capital, Consumption, Communication, and Citizenship: The Social Positioning of Taste and Civic Culture in the United States." *Annals of the American Academy of Political and Social Science* 611(1):31–50.

Lewis Oscar. 1961. *The Children of Sanchez: Autobiography of a Mexican Family.* New York: Random House.

Lewis Oscar. 1966. *La Vida: A Puerto Rican Family in the Culture of Poverty in San Juan and New York.* New York: Random House.

Liebow, Elliot. [1967] 2003. *Tally's Corner: A Study of Negro Streetcorner Men.* New York: Rowman and Littlefield Publishers.

Lively, Kathryn. 2000. "Reciprocal Emotion Management: Working Together to Maintain Stratification in Private Law Firms." *Work and Occupations* 27(1):32–63.

Lizardo, Omar. 2006. "How Cultural Tastes Shape Personal Networks." *American Sociological Review* 71(5):778–809.

Lizardo, Omar. 2013. "Variety in Cultural Choice and the Activation of Social Ties." *Social Science Research* 42(2):321–330.

Lizardo, Omar and Michael Strand. 2010. "Skills, Toolkits, Contexts, and Institutions: Clarifying the Relationship between Different Approaches to Cognition in Cultural Sociology." *Poetics* 38(2):204–227.

Lovaglia, Michael and Jeffrey Houser. 1996. "Emotional Reactions and Status in Groups." *American Sociological Review* 61(5):867–83.

Lubrano, Alfred. 2004. *Limbo: Blue-Collar Roots, White-Collar Dreams.* Hoboken, NJ: John Wiley and Sons.

Mare, Robert. 1980. "Social Background and School Continuation Decisions." *Journal of the American Statistical Association* 75(370):295–305.

Mare, Robert. 1991. "Five Decades of Educational Assortative Mating." *American Sociological Review* 56(1):15–32.

McFarland, Daniel and Heili Pals. 2005. "Motives and Contexts of Identity Change: A Case for Network Effects." *Social Psychology Quarterly* 68(4):289–315.

McLanahan, Sara and Gary Sandefur. 1994. *Growing Up with a Single Parent: What Hurts? What Helps?* Cambridge, MA: Harvard University Press.

Merton, Robert. 1941. "Intermarriage and the Social Structure: Fact and Theory." *Psychiatry* 4:361–374.

Miller, Jean Baker. 1983. *The Construction of Anger in Women and Men.* Wellesley, MA: Stone Center for Developmental Services and Studies, Wellesley College.

Moore, Mignon. 2011. *Invisible Families: Gay Identities, Relationships, and Motherhood among Black Women.* Berkeley: University of California Press.

Morin, Rich. 2012. "Rising Share of Americans See Conflict Between Rich and Poor." Pew Research: Social and Demographic Trends.

Morris, Martina and Bruce Western. 1999. "Inequality in Earnings at the Close of the Twentieth Century." *Annual Review of Sociology* 25:623–657.

Mullen, Ann. 2010. *Degrees of Inequality: Culture, Class, and Gender in American Higher Education*. Baltimore, MD: Johns Hopkins Press.

Murray, Charles. 2012. *Coming Apart: The State of White America 1960–2010*. New York: Crown Forum.

Musick, Kelly, Jennie Brand, and Dwight Davis. 2012. "Variation in the Relationship between Education and Marriage: Marriage Market Mismatch?" *Journal of Marriage and Family* 74(1):53–69.

Oakes, Jeannie. 1985. *Keeping Track: How Schools Structure Inequality*. New Haven, CT: Yale University Press.

O'Rand, Angela and Robert Ellis. 1974. "Social Class and Social Time Perspective." *Social Forces* 53(1):53–62.

Ortner, Sherry. 2003. *New Jersey Dreaming: Capital, Culture, and the Class of '58*. Durham, NC: Duke University Press.

Ostrove, Joan. 2003. "Belonging and Wanting: Meanings of Social Class Background for Women's Constructions of their College Experiences." *Journal of Social Issues* 59(4):771–784.

Pahl, Jan. 1994. "The Allocation of Money and the Structuring of Inequality within Marriage." *The Sociological Review* 31(2):237–262.

Pakulski, Jan, and Malcolm Waters. 1996. *The Death of Class*. London: Sage.

Pattillo, Mary. 2005. "Black Middle-Class Neighborhoods." *Annual Review of Sociology* 31: 305–329.

Pattillo, Mary. 2007. *Black on the Block: The Politics of Race and Class in the City*. Chicago: University of Chicago Press.

Peterson, Richard and Roger Kern. 1996. "Changing Highbrow Taste: From Snob to Omnivore." *American Sociological Review* 61(5):900–907.

Petev, Ivaylo. 2013. "The Association of Social Class and Lifestyle Persistence in American Sociability, 1974 to 2000." *American Sociological Review* 78(4):633–661.

Popkin, Susan, Laura Harris, and Mary Cunningham. 2002. "Families in Transition: A Qualitative Analysis of the MTO Experience." The Urban Institute, Washington DC.

Pyke, Karen. 1996. "Class-Based Masculinities: The Interdependence of Gender, Class, and Interpersonal Power." *Gender & Society* 10(5):527–549.

Reardon, Sean and Kendra Bischoff. 2011. "Income Inequality and Income Segregation." *American Journal of Sociology* 116(4):1092–1153.

Ridgeway, Cecilia and Cathryn Johnson. 1990. "What Is the Relationship Between Socioemotional Behavior and Status in Task Groups?" *American Journal of Sociology* 95(5):1189–1212.

Ridgeway, Cecilia and Lynn Smith-Lovin. 1999. "The Gender System and Interaction." *Annual Review of Sociology* 25:191–216.

Rist, Ray. 1970. "Student Social Class and Teacher Expectations: The Self-Fulfilling Prophecy in Ghetto Education." *Harvard Educational Review* 40:411–451.

Rivera, Lauren. 2011. "Ivies, Extracurriculars, and Exclusion: Elite Employers' Use of Educational Credentials." *Research in Social Stratification and Mobility* 29(1):71–90.

Rivera, Lauren. 2012. "Hiring as Cultural Matching: The Case of Elite Professional Services Firms." *American Sociological Review* 77(6):999–1022.

Rivera, Lauren. 2015. *Pedigree: How Elite Kids Get Elite Jobs.* Princeton, NJ: Princeton University Press.

Robinson, John and Geoffrey Godbey. 1997. *Time for Life: The Surprising Ways Americans Use Their Time.* University Park: Pennsylvania State University Press.

Roksa, Josipa and Daniel Potter. 2011. "Parenting and Academic Achievement: Intergenerational Transmission of Educational Advantage." *Sociology of Education* 84(4):299–321.

Rosenfeld, Michael. 2008. "Racial, Educational and Religious Endogamy in the United States: A Comparative Historical Perspective." *Social Forces* 87(1):1–31.

Rubin, Lillian. 1976. *Worlds of Pain: Life in the Working-Class Family.* New York: Basic Books.

Rubin, Lillian. 1994. *Life on the Fault Line: America's Working-Class Speaks about the Family, the Economy, Race and Ethnicity.* New York: Harper Collins Publishers.

Ryan, Jake and Charles Sackrey. 1984. *Strangers in Paradise: Academics from the Working Class.* Boston: South End Press.

Sayer, Liana. 2005. "Gender, Time, and Inequality: Trends in Women's and Men's Paid Work, Unpaid Work, and Free Time." *Social Forces* 84(1):285–303.

Schieman, Scott, Yuko Kurashina Whitestone, and Karen Van Gundy. 2006. "The Nature of Work and the Stress of Higher Status." *Journal of Health and Social Behavior* 47(3):242–257.

Schneider, Barbara and David Stevenson. 1999. *The Ambitious Generation: American Teenagers, Motivated by Directionless.* New Haven, CT: Yale University Press.

Schoen, Robert and John Wooldredge. 1989. "Marriage Choices in North Carolina and Virginia: 1969/1971 and 1979/1981." *Journal of Marriage and Family* 51(2):465–481.

Schoeni, Robert and Karen Ross. 2005. "Material Assistance from Families during the Transition to Adulthood." Pp. 396–416 in *On the Frontier of Adulthood*, edited by Richard Settersten Jr., Frank Furstenberg Jr., and Ruben Rumbaut. Chicago: University of Chicago Press.

Schwartz, Christine. 2010. "Earnings Inequality and the Changing Association between Spouses' Earnings." *American Journal of Sociology* 115(5):1524–1557.

Schwartz, Christine and Nikki Graf. 2009. "Assortative Matching Among Same-Sex and Different-Sex Couples in the United States, 1990–2000." *Demographic Research* 21:843–878.

Schwartz, Christine and Robert Mare. 2005. "Trends in Educational Assortative Marriage from 1940 to 2003." *Demography* 42(4):621–646.

Seidman, Steven. 2011. "Class Matters, But How Much? Class, Nation, and Queer Life." *Sexualities* 14(1):36–41.

Sennett, Richard and Jonathon Cobb. [1972] 1993. *The Hidden Injuries of Class.* New York: W.W. Norton and Company.

Shauman, Kimberlee and Mary Noonan. 2007. "Family Migration and Labor Force Outcomes: Sex Differences in Occupational Context." *Social Forces* 85(4):1735–1764.

Shows, Carla and Naomi Gerstel. 2009. "Fathering, Class, and Gender: A Comparison of Physicians and Emergency Medical Technicians." *Gender & Society* 23(2):161–187.

Simon, Robin and Leda Nath. 2004. "Gender and Emotion in the United States: Do Men and Women Differ in Self-Reports of Feelings and Expressive Behavior?" *American Journal of Sociology* 109(5):1137–1176.

Skeggs, Beverly. 1997. *Formations of Class & Gender: Becoming Respectable.* London: Sage Publications.

Skopek, Jan, Florian Schulz, and Hans-Peter Blossfeld. 2009. "Online Mate Search—Education-Specific Mechanisms of Choosing Contact Partners." *Kolner Journal of Sociology and Social Psychology* 61(2):183–210.

Smock, Pamela and Fiona Greenland. 2010. "Diversity in Pathways to Parenthood: Implications, and Emerging Research Directions." *Journal of Marriage and Family* 72(3):576–593.

Song, Miri. 2009. "Is Intermarriage a Good Indicator of Integration?" *Journal of Ethnic and Migration Studies* 35(2):331–348.

South, Scott. 1991. "Sociodemographic Differentials in Mate Selection Preferences." *Journal of Marriage and Family* 53(4):928–940.

Stearns, Carol and Peter Stearns. 1986. *Anger: The Historical Struggle for Emotional Control in American's History.* Chicago: University of Chicago Press.

Steinbugler, Amy. 2012. *Beyond Loving: Intimate Racework in Lesbian, Gay, and Straight Interracial Relationships.* New York: Oxford University Press.

Stempel, Carl. 2005. "Adult Participation Sports as Cultural Capital: A Test of Bourdieu's Theory of the Field of Sports." *International Review for the Sociology of Sport* 40(4):411–432.

Stephens, Nicole, Hazel Markus, and Sarah Townsend. 2007. "Choice as an Act of Meaning: The Case of Social Class." *Journal of Personality and Social Psychology* 93(5):814–830.

Stone, Pamela. 2008. *Opting Out?: Why Women Really Quit Their Careers and Head Home.* Berkeley: University of California Press.

Strauss, Anselm and Juliet Corbin. 1998. *Basics of Qualitative Research: Techniques and Procedures for Developing Grounded Theory*. London: Sage Publications.

Streib, Jessi. 2011. "Class Reproduction by Four Year Olds." *Qualitative Sociology* 34(2):337–352.

Stuber, Jenny. 2005. "Asset and Liability? The Importance of Context in the Occupational Experiences of Upwardly Mobile White Adults." *Sociological Forum* 20(1):139–166.

Stuber, Jenny. 2011. *Inside the College Gates: How Class and Culture Matter in Higher Education*. New York: Lexington Books.

Swidler, Ann. 1986. "Culture in Action: Symbols and Strategies." *American Sociological Review* 51(2):273–286.

Swidler, Ann. 2001. *Talk of Love: How Culture Matters*. Chicago: University of Chicago Press.

Taylor, Patricia, and Norval Glenn. 1976. "The Utility of Education and Attractiveness for Females' Status Attainment through Marriage." *American Sociological Review* 41(3):484–498.

Tichenor, Veronica. 2005. *Earning More and Getting Less: Why Successful Wives Can't Buy Equality*. New Brunswick, NJ: Rutgers University Press.

Tokarczyk, Michelle and Elizabeth Fay. 1993. *Working Class Women in the Academy: Laborers in the Knowledge Factory*. Amherst: University of Massachusetts Press.

Torche, Florencia. 2011. "Is a College Degree Still the Great Equalizer? Intergenerational Mobility across Levels of Schooling in the United States." *American Journal of Sociology* 117(3):763–807.

Townsend, Nicholas. 2002. *Package Deal: Marriage, Work, and Fatherhood in Men's Lives*. Philadelphia: Temple University Press.

Tucker, Robert, ed. 1978. *The Marx-Engels Reader*. New York: W. W. Norton and Company.

Turner, Jonathan. 2010. "The Stratification of Emotions: Some Preliminary Generalizations." *Sociological Inquiry* 80(2):168–199.

Upright, Craig. 2004. "Social Capital and Cultural Participation: Spousal Influences on Attendance at Art Events." *Poetics* 32(2):129–143.

Van Eijck, Koen. 1999. "Socialization, Education, and Lifestyle: How Social Mobility Increases the Cultural Heterogeneity of Status Groups." *Poetics* 26(5–6):309–328.

Vincent, Carol and Stephen Ball. 2007. "Making Up the Middle-Class Child: Families, Activities, and Class Dispositions." *Sociology* 41(6):1061–1077.

Walkerdine, Valerie, Helen Lucey, and June Melody. 2001. *Growing Up Girl: Psychosocial Explorations of Gender and Class*. New York: New York University Press.

Walzer, Susan. 1998. *Thinking about the Baby: Gender and Transitions into Parenthood*. Philadelphia: Temple University Press.

Weber, Max. [1905] 2001. *The Protestant Ethic and the Spirit of Capitalism.* New York: Oxford University Press.

Weber, Max. [1946] 1994. "Status Groups and Classes." Pp. 142–145 in *Social Stratification: Class, Race, & Gender in Sociological Perspective,* edited by David Grusky. Boulder, CO: Westview Press.

Weininger, Elliot and Annette Lareau. 2009. "Paradoxical Pathways: An Ethnographic Extension of Kohn's Findings on Class and Childrearing." *Journal of Marriage and Family* 71(3):680–695.

Wharton, Amy and Deborah Thorne. 1997. "Why Mothers Matter: The Effects of Social Class and Family Arrangements on African American and White Women's Perceived Relations with their Mothers." *Gender & Society* 11(5):656–681.

Wilkins, Amy. 2008. *Wannabes, Goths, and Christians: The Boundaries of Sex, Style, and Status.* Chicago: University of Chicago Press.

Willis, Paul. 1977. *Learning to Labor: How Working-Class Kids Get Working-Class Jobs.* Aldershot, UK: Gower.

Williams, Joan. 2010. *Reshaping the Work-Family Debate: Why Men and Class Matter.* Cambridge, MA: Harvard University Press.

Wingfield, Adia. 2010. "Are Some Emotions Marked 'Whites Only'? Racialized Feeling Rules in Professional Workplaces." *Social Problems* 57(2):251–268.

Wright, Erik Olin. 1985. *Classes.* London: Verso.

Yancey, George and Richard Lewis Jr. 2009. *Interracial Families: Current Concepts and Controversies.* New York: Routledge.

Zelizer, Viviana. 1989. "The Social Meaning of Money: 'Special Monies.'" *American Journal of Sociology* 95(2):342–377.

Zweig, Michael. 2000. *The Working Class Majority: America's Best Kept Secret.* Ithaca, NY: Cornell University Press.

INDEX